Sustainable Organizations - Models, Applications, and New Perspectives

Edited by Brizeida Hernández-Sánchez and Jose C. Sánchez-García

Published in London, United Kingdom

IntechOpen

Supporting open minds since 2005

Sustainable Organizations - Models, Applications, and New Perspectives
http://dx.doi.org/10.5772/intechopen.91607
Edited by Brizeida Hernández-Sánchez and Jose C. Sánchez-García

Contributors
Reynaldo Bontuyan Inocian, Muhammad Auwal Abdullahi, Zainalabidin Mohamed, Mad Nasir Shamsudin, Juwaidah Sharifuddin, Fazlin Ali, Ihor Katernyak, Viktoriya Loboda, Zainuddin Manan, Sharifah Rafidah Wan Alwi, Nkemdilim Iheanachor, Oluwayemisi Adebola Abisuga, Oluwabunmi Adejumo, Ngunan M. M. Ikpaya, Ikpaya Ikpaya, Eseoghene Ovie, Chisom Grace Nwokike, Sesugh Nongo, Godwin Ogor-Igbosuah, Katundu Imasiku, Xiaoyao Yue, Abul Hassan, Kassu Jilcha Sileyew, Ruixuan Ji

First published in London, United Kingdom, 2021 by IntechOpen
IntechOpen is the global imprint of INTECHOPEN LIMITED, registered in England and Wales, registration number: 11086078, 5 Princes Gate Court, London, SW7 2QJ, United Kingdom
Printed in Croatia

British Library Cataloguing-in-Publication Data
A catalogue record for this book is available from the British Library

Additional hard and PDF copies can be obtained from orders@intechopen.com

Sustainable Organizations - Models, Applications, and New Perspectives
Edited by Brizeida Hernández-Sánchez and Jose C. Sánchez-García
p. cm.
Print ISBN 978-1-83880-962-1
Online ISBN 978-1-83880-963-8
eBook (PDF) ISBN 978-1-83880-964-5

For EU product safety concerns:
IN TECH d.o.o., Prolaz Marije Krucifikse Kozulić 3, 51000 Rijeka, Croatia, info@intechopen.com or visit our website at intechopen.com.

Meet the editors

Brizeida Hernández-Sánchez. Ph.D. from the University of Salamanca. She received the Extraordinary Prize for doctoral research. She has a Master in Psychopedagogy; Education for Diversity and a Master in Information Technology and Communication, both from the Specialized University of the Americas. She is an Associate Professor at the University of Salamanca, Faculty of Education. She is the academic coordinator of the Extraordinary Chair in the Entrepreneurship Training Program at the University of Salamanca. She has been a career coordinator at the graduate level. She is the coordinator of different international postgraduate (master) programs in the General Secretariat of the International Network for Training and Research AFIDE. Member of the GIR-IDEM- University of Salamanca. She is the author of numerous articles published in high impact international journals. She is the author of books and book chapters of a national and international nature. She is also a member of several different editorial committees of international journals.

José Carlos Sánchez-García. Doctor in Psychology from the Autonomous University of Madrid. He achieved his Master's degree in Clinical Psychology and his Master's degree in Industrial Psychology, from the Complutense University of Madrid. He is a Professor of Entrepreneurship at the University of Salamanca. He has been the Dean of the Faculty of Psychology at the University of Salamanca for eight years. Currently he is the Director of the Doctorate Program in Psychology at the University of Salamanca. He is also the Director of the Entrepreneurship Chair at the University of Salamanca and the Director of different international postgraduate programs (masters degrees) in entrepreneurial development and innovation. He is the President of AFIDE (Association for Training, Research and Development of Entrepreneurship). He was awarded the OPA Award for his research and promotion of entrepreneurship at the university, as well as the Juan Huarte de San Juan Award for his career as a psychologist and promotion of psychology. He also received an award from the Municipality of Osorno (Chile) for promoting entrepreneurship in this region. He is the author of numerous articles published in international high-impact journals. He is also the author of books and book chapters of a national and international character. He is a member of different editorial committees of international magazines as well as a member of different international associations in the field of psychology and entrepreneurship. He is a visiting professor at different European and Latin American universities

Contents

Preface

The global environmental crisis, on the one hand, and the economic and social crises, on the other, are the main causes for the theoretical questioning of current development models, and consequently, the formulation of proposals for a paradigm shift known as sustainable development (or sustainability). Sustainable entrepreneurship is, in essence, the implementation of a sustainable innovation aimed at a mass-market that provides benefit to a large part of society. From the environmental point of view, entrepreneurs and companies that make environmental progress engage in "sustainable entrepreneurship", generating new products, services, techniques and modes of organization that substantially reduce the impact on the ecosystem and increase the quality of life, generating employment and social value.

The term sustainable development was used for the first time in a public document in 1980, in the World Conservation Strategy and gained popularity in 1987 in the World Commission on Environment and Development Report where it was defined as development that meets the needs of present generations without compromising the ability of future generations to meet their needs.

Previously, sustainability was related to environmental issues, however, it is currently addressing the inclusion of social and environmental aspects in business activities and in interactions with stakeholders.

At the international level, in recent years there have been several global initiatives that promote sustainable development, such as the United Nations (UN) Millennium Development Goals; UNESCO's Implementation Plan, named Decade of Education for Sustainable Development; the United Nations Development Program (UNDP)'s Sustainable Development Goals, etc. On the other hand, other initiatives are specifically referred to the business world, such as Business for Social Responsibility (BSR), created by North American businesspersons in the 1990s; the World Business Council for Sustainable Development (WBCSD), created from the merger of the Business Council for Sustainable Development and the World Industry Council for the Environment; the United Nations Global Compact, an instrument created by the UN and the Earth Charter of The Hague, just to mention some of the most relevant.

Sustainable entrepreneurship implies a process where the purpose is to achieve sustainable development through the discovery, evaluation, and exploitation of opportunities; and the creation of value that causes economic prosperity, social cohesion, and the protection of the environment. Social, environmental, and commercial entrepreneurship coexist.

It is necessary to understand the great complexity that the management of this type of business can entail, since there is a great difference between a company with a purely financial orientation and a sustainable company, which is multidimensional. For this, it is necessary to integrate different perspectives in the study of sustainable entrepreneurship, since the existing literature generally refers to economics, especially to market failures, and only to a lesser extent, the role of government and institutions.

Given the multidisciplinary nature of the object of study, we have divided this book into 12 chapters. From Chapter 1 to Chapter 4 we have explored all the necessary content to learn how to start and create a business from a modern and updated approach based on sustainability. New trends in innovative and inclusive business models are added to the classic aspects of entrepreneurship, emphasizing the three values of sustainability: economic, social and environmental. All these models serve to define and scale the triple value proposition aimed at all stakeholders and offer a global and integrated vision of the enterprising, highlighting social and green enterprises for their current relevance.

In Chapter 5 we deal with the issue of gender equality. The realization of this right is the best opportunity there is to face some of the most pressing challenges of our time, from the economic crisis and lack of healthcare to climate change, violence against women, and escalating conflicts. Not only are women more seriously affected by these problems, but they also have the ideas and leadership skills to solve them. Gender discrimination, which continues to hinder women, is also an obstacle in our world.

Furthermore, women constitute half of the world's human capital and represent one of its most underutilized resources. Sustainable economic growth at the national and global levels depends on the participation of women in the workforce and the full use of their skills and qualifications.

The 2030 Agenda for Sustainable Development, and its 17 Sustainable Development Goals (SDGs), approved in 2015, propose a roadmap to achieve the corresponding level of sustainable progress that leaves no one behind. Achieving gender equality and the empowerment of women is an integral part of each of the 17 SDGs. Ensuring respect for women's rights through all of these goals is the only way to obtain justice, achieve inclusion, create economies that benefit all people, and care for our environment, now and for generations to come.

The chapters that follow provide guidance to help translate sustainability strategies across cultures. In particular, Chapters 6, 7, 8, and 9 address the problem of the absence of a sustainable economic development model in South Africa, Nigeria, and in Islamic cultures, caused by the lack of managerial training aimed at addressing environmental impact in the transformation processes of materials.

These processes are analyzed through the Triple Bottom Line perspective that effectively describes the primary objectives of sustainability. This paradigm has significantly highlighted some of the key relationships between cultural, social, and economic institutions in relation to environmental goals, leading to the realization that we need more analytical thinking about the economy and markets if we are to achieve global sustainability.

The final chapters of the book (Chapters 10, 11, and 12) analyze current trends in sustainable development at the local level, which clearly points to education as a powerful tool to facilitate the transition to more sustainable forms of development. In other words, it has a fundamental role as an articulator of a process of change of attitudes and values in the education of students, understanding sustainability as a new positive social value of social transformation. Faced with this challenge, education, from a skill training model, can integrate basic knowledge for sustainability to be developed in formal and non-formal educational institutions and at different educational levels from kindergarten to university, taking into account the ethical models from which to start to promote sustainable human development from an environmental and social point of view.

Through these chapters, we guide the reader through the understanding of theoretical concepts, and examples of sustainable enterprises are made available to the reader that serves as a reference and that allow the development of practical activities. For this reason, companies have been selected that not only practice socially responsible actions, but also base their business model on corporate sustainability, including companies for the common good and social enterprises. In this way, the development of competitive advantages based on sustainability arguments is proposed, aligning entrepreneurship with the goals of sustainable development (SDG).

Brizeida Hernández-Sánchez and José Carlos Sánchez-García
University of Salamanca,
Salamanca, Spain

Chapter 1

Organizational Insights, Challenges and Impact of Sustainable Development in Developing and Developed Nations

Katundu Imasiku

Abstract

While developed nations can fully explore various sustainable business models to achieve sustainability, this might not be easy for developing nations because of poor governance systems, characterized by inequality, patronage, and corruption and other challenges. This chapter evaluates organizations as developing and developed nation blocs by first providing insights on how organizations can contribute to the social and environmental sustainability, and second, by highlighting the challenges and approaches for sustainable development. The chapter further unravels the potential for both blocs to grow and achieve sustainability through technology and innovative strategies alongside the opportunities offered by having fast-growing populations and natural resources. To achieve sustainability, a twofold approach comprising the 360-organizational sustainability approaches and advanced sustainability system analysis approach is used. The key societal driving forces in both blocs for exploiting sustainable business practices are governance and institutions, technology and innovation, economy and society, population and behavior, and financing for development which can unlock sustainable business opportunities for sustainable development. To address the business climate challenges, it is inferred that organizations can achieve global sustainability by integrating sustainable production and consumption, biodiversity and ecosystem services, equity and resilience sectors to attain an environmentally and socially governed systems globally.

Keywords: organization, sustainable development, models, challenges, innovation, technology, good governance, developing and developed nations

1. Introduction

The Brundtland Commission defines sustainable development as development which keeps in check the present generation's needs without neglecting the future generation's capability to address their needs [1]. In the long run, sustainable development can provide a solution to how the world plans its economic activities and growth without damaging the environment and to ensure a safer habitat is maintained for the succeeding generations, to also build up their economies and societies without neglecting the environment. Apart from sustainable development fulfilling peoples' needs without discouraging the chances of others, it covers a lot of more extensive issues like ecological, social, and financial advancement which are critical to the social prosperity of all [2, 3].

While conceding that great advancement has been accomplished this far, yet its lopsidedness all-inclusive is as yet a stressing factor. Quick development in some developing nations has diminished high living standards and exacerbated poverty and inequalities. These inequalities sabotage the inclusiveness, social protection, and even sustainable development since it diminishes interests in health systems and training frameworks and counterbalances financial and political stability [4].

Although fast-growing population dynamics can improve the labor market, it conjointly can expand inequalities in both developing and developed nations and globally contingent upon the readiness by the country being referred to. Expanded urbanization, population growth, and population aging may likewise rise thriving in certain countries, but it might likewise cause significant stress on national infrastructures and public finance, education, and health-care systems [5].

To attend to these barriers globally and gain sustainable development positioning, there is a need to advance plans that encourage change the way governments are administered, the way products and services are delivered, employments creation, global consumption trends, and how the management of natural resources is done. Embracing the "business as usual" motto presents clear dangers because there is adequate proof that they are answerable for the worldwide megatrends that set as dangers to sustainability [6].

2. Global trends for sustainable development challenges

The challenges to sustainable development are influenced by socioeconomic, demographic, technological, and environmental trends which are seen to be the primary changes that transform society and considerably sway onto individuals. The formative advancement accomplished as of late combined with the unpredictable global economic changes have resulted in the following trends [4];

i. In a global financial crisis, the international community needs to put up development strategies to address impoverishment and sustainable development. If the socioeconomic progress stays lopsided, more costs are likely to be incurred because of environmental degradation.

ii. The variety of socioeconomic, population, technology, and environment-driven trends causing the sustainable development challenges are inequality, globalization, environmental degradation, and population diversity.

iii. These trends complement each other in manners which pose several challenges. Rapid urbanization in developing nations, financialization, and globalization are recipes for inequality and introducing nations to high food and nutrition risks, environmental degradation, and energy security because of high demand for land and water.

iv. Since environmental degradation has so far reached a crucial stage, the casual business as usual approach is highly discouraged for transformative change to occur at a community level, country level, and even at a global level to attain sustainable development.

3. Strategies for sustainable inclusiveness

The outcome document of the UN Conference on Sustainable Development gives direction to accomplishing the progress to sustainable development as approaches for increasing the prosperity of current and future generations. Sustainable development strategies should be comprehensive and take extraordinary consideration of the requirements of the poor and vulnerable. Strategies should be goal-oriented, action- and community-based, considering distinctive national conditions [7].

The strategies should systemically transform usage and creation structures and may include, inter alia, colossal value corrections, empower the protecting of typical blessings, lessen inequalities, and strengthen the fiscal organization. Such a strategy should restrain such use and creation that have negative externalities, while at the same time trying to expand the kinds of utilization and creation that make positive externalities. Examples of restricting negative externalities include a decrease of ecological contamination, while instances of positive externalities incorporate, for instance, innovation adjustment, a decrease of food waste, and improve overall nutritional value.

Technology will positively assume a significant job in addressing the consumption patterns to drive the formation of innovations and advancements that are important for sustainability. Accomplishments in achieving these progressions will require a significant redesign of the economy and society and changes in ways of life. Economic and finance-related impetuses for the creation and reception of new technological advances will be required alongside innovative policy changes. The all-embracing objectives of the essential requirements for sustainable development comprise; combating poverty, unsustainable consumption and production, and ensuring that natural resources are well managed and protected.

In today's global world, climate and environmental protection need to be taken as a universal goal by all. The current trend of relocating the manufacturing sector and other services to developing nations demands that developed nations will also offer both technical and financial support to the developing nations.

Sustainable development transformation entails, change involves, inter alia, noteworthy value redresses, a solid promise to safeguarding natural endowments, a decrease of inequalities, accounting for the environmental, public sector strengthening, and investment for development and profit-sharing, thereby improving poor people's livelihood and socio-well-being.

Sustainable development strategies in developing nations will keep on offering need to human development, with a focus on reducing impoverishment. While human development needs more notice taken to toward people's quality of life and other issues at country-level, its achievement depends to a large degree on utilizing the open doors made by globalization and on restricting its contrary effects. In this circumstance, better organization of capital streams and macroeconomic guidelines may be indispensable and sufficiency between country-specific development strategies and global decision-making is significant. Overall organizations need to oblige the novel needs of developing countries, especially those of the creating countries. The global plan will similarly need to take as being of great importance to avoidance clashes, human rights abuse, guaranteeing that great administration wins and a decreased inequality.

4. Global challenges for sustainable development

Today, it is imperative to take note of that sustainable development is similarly substantial in developing and developed nations, despite them managing polarly inverse sides of the range. Although developed nations might be developed, that does not infer that they are sustainable. However, the primary objective of these nations should be to free their general public of issues like social inequalities, poor waste management and poor environmental management [4].

i. Having poor or no capital budget to plan and complete economic activities.

ii. Having a business climate which is characterized by civil war makes sustainable development difficult because of misplaced priorities.

iii. Natural calamities, like earthquakes, tremors and floods, can present a danger to sustainability because they can affect the flow of water and even cause damage to infrastructure or disturb arable land or habitable land. In Ramche, a rural settlement in Nepal, an earthquake struck the river that supplied water, leaving Ramche in a water crisis that forces the villagers to use E-Coli infected water. Similarly, in Canada, E. coli water contamination forced a 10-year evacuation plan of the Kashechewan area. This forced people to drink and cook out of desperation [8, 9]. For instance, the 2004 tidal waves in South East and Eastern Asia danged a lot of infrastructures and claimed close to 226,000 lives in Africa and Asia. For instance, the damage of Japan's open-vehicle approach is a good example [10].

iv. The prevalence of clashes between long-term sustainable investment and immediate gains or profits with governments is a source of concern and worry. Although politically motivated to win votes in south Poland, a legislative orders to finance sustainable energy resources for energy production in the mining sector is approved instead of promoting dirty coal power generation which currently accounts for about 80% of the generated power in Poland [11, 12].

v. Public goods abuse by public officers or any act of bribery that deviates from the acceptable standards of society for personal gains is corruption and one of the greatest barriers to sustainable development [13]. Nepal's foreign grants are mainly provided by the UK unraveled that because of corruption and bureaucratic systems in Nepal, the development projects by NGOs can never pass or be approved without bribing the government ministers alongside huge administration fees demanded by the Nepal government essentially hinders progress [14].

In Africa, the UNECA reports that corruption impedes economic growth because it discourages foreign investments, distorts resource distribution public spending and market competition, increases the production costs. The consequence of these vices is that the quality of services and public infrastructure and the amount of tax returns are drastically reduced alongside a rising misappropriation and misallocation of scarce resources. Politically, it undermines the rule of law, human rights, accountability and transparency and this makes government wings weak [15].

vi. Poor municipal service delivery. Poor municipal services which include sewerage and other waste management and disposal in the cities and rural areas poses a threat to human health.

vii. Climate change is another enemy to sustainable development and needs frantic efforts to mitigate and adapt so that ecological systems are maintained to reduce the secondary effects like global warming, skin diseases, floods, drought and other extreme weather events.

viii. While hunger and malnourishment, is an issue of the past in developed nations and diminishing in developing nations, it persists in some nations, and this presents a threat to food security.

ix. The existing disparity in the per capita income within and outside inside nations is a source of possible tension and conflict.

x. The rapid urbanization experienced in developing nations has posed large pressure on municipal services and this demands that infrastructure be improved in both public and private sectors of society.

xi. As long as the current sustainable energy demands are not met at the household level, the future and projected demands will remain neglected which even increases the energy deficit.

xii. The recurrence of global financial crises can reduce access to long-term development finance and sustainable investments.

xiii. Pandemics like the 2020 COVID-19 can also retard sustainable development because it can lead to reduced access to long-term development finance and sustainable investments.

xiv. Unsustainable consumption and production are a significant sustainable development challenge that has emerged and developed in developed nations, while the developing nations have progressively followed these unsustainable ways. This has made the per capita carbon emission levels in developed countries 20–40 times higher than would normally be appropriate for air steadiness or atmospheric stability and the per capita ecological footprints being 4–9 times higher than their bio-capacity in developed countries [4].

In summary, developing nations have in actuality advanced sustainability actions which are more developed than those actualized in developed countries to date. For example, Ecuador and the Plurinational territories of Bolivia honor their nature to the extent of protecting it using the constitution [16, 17]. Currently, most developing countries are building up sustainable consumption ways, through optimistic model development. Drawing on their traditional know-how, many countries can leapfrog cleaner approaches of producing goods, thereby greening agribusiness and industry sectors. All nations globally should encourage the use of suitable approaches like the deployment of technology and all the innovation and services that come with it to make both developed and developing nations go into an upright pattern of participation and commitment among all stakeholders at individual, private and public, and international levels to achieve global sustainable development. One positive strategy to achieve this is the transformation toward sustainable cities and nations globally [18].

5. A pathway to global sustainable cities

Although urbanization creates employment and other opportunities to many people globally, it has also brought about poverty because rapid urbanization increases pressure on resources, especially food, water, energy and sanitation services and public services like education and health. More than 50% of the population globally lived in the urban cities in 2007 but this percentage is projected to be greater than 70% by the year 2050. Further, 80% of the global population ramp from urbanization is expected to occur in developing nations, particularly in urban cities in Asia and Africa [18, 19].

Between 1950 and 2010, medium cities and large cities had added 632 million and 570 million people, respectively. This population ramp in cities over a 15- to 20-year period is worth noting because it has some significant policy implications. Since future rapid urbanization is expected to occur in developing nations, there is a need to prepare to boost resources, increase the developmental capacity for the municipalities to avoid being overwhelmed with the anticipated pressure. Some of the causes of this constant evolution in major cities include the individual's mobility, a high birthrate, ecological changes, socioeconomic development alongside local, national and international policy reforms [18, 19].

The cities in developing nations have inadequate public services like health care, clean water and sanitation and electricity and this is worsened by the lack of municipal capacities to improve access decent jobs, health systems and basic infrastructure that would help reduce vulnerability to contamination, environmental degradation, diseases, climate change and natural calamities.

Although developed nations already have access to these amenities and most basic public services, they too still face challenges of sustenance and increased efficiency especially in the energy generation and water supply, which may require loss and waste management and recycling systems. Failure to manage these resource systems properly would increase the ecological footprints in cities.

Most cities globally are vulnerable to climate change impacts and this puts pressure on the poor people's capacity to adapt, regardless of whether that nation is highly industrialized or has a higher per capita income. The recurrence of global economic crises increases unemployment rates, especially among the educated young men and women in the cities. The prevalent inequalities between urban and rural areas and within urban communities are mainly persistent in developing nations. The growing disparities between rural areas and urban areas alongside high inequality rates in urban areas have continued to exist in developing nations with more than 1 billion people still live in the inner-city slums which lack clean water, sanitation facilities, health and education and basic infrastructure. On a more saddening note, from the current trends, it is estimated that 3 billion people will still live in slums by 2050 unless sustainable measures are taken to address this issue [18, 19].

This points to the need to effectively manage the urban cities as a condition for sustainability using sustainable organization frameworks like the 360-organization sustainability model. The 360-organizational sustainability is not just an organizational performance tool and a public relations mode of disseminating organizational corporate social responsibility messages but also a vision that has a clear strategic plan with measurable employee performance objectives and shared values [20, 21].

6. 360-organizational sustainability approach

To meet the 360-organizational sustainability criteria, the management team of the organization must have "Yes" as an answer all the following series of questions [20, 21]:

i. Is the organizational development and exploitation of human resources done sustainably?

ii. Are the worker's socio-well-being incentives suitable for all?

iii. Are the ways of life and aspirations of the workers sustainable and achievable considering the amount of time spent outside the firm?

iv. Is the community, country or global society in which our organization operates, desirable and sustainable?

v. Is our organization environmentally neutral concerning all our operations in the supply chain network?

vi. Is our organization achieving economic growth?

This chapter proposes that implementing a 360-organizational sustainability approach is a highly desirable type of organization needed to bring about the transformation in cities, rural area and globally. It should be every government, firm, community or persons desire to deploy the 360-organizational sustainability model. **Figure 1** shows the four main elements of the 360-organizational sustainability model as modified from Mark Hollingworth [20].

Figure 1 shows that the sustainability analysis elements are arranged into four categories, namely: (a) the biosphere, (b) internal and external human resources, (c) the community, and (d) the organization.

The underlying response to being tested to thoroughly consider the focal point of the 360-organizational sustainability approach is to increase the phantom of the expanded expenses related to doing as such. Most likely, any endeavors to develop the 360-organizational sustainability will bring about higher monetary expenses to the firm. This might be valid on both a short and long-term basis. Notwithstanding, today, while we look to keep away from those possible costs, we incur, our firms, societies and the whole biosphere into a circular drive of non-sustainability, with an exceptionally strong block divider at its end which might occur any time [20, 21].

Although being "environmentally green" implies that the firm would incur greater expenses at the inception of the concept of environmental sustainability, most leaders in firms like Interface and Bolthouse Foods have indicated that

Figure 1.
The 360-organizational sustainability model, adopted from Hollingworth [20].

focusing on just the biosphere sustainability can really give you a sustainable upper hand—while expanding gainfulness and decreasing business risks. Simply envision what prizes anticipate associations accomplishing 360-organizational sustainability. Further, if the markets are viable, the achievement of sustainability is reflected in a firm's worth or share value which in the long term will be considered to be lower than firms which are not sustainable [21].

The business world is obviously deficient with regards to leadership in the area of sustainability, but the 360-organizational sustainability and former Anglican Arc-Bishop Desmond Tutu famous demands that everyone is in proximity to fill-up a leadership position in society [22]. This implies that a corporate shared value (CSV) norm is needed by those who intend to fill-up the existing leadership vacuum [23].

7. Sustainable transformational research strategies

By 2030, the two blocs—developing and developed nations will need to adopt the key transformational strategies toward developing sustainable socioeconomic frameworks and balanced ecosystem by reforming the policies and governance system; changing human behavior, societal norms, and beliefs; enhancing data analytics using machine learning (ML) and artificial intelligence (AI); and making communities aware of these key drivers of sustainability [24].

Understanding the weight of addressing sustainability challenges worldwide requires coordinated investigations and integrating contradictory sectors of society like production and consumption with biodiversity and ecosystem services to build resilience at the expense of inequality. Achieving this will need an integrated

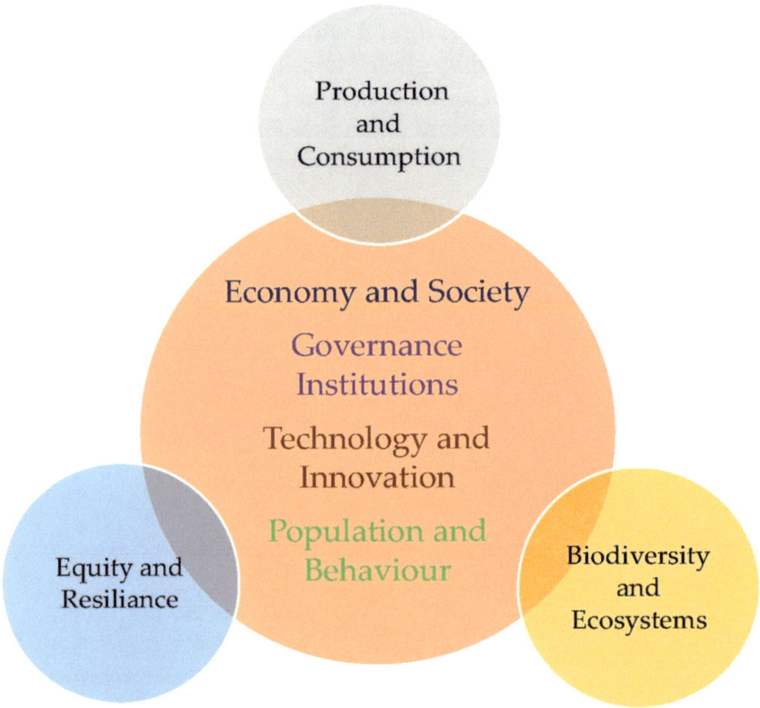

Figure 2.
Primary societal drivers and secondary pressures for sustainable transformations, adopted from IIASA [25].

strategy that brings all these sectors together. **Figure 2** shows synergies across seven key driving sectors to facilitate the development of systems approach sustainability.

Figure 2 shows the primary and secondary drivers of sustainability. While an adaptable multi-model approach at primary level that is concerned with conventional organizational system models, governments are expected to adapted models for theory testing, predictability models to investigate the soundness of societal system dynamics and policy assessment before deployment. Further, at a higher level, the approach may integrate the secondary pressures like equity and resilience, biodiversity and ecosystems and production and consumption to achieve total sustainability. In more detail, all the seven societal drivers that are necessary to help develop cutting-edge model approaches that are country-specific and capable of resolving the sustainability issues.

7.1 System approaches for sustainability

7.1.1 Primary approaches

7.1.1.1 Governance and institutional establishment

Although the world does not view the prevalent governance and administration frameworks as inappropriate for combating the challenges that are related to the climate and the environmental pressures, it is an effective approach, as long as exceptional changes concerning scale, degree, and speed in all system characteristics are made. These characteristics or attributes include; social conduct; administrative, authoritative, and bureaucratic systems; monetary organizations and incentives; and technical or biophysical frameworks. It is evident that our current administration structures of covering and settled establishments, rules, shows, procedures, and systems by which choices are made and actualized are deficient or have been mistranslated and therefore cannot drive the necessary changes, at the national or global level [26, 27].

This acknowledgement is provoking the academic world to take part in a significant reconsideration of its logical approaches, its strategies for science communication and commitment, and its apparent job in the public arena—offering rise to the new space of "transformative science."

7.1.1.2 Innovation and technology development

New innovations and technological development, including digitalization, are now having significant effects across different thematic areas of the economy around the world. They are not just affecting equity, work, production, recreation, conduct, education, and governance, but on the other hand, are expanding cultural and social partitions. Seeing how new technologies converge with and are utilized by society, and the ensuing ramifications of this is basic to outfitting advances to assist social orders and the prosperity of residents. The key challenge is how policies can create possible advantages of innovation and technological advancement as the world transform toward total sustainability [28].

7.1.1.3 Economy and society

Modern society is concerned with how social orders sort out their economic activities and how significant this process is for sustainable transformation. The socioeconomic framework is straightforwardly embroiled in supporting a worldwide challenge as inescapable and developing societal disparities, prevalent impoverishment, and diminished social and cultural flexibility. Additionally, the manner in which the social sector designs and boosts its economic activities has solid ramifications for the change toward dematerialized production and consumption designs, just as the sustainable utilization of land, water, and natural resources [29].

The economy is profoundly inserted in both social and biophysical frameworks and consequently are examined in an integrated manner. This requires a systems examination approach and interdisciplinary exploration structures, containing a scope of different logical approaches and techniques to portray, comprehend, and clarify socioeconomic, political, and environmental progress. Given the current social issues that are driven by current predominant economic frameworks and structures, it is pivotal to find new answers for these issues and show the capability of system thinking in accelerating other socioeconomic points of views and options [29].

7.1.1.4 Population and behavioral change

The socioeconomic and technological improvement over the previous decades has contributed significantly to improving human living standards and prosperity. In any case, these advantages are not uniformly distributed across nations, locales and communities, and populace groups. Such disparities obstruct economic development, economic growth, and subsequently, the accomplishment of sustainability. Besides, a lot of the new difficulties we face today are the outcomes of past pursuit to enhance and improve the human condition. Not exclusively did socioeconomic advancement lead to declining birth rates and expanding life span bringing about populace aging; it likewise prompts ways of life and dietary changes bringing about upward or downward shifts of mortality rates from chronic, non-transmittable, and degenerative sicknesses. Such changes in way of life and consumption exacerbate global climate change, while environmental change thusly influences human and social prosperity [4].

Transformations in the economic and social structures require personal conduct change, which offers impressive potential for moving toward sustainability in cost-effective ways, wider and emerging technological advancement like those from the COVID-19 pandemic. Apparently, the best way to confront such changes is to find out how to inspire the vital wide-scale and predominant behavioral change is to explore integral and blended ways that incorporate social sciences, natural sciences and engineering [4].

7.1.2 Secondary approaches

7.1.2.1 Equity and resilience

People are both the reason for most changes worldwide and are conjointly affected by these changes. This affirms the existence of system risks that are probably going to course across interconnected socioeconomic systems and force insufferable weights that are normally borne excessively by the poor and vulnerable individuals. These risks may emerge from extreme climate weather conditions, forced human movements, food and water deficiencies, pandemics, sea and air contamination, biodiversity loss, and financial disturbances that may cause a financial crisis. Projections indicate that these risks will increment considerably, and likely to bring about a foreseen decrease in societal resilience [6].

Based on this background, it is important to see how populace and socioeconomic pressures, individual and group activities (i.e., values, beliefs, norms, and cultures), and the community diversity (e.g., rural and urban) influence potential intercessions to improve versatility, equality, and the manageability of human societies. It is additionally generally perceived that the polarization of societies mostly brings about policy check or reformulation, a situation that must be resolved by improved collaborations between socioeconomic systems and governance systems [6].

7.1.2.2 Production and consumption

The patterns of resource consumption and production of goods are characterized by inequality and unsustainable consumption. The test for societies is to change the current way of producing goods and consumption of goods makes the economy to decouple the economic growth and social well-being for people from the degradation of the environment, yet in addition, diminishes the earth's resources. This requires a principal pull together by the executives of public and private. Patterns like digitalization can positively or negatively contribute to sustainability, by making the production, transport, and trade sectors increase productivity or increase resource demand. It is important to improve the designs of end-users at large-scale worldwide. There is a need to deploy more integrated tools to cultivate circular economies that are characterized with utilizing less raw materials, components and products to reduce costs and possibly adopt renewable resources [4].

7.1.2.3 Biodiversity and ecosystems

In the specter of changing climate and high resource consumption pressure by humans and animals especially on food, fiber, fodder and other bio-products, the present-day unsustainable land use and water consumption are reducing the quality and levels of fresh-water and ground-water levels, compounding into land degradation, losses in biodiversity, unbalanced ecosystems and contributing 25% of the global greenhouse gas emissions. In the course of the most recent 40 years, both warm- and cold-blooded animals on land and in water have decreased by about 60% and may face extinction. Further, in excess of 800 million individuals are still malnourished and need access to clean water. The United Nations appraises that food creation should increment by half to fulfill the needs of anticipated populace development by 2050, which will likewise build the worldwide demand for water by over half. Creating supportable pathways to land, water, food, and biodiversity the board over all areas and strategy levels are key to overcoming the climate change-related issues that result from losses in biodiversity and ecosystems [30–32].

8. Sustainability drivers from leading firms: insights from stakeholder interviews

Some driving factors that influence sustainability in a firm include; politicking and governance issues, rapid urbanization, high population growth, societal and cultural norms and beliefs and climate change. These factors subsequently take a tore on the global socioeconomic and environmental objectives and interest to sustainably use and preserve natural resources. To successfully manage these driving factors there is need to engaging in stakeholder dialog while creating new reaction options and situations that help analyze the patterns of achieving sustainability. **Figure 3** shows the driving factors of sustainability dynamics model.

From the stakeholder interviews by Ernst and Young audit firm on a global audience of 1661 leaders and practitioners from 69 countries using a conference survey Approach showed that the trends that influential to sustainability include (a) insufficient gains from resource productivity, (b) extension of clean technologies

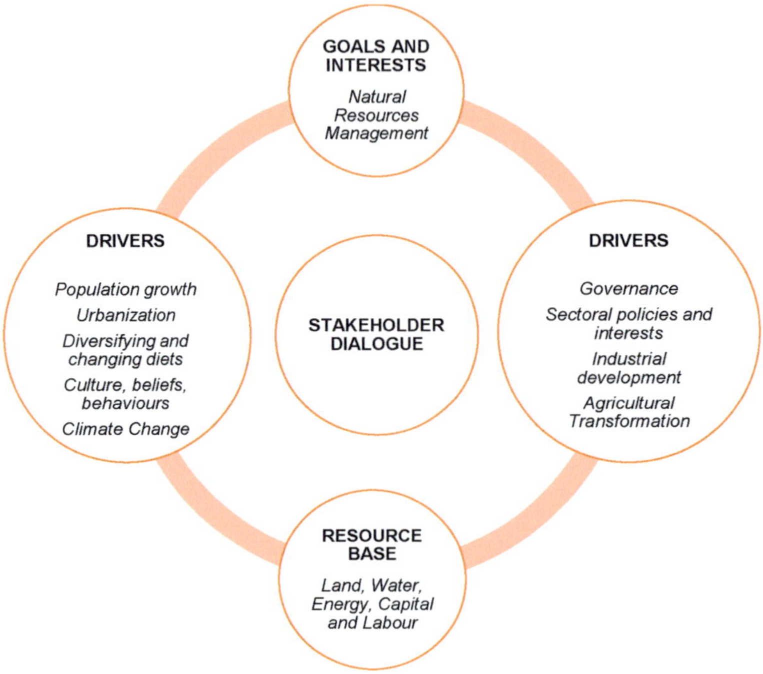

Figure 3.
Driving factors for sustainability dynamics, adopted from FAO [33].

approaches, (c) stiffer guidelines, (d) evaluating financial risks, (e) digitalization, (f) varying demands of clients, (g) war for ability, and (e) climate change, as assumed in **Figure 3** [34]. To reduce the financial risks to sustainability, there is a need to improve financing mechanisms for sustainable development.

9. Financing for sustainable development: new approach and commitment

Financing for sustainable development entered another era in July 2015, when the world consented to the Addis Ababa Action Agenda, a system and set of duties for financing the United Nations Sustainable Development Goals. Since this will require unquestionably more capital funds than help, in form of grants, the World Bank Group, along with other multilateral banks and the International Monitoring Fund (IMF), resolved to utilize billions in investment financing, aid and grants, in inventive approach to catalyze trillions in financing development programs. In 2017, in Hamburg, the world's G20 nations strengthened the task of catalyzing development finance by Multilateral Development Banks (MDBs), alongside public-private partnerships (PPPs) to newer forms of finance, including blended finance, as well as new bond instruments such as green bonds (GBs), social impact bonds (SIBs), and development impact bonds (DIBs). These new budgetary instruments are planned for expanding the flexibly of private cash-flow to developing countries and offer the critical potential to close the financing gap that right now exists in the developing countries. Specifically, mixed-finance is probably going to turn into a key segment in the financing for developed strategy and one of the primary mainstays of the global financing system created to help the post-2015 sustainable development agenda [35]. The Official Development Assistance (ODA), then again, is probably going to still be very important for developing nations since it gives 40% of money financial resource and, truth be told, the largest financer [36].

Notwithstanding worldwide public resources as ODA providing an essential input, nations have the essential obligation to progress and self-finance their own development. Nations must add to the progressions of Domestic Resource Mobilization (DRM)—as expenses, taxes, or other accessible assets—and guarantee that local policies like (legal, tax, institutional, economic, regulative, etc.) upgrade the viability of DRM, to maximize the utilization of this subsidy through national, provincial, at the city level, and down to municipal councils.

Further, to move from the "billions" in ODA to the "trillions" required for the implementation of the SDGs, the communities worldwide and especially in developing nations need to use various types of investment—including private, public, country, and international—and exploit the particular qualities and strengths of all the sources [35]. The following seven steps can serve as key enablers of the financing for development [37]:

i. Financial Resource Mobilization for increased impact using integrative thinking and creative approaches.

ii. Leveraging public finance by using scarce financial international and domestic resources where they have the greatest impact and this catalyzes other domestic financial resources.

iii. Overcrowding the private sector finances for development can help improve investment capacity to drive innovative programs and their delivery.

iv. Strengthening the multilateral development banks (MDBs) by utilizing their accounting reports and financial platforms catalyze private capital and other financial flows.

v. Technology and innovative business models offer extraordinary opportunities to rethink and quicken ways to development by making conceivable, a world with all-inclusive access to financial services and government services and global financial markets.

vi. Improving investment information, using big data, and innovative diagnostic devices are capable of evaluating investment risks and investment returns in developing countries.

vii. Enhancing development finance associations and building multi-partner forums. Another degree of joint effort is required over a scope of partners to address financing challenges.

10. How to operationalize countries with integrated financing models?

The four main stages for the design and operation of financing models comprise (a) evaluation and diagnostics, (b) the financing procedure, (c) monitoring and review, and (d) governance and coordination. **Figure 4** shows the stages of operationalizing financing mechanisms. **Figure 4** shows the stages of operationalizing financing mechanisms.

Figure 4 shows the operationalizing financing mechanisms that vary by nation, reflecting national limits and preferences. For instance, vulnerable nations may

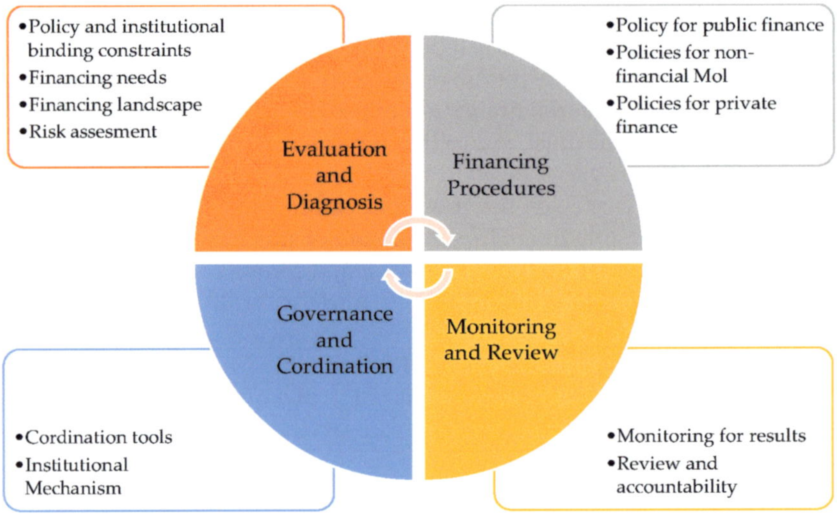

Figure 4.
Integrated operational financing model, adopted from Addis Ababa action agenda resolution [37].

underscore the significance of possible financing choices to have the option to react to financial stuns or shocks. Nations increasingly dependent on the arrangement of concessional funding may address arrangement of the development collaboration with country-specific needs. Nations with limited capacity may need to give priority to steps to reinforce their essential institutional capacities in key financing sectors, before attempting to actualize progressively to more complex tools. Expanding domestic resource mobilization is supposed to be every nation's priority, however, the approaches deployed are likely to vary to reflect the existing capacities and constraints [37, 38].

The stage of integrating the national finance models should be created iteratively, with each progression advising the others. The preferences communicated in the sustainable development financing procedures give the premise to the need's evaluation. Worth noting is that this evaluation is affected by the kind of financing. For instance, the expenses of private and public finance vary, because of having different rates of financing. Likewise, the financing system also affects the requirements for evaluation. For instance, policies that enhance economic activities may raise public resources, and this helps to bring down the financing gap. The monitoring and review sector give feedback, that can educate the evaluations and lead to various preferences. Then again, feeble monitoring and review can lead to policies becoming ineffective, increased need for financing and consequently influencing future policymaking. Further, this also leaves unlearned lessons. Finally, strong and good governance is significant because it offers a coordination instrument that manages this procedure all through the entirety of its stages [37, 38].

11. Conclusions

As the world faces several difficulties within the economic, social, and environmental sectors, the number of people who are still impoverished exceeds 1 billion. As if this is not enough, inequality, unsustainable consumption, and production have also been on the increase, and this has led to large economic and social costs that pose a threat to human and plant life on earth. Accomplishing global sustainable development requires the world to act toward the global goal to drive socioeconomic development strategically through enhanced financing and business opportunities that enhance economic growth and create more employment opportunities, while emphasizing the reinforcement of environmental protection.

The strategies toward sustainable social-economic and environmental systems through drivers and pressures, such as insightful policy reforms in institutions and governance systems, changing human behavior and societal norms, having strong data innovations and systems analytic capabilities, and changing ways of consumption and production, as well as widespread societal awareness building and mobilization should be highly upscaled globally to transform toward sustainability and achieve sustainable development. Sustainable development should be comprehensive and take into consideration the needs of vulnerable and poor people. The strategies developed or deployed should be goal-oriented and community-oriented to manage various degrees of development. They should fundamentally change their consumption and production patterns, inequality, and reinforce biodiversity restoration programs and this may involve, among other things, huge price/cost adjustments, safeguarding natural resources, decreasing existing disparities, and strengthening economic growth and improved governance systems using financing models for development. This points to Environmental Social Governance (ESG) investment approach as a powerful strategy for sustainable development investment. Recently, the Environmental Social Governance investing has gained traction and entails researching and factoring in environmental, social, and governance issues in addition to the usual financials because it reduces portfolio risk, generates competitive investment returns, and makes investors feel secure about their stocks in both developing and developed nations. It is recommended that ESG, financing for development, and 360-organizational sustainability should be adopted as core strategies by global investors and countries, respectively, to cultivate corporate shared values (CSVs) among all stakeholders and desist from the "business as usual" approach, which works against sustainable development.

In summary, it can be stated that for an organization to be sustainable and meet their objectives profitably, they should adopt the mid-path that ensures an adequate balance between profitability and sustainability. Thus, companies must be innovative and agile to changes. For this, a clear set of sustainability and resilience criteria will help the companies to improve, while leaving room to respond to these pressures with different options and sustainable models. The significance of these models is that they provide insight to policymakers to achieve sustainable development change using development financing models that enhance acceptable attitudes, sustainable production and consumption, and a clean environment while ensuring that companies still operate profitably.

Acknowledgements

I recognize and acknowledge Professor Valerie M. Thomas of Georgia Institute of Technology, USA, and the African Centre of Excellence in Energy for Sustainable Development at the University of Rwanda for their support.

Conflict of interest

The author declares no conflict of interest.

Author details

Katundu Imasiku
University of Rwanda, Kigali, Rwanda

*Address all correspondence to: katunduimasiku@gmail.com

References

[1] Brundtland Commission. Our Common Future: Report of the World Commission on Environment and Development. UN Documents Gathering a Body of Global Agreements. New York: Oxford University Press; 1987

[2] Department of Agriculture Water and the Environment – Australia. Ecological Sustainable Development. 1992. Available from: https://www.environment.gov.au/about-us/esd [Accessed: 23 July 2020]

[3] Freedman B. Ecologically sustainable development. In: Environmental Science Subtitle: A Canadian Perspective. Ontario: Open Library Publishing Platform; 2018

[4] United Nations. World Economic and Social Survey 2013 Sustainable Development Challenges. New York: United Nations; 2013

[5] Soyka PA. Creating a Sustainable Organization: Approaches for Enhancing Corporate Value through Sustainability. New Jersey: Pearson Education, Inc. Publishing; 2012

[6] Jütting JP, de Laiglesia JR, editors. Is Informal Normal? Towards More and Better Jobs in Developing Countries. Paris: OECD; 2009

[7] Sustainable Development Goals Platform. United Nations Conference on Sustainable Development, Rio+20. 2012. Available from: https://sustainabledevelopment.un.org/rio20. [Accessed: 23 July 2020]

[8] Government of Nepal - National Planning. Post Disaster Needs Assessment. Ontario, Canada: Western University in London; 2015. Available from: https://iveybusinessjournal.com/publication/building-360-organizational-sustainability/

[9] Cultural and Survival. Water Crisis Forces Government Action. 2018. Available: https://www.culturalsurvival.org/news/water-crisis-forces-government-action [Accessed: 23 July 2020]

[10] Pierre O, Longueville F. The tsunami in South-East Asia – A retrospective analysis of the management of an apocalyptic natural disaster. European Journal of Geography. [Online], Environment, Nature, Landscape, document 321. 2011. DOI: 10.4000/cybergeo.3081. Available from: http://journals.openedition.org/cybergeo/3081

[11] Kublik A. The Government Is Pouring Billions of Zlotys on Mining, Public Media and Morawiecki's Agencies; 2018. Available from: https://wyborcza.pl/7,155287,22566805,rzad-sypnie-miliardami-zlotych-na-gornictwo-media-publiczne.html

[12] Mikulska A, Eryk K. Explaining Poland's Coal Paradox. 2018. Available from: https://www.forbes.com/sites/thebakersinstitute/2018/03/28/explaining-polands-coal-paradox/#6abd71f04867 [Accessed: 21 July 2020]

[13] Andvig JC, Odd-Helge F, Amundsen I, Sissener T, Søreide T. Corruption: A Review of Contemporary Research. Bergen: Norwegian Institute of International Affairs; 2001. Available from: http://hdl.handle.net/11250/2393361

[14] UKaid. Development Tracker. 2020. Available from: https://devtracker.dfid.gov.uk/countries/NP [Accessed: 23 July 2020]

[15] UNECA. Combating Corruption, Improving Governance in Africa. Addis Ababa: UNECA; 2016

[16] Rapid Translation Alliance. Buen Vivir: The Rights of Nature in Bolivia and Ecuador. 2018. Available from: https://www.rapidtransition.org/stories/the-rights-of-nature-in-bolivia-and-ecuador/ [Accessed: 25 July 2020]

[17] Hammond JL. Indigenous community justice in the Bolivian constitution of 2009. Human Rights Quarterly. 2011;**33**(3):649-681

[18] Cedric P. Sustainable Cities in Developing Nations: Theory and Practiceatthe Millennium. London: Earthscan PublicationsLtd; 2000

[19] Peris-ortiz M, Bennett DR. Sustainable Smart Cities: Creating Spaces for Technological, Social and Business Development. Valencia: Springer; 2017

[20] Mark H. Building 360 organizational sustainability. Product Number: 9B09TF07. Ivey Business Journal. 2000:1-10. Available from: https://iveybusinessjournal.com/publication/building-360-organizational-sustainability/ [Accessed: 11 January 2009]

[21] Melkonyan A, Gottschalk D, Vasanth KV. Sustainability assessments and their implementation possibilities within the business models of companies. Sustainable Production and Consumption. 2017;**12**:1-15

[22] Rensburg R. Archbishop Desmond tutu as moral sage and servantleader: A compassionate zealot. Verbum et Ecclesia. 2002;**23**(3):1-16

[23] Chatterji M. Why is Sustainability the Need of the Hour for Businesses. Entrepreneur India. 2017. Available from: https://www.entrepreneur.com/article/302070 [Accessed: 20 June 2020]

[24] Imasiku K, Thomas V, Etienne N. Unraveling green information technology systems as a global greenhouse gas emission game-changer. Administrative Sciences. 2019;**9**(43):1-29

[25] IIASA. Reducing Footprints, Enhancing Resilience Systems Science for Transformations to Sustainability IIASA Strategy 2021-2030. Vienna: IIASA; 2021

[26] Greenwood R, Oliver C, Lawrence TB, Meyer RE, editors. Tha SAGE Handbook of Organizational Institutionalism. 2nd ed. Los Angeles, London, New Delhi: SAGE; 2017

[27] Lozano R, Garcia I. Scrutinizing sustainability change and its institutionalization in organizations. Frontiers. 2020;**1**(1):1-16

[28] Walker J, Alma P, Gordon W, editors. Sustainable Development Goals: Harnessing Business to Achieve the Sustainable Development Goals through Technology, Innovation and Law Reforms. Wiley, New Jersey: Sussex; 2019. pp. 1-432. ISBN: 978-1-119-54180-6. Available from: https://books.google.rw/books/about/Sustainable_Development_Goals.html?id=UKCkDwAAQBAJ&redir_esc=y

[29] Filho WL, de Brito PRB, Fernanda F, editors. International Business, Trade and Institutional Sustainability. Cham, Switzerland: SAGE; 2019

[30] FAO. State of the World's Forests and Agriculture: Land-Use Challenges and Opportunities State of the World's Forests. Rome: FAO; 2016

[31] FAO. World Deforestation Slows down as More Forests Are Better Managed. 2016. Available from: http://www.fao.org/news/story/en/item/326911/icode/ [Accessed: 24 July 2020]

[32] Alcamo J et al. Ecosystems and Human Well-Being: A Framework for Assessment. Washington, DC, London, Covelo: Island Press; 2003. ISBN 1-55963-403-0

[33] FAO. Food and Agriculture Organization: Driving Action across the 2030 Agenda for Sustainable Development. Rome: FAO; 2017. p. 2020. Available from: http://www.fao.org/3/a-i7454e.pdf [Accessed: 01 July 2017]

[34] Ernst and Young. Sustainability Reporting — The Time Is Now. London: Ernst and Young; 2014

[35] OECD. Blended Finance Vol. 1: A Primer for Development Finance and Philanthropic Funders. Cologny: OECD; 2015

[36] United Nations. Report of the Intergovernmental Committee of Experts on Sustainable Development Financing, See Note 5, 14. United Nations; 2014

[37] World Bank. Financing for Development at the World Bank Group; 2018

[38] United Nations. Financing for Sustainable Development Report. United Nations; 2019. p. 2019

Chapter 2

Workplace Innovation for Social Sustainable Development

Kassu Jilcha

Abstract

The purpose of this chapter is to discuss the importance of workplace innovation to sustainable development of the organizational change process. Workplace innovation has been distinguished from the technical innovation and its significance to intangible service improvements. It has addressed how sustainable development is affected by workplace safety, health, productivity, and wellbeing at the workplace. The chapter also attempted to see the three pillars of sustainable development against the six pillars of sustainable development dimensions from prospective points of the previous studies. The previous studies' findings considered sustainable development dimensions as economic, social, and environmental dimension, while the recent study has introduced additional three new sustainable development dimensions emanating from the existing dimension such as cultural, political and technological dimensions. Therefore, the paper tried to address the workplace innovation, its importance, model, and its impact on sustainable development of the global society.

Keywords: workplace, innovation, sustainable development, workplace innovation, dimensions, pillars

1. Introduction

Due to the growing market of employment, the Workplace issue needs to be given serious attention [1, 2]. Research findings distinguished that workplace organization, layout, human resource management, top management, workers' participation, policy and training were overlooked areas in spite of considering the need for strong workplace safety and health improvements approaches through innovative approaches. At various levels, especially at the national level, OSH problems lack top management commitment, national policy and uniform standards. In addition to these factors, absence of awareness within the enterprise, organizations and at individual employees' level, dearth of cultural norms of workplace health and safety are areas missed unconsidered for the workplace improvement.

The hazards which require innovation at workplace can be classified as health hazards and physical hazards [3]. Health hazards are categorized into; biological hazards such as bacteria, fungi and viral; chemical hazards such as fumes, dusts, smokes, gases, vapors, heavy metals and physical hazards such as noise, temperature, illumination, vibration and radiation. All the mentioned types of workplace hazards which cause stress on our employees can be handled by the science the so-called workplace innovation even though it is a recent emerging workplace improving science.

Workplace in globe is the place where the interaction of people and machine or equipment involves. Unless and otherwise workplace being attractive, safe, healthy and productive for the citizen, it results in disruption of the whole economy and social values in a globe. To bring the workplace productivity and safe workplace to flexible quality, the timely tool is innovation that looks into the mechanism that changes the dynamic workplace movements. The workplace innovation for any organization improvement in productivity and safety of well-being is one of the key variables. This leads the globe and citizens to sustainable development. The outbreaks like COVID-19 have more negative impact on workplace and productivity of the employees. To curb such sudden and unpredictable outbreaks, workplace innovation is very important in setting a new mechanism how to work in controlling such outbreaks to sustain the economy of globe. Therefore, this chapter helps to show new focus points were our globe is changing dynamically with outbreaks. The outbreaks such as COVID-19 or other that may arise in the future should have to be addressed how to challenge this at workplace before it emerges. That is an important issue to consider workplace innovation and consider sustainable development of the society.

2. How to designate workplace

Workplace is the environment where people participate and do their operation in their day to day life activities. Workplace can be related with organizational behavior, organizational culture, organizational motivation and conflict. Among the most important variables and considerations of workplace one is workplace safety and health (WSH). WSH issue is remained a neglected socio-economic development priority, particularly in developing countries including Africa. Occupational safety and health (OSH) are becoming priority areas of concern within the spheres of industrialization and the labor market that requires workplace revolution. This is because of industrialization all over the world is developing at a debauched rate and the labor market continues to upsurge. Due to the growing market of employment, the OSH issue needs to be given serious attention [2] at workplace environment. In this chapter, we can distinguish and see that workplace organization, layout, human resource management, top management, workers' participation, policy and training are some of the areas were overlooked in previous studies that are under studied in spite of considering the need for strong WSH improvements approaches. At various levels, especially at the national level of developing countries, OSH problems lack top management commitment, national policy and uniform standards implementation. In addition to these factors, absences of awareness within the enterprise, organizations and at individual employee's level, dearth of cultural norms of WSH are areas missed and unnoticed in the workplace improvement process.

It can be seen that occupational health and safety is the concern of human wellbeing that, this day, industrialization and service giving sectors development is accelerating resulting in workplace health problems. WSH existence is in line with the sayings that "Health is Wealth" [4, 5]. In recent years, the quality of health and safety requirements in many countries have been more stringent than was the case before. Hence, pressures from communities have led to the enactment of various safety legislations and safety standards in different countries and regions for different industries [6]. Despite the fact that people are working and spending most of their working hours at the workplace, little attention and resources are accorded to health and safety at workplace [7, 8].

In emerging economies, workplace has been overlooked in their industrial development policies and strategies. They are mostly focused on the production volume or profit undermining the latent effect of unsatisfactory working environment. For instance, in some of African countries like Ethiopia, there had been no workplace policy standing alone for the manufacturing industries and other sectors that enforce WSH of employees and working equipment. Healthy people are expected to contribute more to productivity and innovation. Workplace accidents and absenteeism from workplace site causes productivity loss [8, 9]. The productivity directly related to workplace comfort and work behavior in the organization. Specially, employee productivity and performance increase when there is less conflict, high motivation, good workplace culture, dynamic teamwork and social interaction.

Workplace design and hazards interventions have been seen as barriers in researches. Miroslav et al. [10] found in their studies that barriers identified in manufacturing industries, which need innovation. In this chapter, the barriers identified to intervention of workplace safety and health were negative managements' attitude, negative workers attitudes, ineffective or excessive legal requirements, bureaucracy, lack of time, lack of training, lack of economic resources, lack of economic results, presence of geographical delocalized activities, and workers participation [11].

While research conducted on WSH spans across disciplines in medicine, public health, engineering, psychology, and business, researches to date have not adopted a multilevel theoretical perspective that integrates theoretical issues and findings from various disciplines [7]. Nowadays, researches require improving workplace as time bringing new scenarios. The emergency of COVID-19 is one of good example that is changing the global economic and social set up. The workplace innovation is, therefore, very important with regard to this COVID-19 to learn and prepare ourselves to tackle such pandemic situation. Hence, a learning organization is very important in the future global development process to keep sustainable development environment. Learning organization is an organization that promotes management tools concerned with the improvement of individual and organizational learning [12]. This learning organizational process helps the globe to predict new ventures that may happen suddenly and change the global economic, social, cultural, technological, political and environmental dimensions. According to the study of Agneta et al. [13] implementing social sustainable innovation is important for industrial development of workplace environment.

3. Innovation for workplace safety

Under this subtopic, it can be seen in subsection of innovation and workplace innovation. This section is presented to show the clear description of innovation, workplace innovation and safety at workplace.

3.1 Innovation

Studies have shown that innovation was first introduced by Joseph Schumpeter in 1934 and the researchers call this man as father of Innovation [14]. As researchers put forward their point that Schumper argued that economic development is driven by innovation by a process of "creative destruction." They said that he argued innovations could be considered "radical" when people generate major disruptive changes, while if these innovations produced small improvements generating a slow change process that people could be considered "incremental." Joseph Schumpeter [14] finally proposed five types of innovations which are (1) introduction of new products, (2) introduction of new methods of production, (3) opening new markets, (4) development of new sources for raw materials or other inputs; and

(5) creation of new market structures in an industry. In this study, we can understand that more of the discussion and division focuses more on product process that unnoticed the workplace services and intangible environmental factors innovation.

The Oslo Manual defines innovation as the implementation of a new or significantly improved product (good or service), or process, a new marketing method, or a new organizational method in business practices, workplace organization or external relations. Thus, the manual moves away from Shumpeter's typology and reduces it to four types which are (1) product and services innovations; (2) process innovations; (3) organizational innovation; and (4) marketing innovations. Here, we can also see that social innovation or workplace innovation is less considered.

According to the previous researchers finding, innovation was considered as a phenomenon which for centuries serves the only purpose of making human beings' lives more comfortable [15]. The same study has considered it as a history, supporting, generating and implementing innovation has been of outstanding importance not only for the well-being but sometimes the survival of individuals, entities and even for whole civilizations and nations. However, innovation is the process of creation, improvement, or adopting new ideas that does not exist in another workplace.

3.2 Workplace innovation (WPI)

Workplace innovation (WPI) definition is adopted from Pot [16] that is defined WPI as the implementation of new and combined interventions in the fields of work organization, human resource management and supportive technologies. He added that it is a complementary to technological innovation even though it was unnoticed as being a basic workplace environment comfort forming process.

Workplace innovation (WPI) brings radical change in the workers' environment, thereby enhancing the profitability of companies [1]. It can be said that the term workplace innovation refers to how people are deployed in order to improve performance and also to create good quality jobs [17].

Study also defined workplace innovation (WPI) as conceptualized, developed and implemented practice or combination of practices that structurally makes division of labor and/or culturally focuses on empowerment enabling employees to participate in organizational change and renewal to improve quality of working life and organizational performance [7, 18, 19]. WPI is narrowed down as an 'HR-toy' which is resulted decision makers on technological innovation, business model innovation and marketing innovation underestimate and underuse the potential of WPI, as they are largely unaware of the role of organization and people to make nontechnical innovations a success [6, 8]. They stated that within organizations, HR-managers and line- and operational managers too strongly function within separate silos. The technological and economic innovation alone is insufficient to solve today's social issues, like poverty, environmental pollution, climate control, and geopolitical tensions [20, 21]. WPI is defined as designate new and combined interventions in work organization, human resource management, labor relations and supportive technologies [22]. Workplace Innovation is defined as a social process which shapes work organization and working life, combining their human, organizational and technological dimensions. We can see examples which are including participative job design, self-organized teams, continuous improvement, and high involvement in innovation and employee involvement in corporate decision making. Such interventions are highly participatory, integrating the knowledge, experience, and creativity of management and employees at all levels of the organization in a process of co-creation and co-design. This simultaneously results in improved organizational performance and enhanced quality of working life. It is important to see Workplace Innovation not as an end state but as a dynamic, reflexive process in which all stakeholders are continually engaged in reflecting on, learning about and transforming work processes and employment practices in response to both internal and external drivers. Workplace Innovation is to contribute to sustainable economics, ecological and social change by fostering the innovative capacity of organizations and individuals. Workplace Innovation is considered a necessary enabler of effective technological innovation. Developing and deploying human talent and fostering a willingness to cooperate are an indispensable component of a versatile network economy, relying heavily on participation, dialog and self-organization by engaged individuals working in and between organizations.

3.3 Workplace safety innovation importance and OSH influence

3.3.1 Workplace innovation importance

Workplace innovation was defined as the process of improving or creating workplace interaction confortable for the organizations. Workplace safety and health needs to be prior area for productivity, workplace comfort and wellbeing improvement. Industrial safety is the focuses on multiple improvements were over all organization involvement based on. In workplace there are numbers of challenges like conflict, health issue, safety, performance and grievance. In general to solve organizational behaviors that results in ill health and performance reduction, workplace innovation has importance. Some of the importance of workplace innovations are sustainability for financial success strategically implementing the social innovation dimension as an integrated part of business operations; sustainable development, increasing the quality of human resources which is a key competitive issue, requiring constant management attention to several dimensions of economic, social, and environmental change; workplace innovations complement economic innovations and are focused primarily on achieving social welfare [23]; improve service of workplace. Innovative workplace helps in increasing workers performance, creating bonds among workers and amendment of managements, upgrading productivity, insuring health and safety of employee, reducing safety cost due to accidents and injuries at work, improving organizational culture toward hard work, building the organization to team up in solving innovative problems, reducing conflicts and increasing motivation, enhancing environmental protection through social corporate integration and enhancing technical innovation success. Therefore, workplace innovation covers broader areas of improvement even though it not defined as technical innovation that commercialize product to the market.

3.3.2 Workplace innovation and its influence on OSH

As stated in the previous sections, innovations have the score to optimize manufacturing processes in workplaces in organizations and develop employees' general experience of work. Here, employers' association, employer and trade unions have a significant part to play in promoting work organization innovations, which can provide win–win benefits for employees and employers. Change comes when we are working smarter, not harder [3, 24]. Higher productivity goes hand in hand with better communication and higher employability, resulting from both a decrease in absenteeism and an increase in social and vocational competences [25]. **Figure 1** indicates that WPI empowers performance of work organization, and employee relationship increasing well-being and OSH final achievement of health condition. The intersection of OSH and WPI is the overall improvement of well-being.

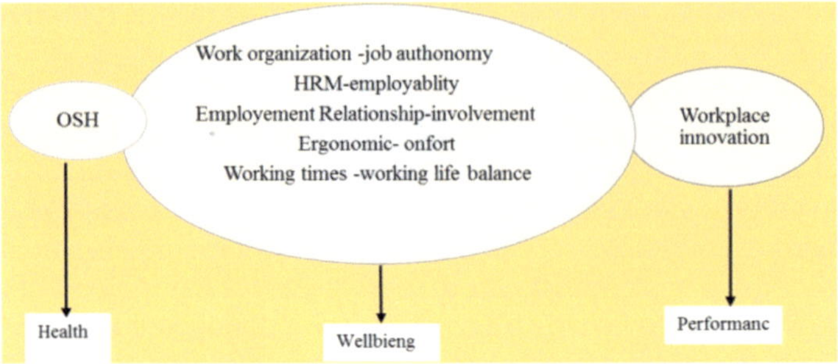

Figure 1.
Overlap of OSH and workplace innovation (Leiven, 2012).

WPI and OSH have different policies with different objectives and instruments. It should not mix up as WPI is not directed at fewer OAs or ODs or less absenteeism, but it might help. OSH policies refer to healthy and productive jobs. Health is a value in itself. Additionally, healthy people are expected to contribute more to productivity and innovation. Absenteeism causes productivity loss [22]. A healthy workforce is a prerequisite for social and economic development and for productivity. Protecting the health of the workforce through access to decent jobs, universally available health services, and social health protection contributes both to sustainable development as well as to worker productivity [26]. Hazardous working conditions and unemployment currently contribute to a very large avoidable burden of disease and loss of income-earning potential [27]. In the discussions made previously, workplace innovation contribution is remarkable.

In solving OSH problems, one of the methods is workplace innovation (WPI). WIP is different from technical innovation (scientific technologies) in which new end product or a service development process is undertaken, rather than nontechnical innovation (supportive technologies). It is defined by Pot [16] as the implementation of new and combined interventions in the fields of work organization, human resource management and supportive technologies. It is a complementary to use technological innovation. The chapter stresses new and combined interventions, by which new is understood as innovation and combined as a bundle of measures referring to work organization, human resource management and supportive technologies. Thus, innovation is not a goal but a means in which it improves a process performance [3]. There is a growing importance of nontechnical factors to foster economic growth; implying technological innovation alone is not enough to make renewal of an organization's work. It needs efforts of looking into overall process optimization and changing organizational systems. Innovations considered as nontechnical factors are for, instance, high performance work systems and new ways of working. Such nontechnical innovations are considered by studies interchangeably as organizational innovation [20, 28], workplace innovation [16, 22], and social innovation in the workplace [24, 25, 29, 30]. These innovations are neither the end products (new products or services), nor the Research and Development expenditures. But they deal with renewal and improvement of the deployment of people, management, human resource, organizational structure, primary process, marketing methods, production methods, organizational policies, redesigning, workplace improvements and refreshment of systems.

The major problems which are not addressed in workplace improvement are workplace innovation and the meaning it conveys in recent times. Innovation was painstaking and it is the only new idea creation and/or new product development process as discussed under many literature reviews. Hence, workplace innovation was not stated well in the research findings like that of ordinary innovation [3].

The author of this study has identified workplace innovation being ignored in OSH improvement system one of the remaining improvement factors [1, 25].

This study defined how workplace safety and health is influenced by workplace innovation, and how workplace innovation contributes to workplace overall improvements. The systematic review has summarized the recent scientific evidence on the effectiveness of the innovation impact on workplace safety and health. The review also reflected the relationships between innovation and OSH problem contributing factors [1, 22]. The present systematic review is thus an attempt to address the challenge and fill the gap that exists on the relationship and impact of innovation in relation to workplace safety and health overall characteristics for controlling of occupational accidents and diseases in the workplace.

Competitiveness is not achieved without innovation, technology and the use of science aggregation in workplace safety and health improvement as one of the typical business processes indication [1, 3]. Researchers wind-up their results that in organizational innovation, it is possible to see into workplace arrangement, attractiveness and employee satisfaction with the work they are doing.

In general, workplace innovations were found to play a key role in decreasing workforce and increasing labor productivity; global competition and knowledge based economy (development of competence and skills); making new technology work through innovative work organization [1]. Workplace innovation explains a larger part of innovation success than technological innovation; high performance work systems have a positive effect on performance outcomes (including labor productivity, and innovation levels); diversity and equality systems have a positive effect as well; on reduced employee turnover (considered to be an indicator for employee wellbeing).

Workplace innovation helps to improve workplace performance, quality of working life, human resource management, and policy issues. European countries are initiating these workplace innovation programmes [22]. Therefore, workplace innovation programme is indispensable for the policymakers to improve workplace safety and health. Studies indicate that workplace innovation and safety issues have been ignored in developing countries. Therefore, this calls for the need to continue conducting research in the future to modernize workplace safety and health improvements. At the same time, this section highlights the workplace innovation is one of the methods to OSH improvement approaches (**Figure 2**). This is a section where it is important to come out from the black box and extend our research approaches to diversified factors with different tools looking forward to dynamic changes to meet the demands of globalization. Workplace innovation needs human resources, technology and knowledge. The presences of these drivers

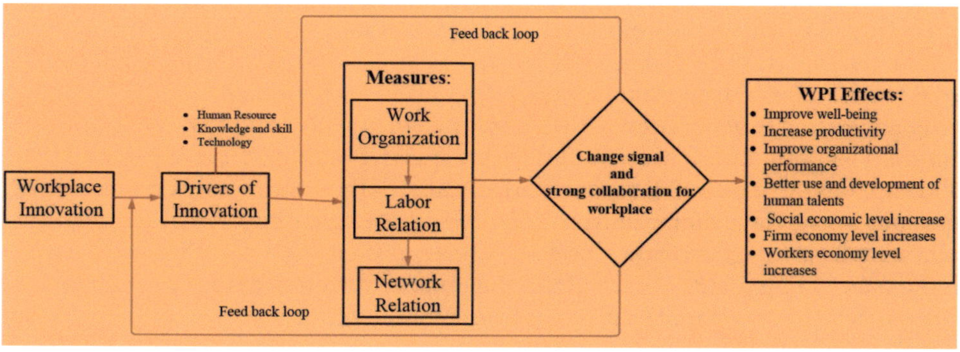

Figure 2.
Modified model of workplace innovation at the organization level [1].

of innovation are the primary inputs of workplace innovation. The measures or initiatives within the model of workplace innovation are divided into three elements; namely work organization, labor relations and network relations. Work organization focuses tasks to be accomplished with autonomy, on opportunities to work either together or independently on employees' choice to determine their working hours in consultation. It means work is facilitated or made flexible by using ICT, among other things and employees spend part of their working hours on developing new ideas, while diverse workforce uses its time and lobor effectively. Meanwhile the logistical processes are organized as efficiently as possible in consultation with employees.

The second element refers to giving high priority to labor relations. This means focusing on employees and management jointly formulating the organization's ambitions, with employees having a say in the organization and its decisions, management and employees encouraging each other to learn innovate and to show creativity, and daring, and most importantly, management and employees trusting each other in undertaking joint endeavors. It also means employees having autonomy in managing their tasks, employees and managers admitting their mistakes and taking corrective measures in time. The third major element is that of prioritizing network linkage both inside and outside the firm. They focus on components within the organization to work with peers and partners such as suppliers, clients, and people in the community, etc. Knowledge organizations are involved to deal with community and social issues by strengthening and multiplying the ties within the networks.

The model then looks at the goals or desired effects of workplace innovation. These effects can be of direct benefit to the organization and/or employees or be indirectly beneficial to society (**Figure 2**). The workplace innovation goals are aimed at to improving organizational, employee and or societal benefits.

The workplace innovation improves workplace condition and employee's moral. The process needs to have cyclical check at each stage of improvement. The approach creates workplace innovation with positive effects. These effects are improved well-being, productivity, organizational performance, better use and development of human talents, and increase in economic levels attributed to firms, workers and the society in general.

4. Sustainable development

4.1 Sustainability development importance and pillars

Sustainable development is the important aspect of the global society to overcome all the challenges of the citizen's health, safety, wellbeing and overall productivity performance. Sustainable can be defined as foundation of the citizens economic, social and environmental set up continuous existence and transition after generation to generation without major change from now onward in the future. This definition is drawn out from prospective point of view of Mirland [31] and Amponsah-Tawiah [32] model. Both of them defined sustainable development depends on the three dimensions or pillars which are economic, social and environmental. The one that make this definition to most of the researchers common is the intersecting points at each dimension in providing a clear picture to their sustainability dimension. For instance, the common area between economic and social dimension is social equity and the common point of economic and environmental dimension is results in sustainable economy of the citizen. The social and environmental intersection ends up with healthy environment that is not polluted and convenient to all life on the earth. The economic dimension includes the jobs, employment, capital assets, investment, creation of worth & prosperity; the environmental dimensions include climate, water, natural resources and biodiversity while that of social dimension encompasses the elements such as health and safety, skilled work force, knowledge workers, community development, inclusion and cohesion. It can be learned that from **Figure 3** the link and the results of the integration of the three dimensions mentioned in the discussion are the indication of sustainable development pillars with the so far studies finding. However, there is another approach which viewed the sustainable development pillars in other angle introducing other factors.

The previous studies conducted on OSH link with sustainable development showed that there are three pillars of sustainable development as economic, environment and society [1]. The studies have unnoticed that culture, politics and technology are the three new pillars as stated by the researches [1]. These researchers tried to include the other three new dimensions to sustainable development pillars mentioned in the previous researchers finding. These were culture, technology and political dimensions.

How culture affect sustainable development of workplace can be described in short. Culture of workplace involvement induces positive or negative effect on productivity, safety and health of the organization. The culture of safety practice and workplace comfort to employees is the one as a dimension. We can say social dimension can consolidate culture but the culture of workplace safety and health improvement to ward productivity improvement was summered by other social factors. For that purpose, culture of workplace safety and health is demanded to stand as individual dimension. The other dimension which is not considered boldly was technological change. The technological development and introduction of new advanced systems enforced the globe to enhance workplace improvement. The technological dimension also considered as a pillar since the chronological changes are bringing to the globe different technological usage and utilization. But the uses and impact of technology was not considered as sustainable development pillar as it was not boldly shown in the researches and practice. The third new dimension introduced as pillar of sustainable development is political dimension. The globe is swaying by the different political challenges. It has not been considered as the one

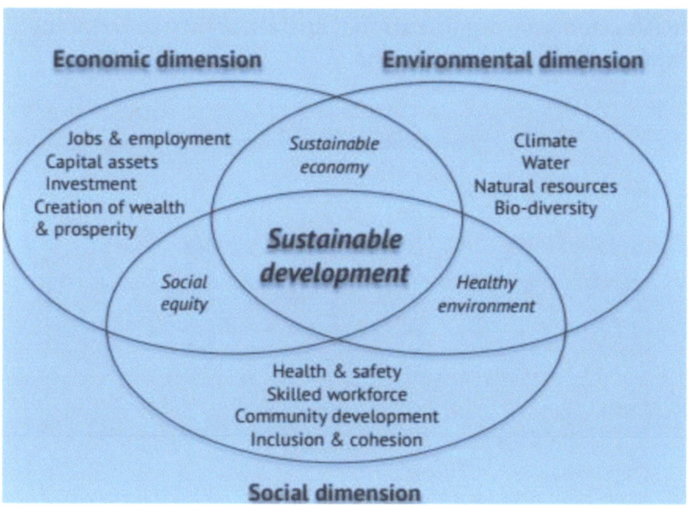

Figure 3.
The three dimensions of sustainable development [31, 32].

of the dimensions that affects sustainable development. The evidences and analysis of these newly introduced factors can be seen in the article cited in [1, 33]. The six pillars introduced and the existing once is indicated in **Figure 4**.

The impact of human behavior (culture) on nature gives increasing rise to public and governmental concern [34]. A learning culture, defined as set of shared beliefs, values and attitudes favorable to learning can be seen as an essential part of the organizational context within which specific organizational design principles and types of work organization are successfully implemented [12].

4.2 Workplace sustainability and workplace safety

It is very important to ask the question what are the key considerations workplace designers take into account when designing and building sustainable workplaces of the future? Sustainability in the workplace has the potential to affect many aspects of an organization, including employee productivity [35]. According to the same study [35] sustainable designers, such as LEED (Leadership in Energy and Environmental Design) professionals, claim that sustainability has numerous positive impacts in the workplace and they impact including fewer employee sick leaves days, increased building occupant satisfaction, and increased employee productivity. The workplace safety matters the organizational productivity increment and wellbeing. The workplace well designed and built, creates high productivity of employees, keep the health of employees and reduce the cost of the organizations that incurred due to the accidents at workplace. This results in increased organizational sustainable economy. A bad office can really impact on output and happiness. The workplaces designed and prepared for employees must meet the mind and physical of the employees so that they are healthy, happy, comfortable and psychological in rest. To create a space that truly encourages a culture of wellness for employees, it is critical to identify the organization's project goals and needs through a process that emphasizes collaboration, consensus building, and innovation. The sustainability of organization is guaranteed when we do have people-oriented workplace design. To make workplace more productive and sustainable for the organization, it is important to focus on the psychological benefits and the wellbeing of workers; how technology integrates and enhances workflow; and the sustainability of the initial build and ongoing maintenance. Hence, the safest workplace design guarantees the employees satisfaction and organizational sustainability in reducing overall costs that comes from multifaceted directions.

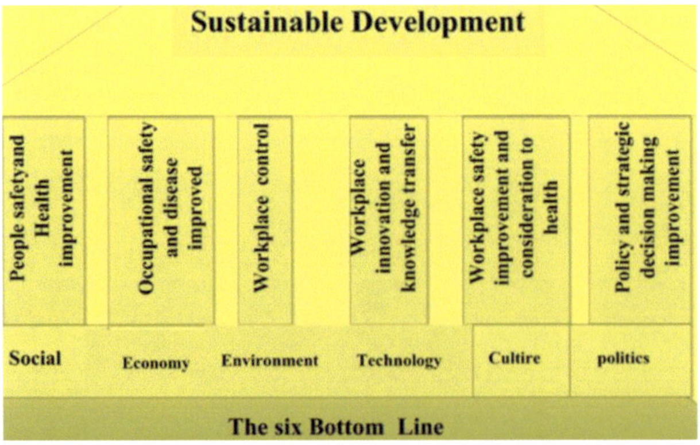

Figure 4.
Pillars of sustainable development and approaches to safety and health [1].

5. Conclusion

In general, we can conclude that this chapter has given the highlight of workplace innovation for sustainable development putting ignition toward in-depth research works by many researchers. It has focused on the workplace innovation and sustainable development in consideration of workplace innovation and technical innovation differences and importance. Sustainable development dimensions are also discussed from the point of three pillars and six pillars with their differences. The dimensions in the previous study mentioned are environmental, social, and economic dimensions. The new three introduced in addition to these are cultural, political, and technological dimensions. These areas are very crucial to focus in the future research to see one by one in detail and their individual advantages and disadvantages. The workplace innovation contribution is also discussed with respect to workplace safety and health, social corporate, and importance in industrial development. The workplace innovation and technical innovation difference and contribution have been considered even though they require further studies.

Conflict of interest

The authors declare that there is no conflict of interest.

Author details

Kassu Jilcha
School of Mechanical and Industrial engineering, Addis Ababa Institute of Technology, Addis Ababa University, Addis Ababa, Ethiopia

*Address all correspondence to: jkassu@gmail.com

References

[1] Jilcha K, Kitaw D. A literature review on global occupational safety and health practice & accidents severity. International Journal for Quality Research. 2016;**10**(2):279-310

[2] Jilcha K, Kitaw D, Beshah B. Workplace innovation influence on occupational safety and health. African Journal of Science, Technology, Innovation and Development. 2016;**8**(1):33-42

[3] Jilcha K. An integrated approach of occupational safety and health practice for Ethiopian manufacturing industries [thesis]. Addis Ababa Institute of Technology: Addis Ababa University. Ethiopia; 2006

[4] Villasor R, Cesar C, Regina S. Health Is Wealth: Measuring the Roles of Income and Spending on Life Expectancy in the U.S. De La Salle University; 2015

[5] Kifle M, Engdaw D, Alemu K, Sharma HR, Amsalu S, Anielski M. The Meaning of Wealth. School of Business. Washington: University of Alberta and ecological economics at the new Bainbridge Graduate Institute near Seattle; 2003

[6] Dejoy DM, Southern DJ. An integrative perspective on worksite health promotion. Journal of Occupational Medicine. 1993;**35**(12):1221-1230

[7] Burke MJ, Signal SM. Workplace safety: A multilevel, interdisciplinary perspective. Research in Personnel and Human Resources Management. 2015;**29**:1-47

[8] Michaels D, Barrera C, Gacharna MG. Economic development and occupational health in Latin America: New directions for public health in less developed countries. American Journal of Public Health. 1985;**75**:536-542

[9] Pot F, Dhondt S, Oeij P. Social innovation of work and employment. In: Franz HW, Hochgerner& J, Howaldt J, editors. Challenge Social Innovation. Potential for Business, Social Entrepreneurship, Welfare and Civil Society. Berlin: Springer Verlag; 2012

[10] Beblavý M, Maselli I, Martellucci E. Workplace Innovation and Technological Change; Working Paper No. 65. Brussels, Belgium: Centre for European Policy Studies; 2014

[11] Podgórski D. Measuring operational performance of OSH management system – A demonstration of AHP-based selection of leading key performance indicators. Safety Science. 2015;**73**:146-166

[12] OECD. Innovative Workplaces: Making Better Use of Skills within Organisations. OECD Publishing; 2010

[13] Sundström A, Ahmadi Z, Mickelsson K. Implementing social sustainability for innovative industrial work environments. Sustainability. 2019;**11**:3402. DOI: 10.3390/su11123402

[14] Vilanova M, Dettoni P. Sustainable Innovation Strategies, Exploring the Cases of Danone and Interface. Barcelona: Institute for Social Innovation, ESADE, Ramol Llull University; 2011

[15] Meissner and Kotsemir. Conceptualizing the innovation process towards the 'active innovation paradigm'—Trends and outlook. Journal of Innovation and Entrepreneurship. 2016;**5**:14. DOI: 10.1186/s13731-016-0042-z

[16] Pot FD. Workplace innovation for better jobs and performance. International Journal of Productivity and Performance Management: 2011;**64**(4):404-415. http://dx.doi.org/10.1108/ 17410401111123562

[17] De Sitter U. Human resources mobilization: Setting the stage for organizational innovation. In: Andreasen LE, Coriat B, den Hertog F, Kaplinsky R, editors. Europe's next step: Organizational Innovation, Competition and Employment. Ilford (Essex), Portland: Frank Cass; 1995. pp. 243-249

[18] Howaldt J, Oeij PRA, Dhondt S, Fruytier B. Workplace innovation and social innovation: An introduction. World Review of Entrepreneurship, Management and Sustainable Development. 2016;**12**(1):1-12

[19] Oeij RA. Workplace Innovation – Social Innovation: Shaping Work Organization and Working Life. Inderscience Enterprises Ltd; 2016

[20] Hage JT. Organizational innovation and organizational change. Annual Review of Sociology. 1999;**25**:597-622

[21] Howaldt J, Schwarz M. Social Innovation. Concepts, Research Fields and International Trends. Sozialforschungstelle Dortmund, ZWE der TU-Dortmund; 2010

[22] Pot F, Totterdill P, Dhondt S. Workplace innovation: European policy and theoretical foundation. World Review of Entrepreneurship, Management and Sustainable Development. 2016;**12**(1):13-32

[23] Konda I, Starc J, Rodicalace B. Social innovations: The way to sustainable development. Faculty of Economics: University of Niš, 17 October 2014. International Scientific Conference; 2014

[24] Eeckelaert L, Dhondt S, Oeij P, Pot F, Nicolescu GI, Trifu A, et al. Review of Workplace Innovation and its Relation with Occupational Safety and Health. Luxembourg: European Agency for Safety and Health at Work: Publications Office of the European Union; 2012

[25] Pot FD, Koningsveld EAP. Quality of working life and organizational performance: Two sides of the same coin? Scandinavian Journal of Work, Environment & Health. 2009;**35**(6): 421-428. DOI: 10.5271/sjweh.1356

[26] WHO. Resolution 60.26. Workers' Health: Global Plan of Action. In: Sixtieth World Health Assembly, Geneva 13-23 May 2007. Geneva; 2007

[27] WHO. Commission on Social Determinants of Health. Closing the Gap in a Generation: Health Equity Through Action on the Social Determinants of Health. Final Report of the Commission on Social Determinants of Health. Geneva; 2008

[28] Lam A. Organizational innovation. In: Fagerberg J, Mowery DC, Nelson RR, editors. The Oxford Handbook of Innovation. Oxford: Oxford University Press; 2004. pp. 115-147

[29] EU DG Enterprise and Industry. Short Meeting Report Supporting Social Innovation in the Workplace. Paper Presented on the European Commission Meeting, Vlaanderen, Actie; 2012

[30] Oeij PRA, Dhondt S, KarolusKraan RV, Pot F. Workplace innovation and its relations with organizational performance and employee commitment. E-journal Lifelong Learning in Europe. 2012;**4**(4): 1-11. Available from: http://www.lline.fi/en/issue/42012/issue-42012

[31] Millard J. How Social Innovation Underpins Sustainable Development.

USA: The Social Innovation Landscape—Global Trends; 1984

[32] Amponsah-Tawiah K. Occupational health and safety and sustainable development in Ghana. International Journal of Business Administration. 2013;**4**(2):74-78

[33] Jilcha K, Kitaw D. Industrial occupational safety and health innovation for sustainable development. Engineering Science and Technology, an International Journal. 2017;**20**:372-380

[34] Casey D, Sieber S. Employees, sustainability and motivation: Increasing employee engagement by addressing sustainability and corporate social responsibility. Research in Hospitality Management. 2016;**6**(1):69-76. DOI: 10.2989/RHM.2016.6.1.9.1297

[35] Nollman MR. Sustainability Initiatives in tshe Workplace and Employee Productivity. 2013. Research Papers. Paper 441. Avaialble from: http://opensiuc.lib.siu.edu/gs_rp/441

Chapter 3

Entrepreneurial Momentum for Sustainable Growth

Ihor Katernyak and Viktoriya Loboda

Abstract

Public and private sectors view entrepreneurship as a movement of active, creative people who exploit opportunities under uncertainty, create new products, jobs, contribute to economic development of region. Entrepreneurs with their 'fresh' vision and agility play an important role in creating the sustainable future for all by overcoming social and environmental challenges. Based on real cases, we illustrate the path travelled by entrepreneurs from identifying the problem and creating the platform for communication with stakeholders to building solution and scaleup. We demonstrate our '4A engine' approach to maintain the momentum for startup consisting of 4 phases: Attention, Actualisation, Attraction, and Action. Even if the start is successful, statistics show that many startups fail between 18 and 24 months. Therefore, we ask startup founders about their practice and biggest surprise they came across, essential choices and important decisions they made. Readers who find this practice useful will reflect by writing a Letter from the Future.

Keywords: entrepreneurship, entrepreneuring, entrepreneurial mindset, startup, sustainable development, best practices

1. Introduction

> *"...the private sector contributes to the achievement of sustainable development and poverty eradication, and <...> partnerships with the private sector play an important role in promoting entrepreneurship, generating employment and investment, increasing revenue potential, developing new technologies and innovative business models and enabling high, sustained, inclusive and equitable economic growth while protecting workers' rights."*
>
> *Entrepreneurship for sustainable development. - Resolution 73/225 adopted by the UN General Assembly on 20 December 2018: https://undocs.org/pdf?symbol=en/A/RES/73/225*

In today's society there is a great demand for entrepreneurial behaviour. Public and private sectors view entrepreneurship as a movement of active, creative people who exploit opportunities under uncertainty, create new products, jobs, contribute to economic development of the region. Entrepreneurs, with their 'fresh' perspective and agility, are able to play an important role in creating sustainable future for all by addressing social and environmental challenges. So currently, entrepreneurship is viewed as a catalyst for sustainable development [1].

The public sector applies entrepreneurial approaches to efficiently develop new types of services for citizens; in particular, social entrepreneurship is developing. Platforms for Communities of Practice are being created (for instance, DESPRO's Community of Practice for Sustainable Development [2]), which promote the culture of management by projects for sustainable development.

Besides, in order to overcome poverty, the public sector is deeply involved in supporting and promoting entrepreneurship ecosystems, the mission of which includes creating favourable conditions for starting business ventures and creating jobs as a return on public investment [3]. But they should understand the entrepreneurial style of thinking and the nature of innovation processes in order to develop ecosystem-building policies for startups (also called '*business incubators*', '*accelerators*' or '*hubs*').

Today it is no longer enough for companies seeking sustainable development to be effective in operation (e.g., reducing waste streams) and successful in the market by constantly improving their products. We also need to make the most efficient use of resources (including energy and materials) to eliminate any harmful effects on the environment, health of a person and a whole community, vitality of future generations throughout the life cycle of products [4]. Therefore, we can define the following criteria for viable innovation: ZERO WASTE, ZERO EMISSION, ZERO TOXIC, ZERO NONRENEWABLE RESOURCES, and ZERO DESCRIMINATION.

In order to compete and scale up, startups equip themselves not only with some technological or product innovations, but also with completely different ways or models of doing business. Investors today look for both solutions (technologies or products) they need and business models that work. From an investor's perspective, it is no longer possible to wait until startups have scaled up, and then invest in the ones that seem to work well. Due to a highly competitive environment in the capital market, investors are forced to invest in a much earlier phase in order to '*qualify*' for later stages.

The recent analytical studies point out the necessity to focus on the early stages of the development of enterprises (ventures), new activities, operational models and practice, in order to determine the factors of sustainable development for entrepreneurial initiatives [5, 6].

Thus, investors have to be able to understand, evaluate and support an enterprise at its early stage, when not only a new product is created, but also certain promising ways of development and the systematic role of the enterprise in the market are determined.

But even if the start of a venture is successful, practice shows that more than half of all startups fail in the first 5 years, and this failure peak occurs during the first 18–24 months after their onset [7].

In this chapter, we first give the definition of who entrepreneurs are, how this definition has acquired different meanings over the last century. We also define the main characteristics of the entrepreneurial 'mindset' and describe the model that helps an entrepreneur to start his/her own venture. Since entrepreneurship is, first of all, a practice, we talk to the founders of startups and learn where the initiative to start their venture came from, what the main reason for creating the startup was, what big surprise they came across in the first 18 months, and what essential choices and important decisions they made.

2. Who are entrepreneurs, and how do they change the world?

The first term we need to define is an "*entrepreneur*". This word comes from a French word '*entreprendre*', which has been used since the 12th century. It literally means: "*go-between*", by finding out the way to provide a product or service to the customers; or "*undertake*", take on certain functions, obligations or complete responsibility for a new venture.

In the middle of the 20th century, entrepreneurs were seen as innovators implementing "*new combinations*" (innovations) to initiate the process of economic development by introducing new quality into the product, new products, finding new demand and new markets, conquering a new source of raw materials and creating a new field of activity. Thanks to Joseph Alois Schumpeter [8], the term '*entrepreneur*' has become widely recognised, and today entrepreneurships is often presented as *a force of 'creative disruption'* [9].

In this regard, Peter Drucker wrote: "*Innovation is the specific tool of entrepreneurs, the means by which they exploit change as an opportunity for a different business or a different service*" [10].

Opportunities and innovation are integral parts of entrepreneurship and, in particular, the act of implementing something new in the face of uncertainty is one of the most difficult tasks of the entrepreneur as it requires determination and perseverance, readiness to manoeuvre. The entrepreneur has to be able not only to create new value and conceptualise new products but also to offer a completely different business model that will demonstrate the potential to scale up. These innovative business models are often the basis of competitiveness for startups, while traditional technological innovations (like transistors or lasers, computers or smartphones) are usually associated with large corporations.

In an effort to fulfil their mission, entrepreneurs must think in a systemic way, move with acceleration and be ready to quickly change both tactics and strategy, perhaps even very dramatically, in response to new environmental challenges.

Thus, entrepreneurship is the accelerated movement of entrepreneurs driven by needs through uncertainty and ambiguity, '*burdened*' with intent and seeking to fulfil their mission as soon as possible: to conquer the market by generating innovations and validating products, to open up new opportunities for localisation of capital, to earn a profit and to '*warm up*' the market itself.

According to G. Onuoha, entrepreneurship is "*the practice of starting new organisations or revitalising mature organisations, particularly new businesses generally in response to identified opportunities*" [11]. Moreover, such creation of an organisation or simply a product occurs in the conditions of uncertainty and ambiguity. Entrepreneurs have to become not only practitioners but also experimenters to minimise the product development cycle and to enter the market as soon as possible with a validated (tested) product. Eric Ries introduces the notion of the Lean Startup [12] as an effective approach for creating and implementing new initiatives, examining customer needs and testing one's vision, adjusting it as quickly as possible by continuously receiving customer feedback [13].

The more modern definition of entrepreneurship is also about people who change (transform) the world by solving urgent problems, creating and presenting innovative products or new systemic solutions.

Thus, an entrepreneur:

- pays attention to the challenges facing humanity, sees critical situations and imagines how everything could ideally be with the same resources used and with minimal impact on nature made;

- selects target groups, determines needs, sees opportunities, and generates ideas;

- perpetuates his/her talent to meet the needs and desires of people in goods, services, experience/impressions, and develops solutions giving preference to systemic transformations;

- accepts the uncertainty on the market, defines the goals for movement in the space of three coordinates: technical feasibility, 'executability', and market perceptibility;
- makes his/her mission attractive to him/herself and to others, by validating both products and business models;
- acts, undertakes (=entreprendre) responsibility, demonstrates determination and push, ingenuity and resourcefulness for passing obstacles;
- generates innovations in the market, 'warms up' the market and creates a place to localise capital and profit;
- creates ventures that both provide the market with products and services, and are also responsible for reducing waste and using resources efficiently.

As stated in this chapter, the leading role played by entrepreneurs in society has historically emerged: they are one of the most important resources and segments of economic growth. But entrepreneurs play the same leading role in the development of social innovation. Therefore, the end result of their actions is associated with a business venture in the private sector, and it is also a driving force for social, public and cultural progress that ensures community health: zero waste, zero emission, zero toxic, zero non-renewable resources, and zero discrimination.

In our understanding, entrepreneurship is about: **people** who transform a problem into an opportunity, success in a dream, construct their future, and accept responsibility for their own choice and destiny; and **freedom** – constructing your life on your own terms, with no bosses, no restricting schedules and no one holding you back.

Entrepreneurs are able to take the first step into uncertainty in order to make the world a better place. Hence, we view *entrepreneurship* as an act of disobedience. Humans are rebels from the first moments of their birth, rebels against what they think is 'wrong'; and some people can see peace only in storms. This is exactly what entrepreneurs are doing as the most powerful transformers in the world.

And today a new term has been coined – Entrepreneuring, which means acting as an Entrepreneur. We define *entrepreneuring* as the art of making practical application of marketing principles and human-centred design thinking, research and innovation, requirements and limitations to solve problems, create new values and design innovative & sustainable business models, and as the process of creating a venture and its scaleup.

Great engineer Theodore von Karman once said, "*Scientists study the world as it is, engineers create the world that never has been*". And today we can continue his thought and say that science studies the world as it is; engineering creates the world that has never been; and entrepreneuring changes the world for the better.

3. How can I maintain momentum for startup?

This section focuses on the issue of how we understand the concept of '*mindset*'. Usually, it can be understood as a way of thinking; that is, a set of beliefs, opinions and thoughts that determine our attitude to the challenges we have received, to our mistakes or our successes, our personal interpretation and our response to events, circumstances and situations; they enable us to create a space for knowledge, for new ideas, for unleashing our talent; they make us thirsty for freedom, cognition and success.

Typical characteristics of individuals with an entrepreneurial mindset include:

- love for freedom and willingness to change the world,
- openness to see opportunities where others see only annoyance and problems,
- courage in actions that correspond to one's values,
- effectiveness, focus on results,
- willingness to learn and not be afraid to experiment,
- take full responsibility for progress, fulfilling one's mission.

The freedom and need for achievement, creativity and innovation, internal locus of control, hard work and reasonable risk taking with possible benefits – all these are integral parts of an entrepreneur's profile. Entrepreneurs can best use available opportunities to solve problems, meet needs even with limited or uncontrolled resources through innovation.

3.1 Attention = everything is possible

If we do not like something, when something annoys us, we can use this situation as an our opportunity to abandon the status quo and change the world around us.

Attention is our level of irritation; and this irritation actually stems from the fact that a person strongly believes that something needs to be done very differently, not the way it is going on now, when excessive resources are wasted and a negative impact is made on nature, health of an individual person or even communities. And this is seen both from the standpoint of those who live in this situation and the entrepreneur who seeks to change it. This requires understanding other people, knowing their values, habits, their problem(s), their 'pain', and searching for alternatives to solve their problem(s).

We might be too self-confident, but our confidence is based on our strengths and beliefs, and we are also directed by intuition which suggests that there should always be another way to do something, in a more effective, interesting, even 'cool' way.

We cannot act like everyone else, which requires us to think differently (expand the horizons of the situation, see new opportunities and set goals), reflect, communicate, generate ideas, put everything into a nice concept (idea) and act decisively (quickly make and timely implement managerial decisions, see their role in overcoming obstacles or through the prism of the expected result), persistently pave our way to the goal, or to get out of it on time in order to start a new venture.

We need to be open to the world; if there are any weaknesses, we should not be ashamed to ask for help, find a common interest and establish a partnership, capture others' interest in our plan (a new approach to meeting needs or a new model for running a business), and it will make us '*smart*'. By '*smart*' we mean being productive, efficient, interesting and competitive.

Now that the opportunities are open, we need to be confident in our actions: that is, always know exactly what we are doing and why we are doing it. For this purpose, we recommend, instead of analysing an idea (or new approach) and focusing on how good it is, turning back to the problem we are going to solve. And it is important to make sure that there is a certain group of people who need an urgent solution to this problem (or 'pain'): i.e., it is necessary to determine the price they pay for living with this problem or even '*pain*'; it is necessary to find out whether they are ready to continue to suffer this '*pain*', and how often they suffer from its '*attacks*'. It is equally important to know what benefits they expect if this problem is solved. Are there any economic, social and emotional benefits that might surprise them? However, if we start not with a problem, but with an idea/new approach, we can end up with the fact that there will be no interest in it. However, when starting with the problem that our potential customers face, there is a better chance to understand the existing contradiction and to create exactly what is in demand; and then we will be able to create an effective business model.

So, on the one hand, we consider current needs, and on the other hand, we may know which technologies should be used, but now we need to focus on the goals we can achieve if we get enough customers and through partnering with them. It should be noted that customers need to be available to us, and they can be sought from potential competitors. If we are able to change the habits of competitors' customers and attract them to us, then this is the most effective way to get '*warmed up*' customers who are willing to pay if we meet their expectations and provide them with what they sacrificed when buying products from our competitor.

3.2 Actualisation = passion

Actualisation is when we focus on an innovative solution to the problem (how to meet the need of potential customers) and our capability of conceptualising, creating and providing a new value onto the market (developing a business model), our vision of systemic transformations.

When we already know what to do and why we need to act, two groups of questions arise:

1. Why Me, and why do I need it? How does this activity, its result correspond to my dreams, my self-realisation? What team do I need to assemble, with what set of necessary skills, competencies and way of thinking?

2. What will I be like when this initiative comes to an end, how will we celebrate our success? That is, we must know not only how to 'commence', but more importantly – how to complete this mission in a sustainable manner.

And thus we come to the conclusion that our goals have actualised our desire to 'immerse' in entrepreneurship. Now we need to be balanced, paying attention to every detail. Each action must be passed through a '*sieve*' of its purpose and expected result. And when you have some activity in the plan, ask yourself: "*What's the point of doing this?*" That is, we have to be sure that we do these actions thoughtfully and for the right reason.

The vision of achieved result and the intention to work hard in conditions of uncertainty stimulate creativity, experimentation, obtaining quick results and learning. Work becomes a passion, admiration and joy. Entrepreneurs do not know exactly what to expect at every turn of their path, however, their worldview is energy, their creativity is a well-chosen route, their product is a means of movement, and their business model is a prospect for scaling up. Constant generation of ideas is a weapon against turbulence and a means of overcoming all kinds of obstacles, while focused attention and active processing of information give the entrepreneur the opportunity to manoeuvre. Entrepreneurs strive to reach the finish line, because this finish is a created value that changes the market, adds value to the company, and makes them successful. But such a huge desire to come to the finish line first can sometimes replace the realisation that sometimes it might be worth getting off the track (route) in time. And it is also an entrepreneurial move: you want to pay the lowest price if your mission fails. Do entrepreneurs like taking risks? In my opinion, they do not. The risk must be calculated and compared with the benefits we want to get.

3.3 Attraction = we are interconnected

We are characterised by valence, we create connections, work hard to build a team and expand our network, build our ecosystem for a startup where we are consulted, motivated, united and stimulated. But in order to remain free, we must refine ourselves, learn, study and improve, never stop to become better or reach high standards. Such benchmarks are a kind of energy level that we have to achieve to leave the comfort (valence) zone and move on.

We are not learning for the future, we are learning for the present, because it is not known what knowledge and skills will be needed in five to ten years, but it is well known what is required today. Besides, skills and experience are placed above knowledge when there is a need for new professionals for your team. We have no choice but to constantly learn and practice, applying knowledge and mastering new skills to support changes in our way of thinking and behaviour.

Now we in the team are '*burdened*' with the idea of how to meet existing needs, what will be the benefit to those who use our offer. And this is not some ingenious idea stuck in our heads: we have created a prototype or even a minimum viable product (MVP) to communicate with potential customers. We need to show the '*traction*' – that is, the monetisation of our offer.

If we are planning to raise capital, we need to have a clear answer to investors' questions: "*How will you make money for us?*", And the answer can only be given when we have a clear, understandable, efficient and even innovative business model, taking into account trends in the industry where we are going to do business, the value created for a specific target group (its size and availability), competitive prices and distribution channels, prospects for expanding our customer base, available resources for organising production, and partners, clear milestones (stages) that allow proving the sustainability of our development, the comparison of cost and revenues – our ability to scale up. Successful entrepreneurs are those who make their customers and partners successful in meeting their needs and achieving their goals.

And of course, we need to be a good salesperson: knowing how to promote ourselves, our ideas, products, our team and our company. Those who will listen to us should not only hear and understand what we say to them, but also resonate with what we strive for and tell others about our initiative.

3.4 Action = the time has come

Once we have started the business, it becomes 100% our commitment, and from now on it depends

1. on how much we have:

    - ambition and passion; whether we trust ourselves and believe in ourselves, whether we believe in the ability of our team and the importance of the mission we perform;

    - confidence in needs; whether we know how to hear our customers and partners, whether we understand their problems and interests;

- willingness to adapt to the situation and make a choice in favour of the best options;
- flexibility – to see multiple opportunities;
- persistence – to reach the finish line;
- positive thinking, drive, striving for the best and change perception of challenges as opportunities to learn, improve;
- determination coupled with a high tolerance for uncertainty and ambiguity, as well as the ability to make quick decisions to save time;
- devotion to victory over competitors or just a desire to do our job well;
- courage, ability to assess risk and reward, willingness to accept well-calculated risk;
- strong desire to learn as soon as possible about the ability to scale up; or fail as soon as possible to give up our passion, 'idée fixe', and pay as little as possible for it; and

2. on how quickly we can accelerate and gain velocity that will create the momentum for take-off of our startup.

In all actions and situations it is necessary to look for lessons to learn from and factors to increase productivity and efficiency, keeping in mind the possible impact on environmental sustainability. Each mistake is a higher level of mobilisation, a new option in the product, adjustments to the business model, or a corrected course of further progress. We need to be smart, insightful, curious and inquisitive. Do not perceive everything as it is; try to look further beyond the horizon. For example, just because you need some light to read a book in the evening does not mean you need a simple light bulb; you probably need a well-thought-out and designed lighting at home. That is, we must learn to look beyond the horizon and anticipate trends, develop competitive advantages under certain constraints, before others can at least begin to understand them.

Thus, the objectives of the *Entrepreneurship Development* is to celebrate such values as freedom and self-confidence, to cultivate a deep awareness of the situation and balance in action, to encourage self-actualisation in life, creativity and the implementation of the most essential first steps. The entrepreneur's task is to learn how to be successful and create an appropriate ecosystem around him/herself where he/she is able to implement own endeavours.

Table 1 presents the 4A approach [14], which we call '4A engine', to maintain the momentum for startup. It consists of 4 phases.

The speed at which your startup develops (scales up) depends, on the one hand, on the type of the market, and on the other hand, on establishing strategic partnerships with customers, suppliers or on entering the network.

Especially in the initial phase of a startup, it is important to prove the viability of the startup's business model – which investors call '*traction*' (or '*grip force*'). Founders demonstrate that their business hypothesis is based on reality, and they seek not just to survive in competition but to influence the market and build a great company. They know their clients very well, and they are constantly experimenting with product features to maximise the profitability from each new group of

Phase / Competences	*Process components*	*Segments*
Attention: Demonstrate the ability to determine a problem /'*pain*' and its cause (core). Demonstrate the ability to see the ideal situation and existing functional contradiction.	high level of irritation – something a needs to be done very differently a problem of a specific target group(s) the target group is accessible for the entrepreneur industry analysis	*Opportunity* for entrepreneurs
Actualisation: Demonstrate the ability to identify a need that will affect a prospect customer's behaviour. Find a system (innovative and comprehensive) solution. Demonstrate the ability to present a solution in a creative way (make a pitch). Make sure that the development of this solution is within our capabilities.	the impact of the need on customer behaviour focus on an innovative solution to the problem benefits for the target group our intention and professional team who believes in the success of your mission competitive advantage, customisation of product	*Capability* of conceptualising and creating something new and in demand
Attraction: Demonstrate the ability to develop a business model (for driving a solution onto the market) as our innovation and competitive advantage.	value for a specific target group customer and delivery price, types of revenue resources, partners and action plan risks; cost and expenses	*Feasibility* of a business model
Action: Demonstrate the ability to discuss business model with potential customers, suppliers, investors, form a partnership. Demonstrate the ability to sell vision. Demonstrate agility and creative approach to business scaleup.	making a compelling offer for our customer planning effective ways of delivering products/ services and getting revenue getting first customers who demonstrate '*traction*' developing a loyalty program	*Validity* –working model and *velocity* to take off

Table 1.
Four phases of maintaining the momentum for startup.

customers they attract. They are able to getting sales in those market segments that they are targeting. Most importantly, they have a lot of data on the direct income and expenses of their startup related to a specific business model and calculated per unit. That is, they know how much it costs to attract one client, and how much they can earn on each of them. Considering the data they receive from these first customers, they can estimate how big the market for their product exists. And now, with all this knowledge, an entrepreneur is in a very good shape to attract venture capital investments and achieve extremely rapid growth.

4. Practicing startup operation and scale-up

In this section, we are going to explore the practice of entrepreneurs seeking to change the world. One of them, Max (29), created a company, which was developing a tool – a '*Smart Glove*' – with the mission of ZERO DISCRIMINATION, to enhance communication of people with hearing impairments who experience communication problems with outer world, using the sign language. Here are his remarks about its purpose:

We wanted to give people who are hard-of-hearing a way to better break out of their communities and to lower their communication barrier, because unfortunately not a lot of people know the sign language. So, for example, if I cannot talk, it's difficult for me to go and do like day-to-day simple functions. For example, if I go to the store, how do I ask a person about the properties of some product? How do I ask for an accommodation I want to get? If I go to a doctor, how do I explain my problems, what's my issue, how it hurts? For instance, in this doctors' situation, usually people need to take someone with them who understands sign language, who can describe their problems to the doctor, which obviously is not optimal for privacy reasons. I do not need other people to know what's wrong with me, medically speaking. So our purpose was to give better tools to people who experience these problems and help them communicate with people around them on a different level.

Our other interlocutor is Mark (35), CTO in a big outsourcing IT company. His passion is making creative ideas come true. He is the core developer and CEO of DigiSCity energy management platform. DigiSCity is the intelligent smart city system, which aims at optimising energy resources and consumption. It can be used by business enterprises and official government municipalities. Using this system, managers can quickly gather the consumption data and deeply analyse energy effectiveness of the buildings as well as respond to the detected anomalies and provide behavioural pattern analysis.

We have conducted interviews with the startup founders approaching them with the following questions:

1. How did you perform in the first 18 months from product, customer, team, brand, partners' perspective and what were the biggest surprises you faced in this period?

Max: - *It was basically a students' project, and at that time me and co-founders did not have much experience in coding and development, none of us had started a startup before. So the biggest surprise was how well-received our project was from the very beginning. Because within 6 months from the start of the development we won Startups competition here in Ukraine, and then within 9 months we went on to head the list in the global software development competition sponsored by large IT corporations. After that, within a year we received a 50 thousand dollar-grant from one of these corporations, which was a tremendous help to us in continuing this project development. So this winning streak and media attention as well as the interest of the community were really surprising and encouraging to us.*

The other surprising thing was that a lot of the investors were really unwilling to look into this project and entertain investing such a technology, because it was not like a 'billion-dollar' market there. So they did not see it as a great business opportunity, more as a social project. This is why they were unwilling to risk investing significant sums of money, as they did not see sky-high rates of return and huge profitability. Obviously, it would never be like another Facebook, or Google, or something like that.

Mark: - *The project was launched in August 2014 at the Smart Energy hackathon – a great choice for starting one's ECO-project. Every city resident might have the feeling that some things in the city could be done better.*

Provision of the energy management systems in Lviv-city was launched in 2005–2006. But the authorities and existing system had already reached the technological threshold, and it was necessary to have some new tools to convert them into a real SmartTech. So the idea of DigiSCity project deals with a smart grid level energy management system. It helps us to collect and organise energy consumption data and other related things: processes in buildings, replacement of appliances, resident behaviour which can be anonymously implicitly extracted and analysed in order to understand energy consumption.

The very first steps were completed with the core team. Specialists experienced in data science, machine learning and full-stack development quickly created the prototype and platform ready for demos. We were working for ourselves just being excited about the idea. After completing that stage, I hired several developers and QA's to support the DigiSCity. Actually, that was a starting point of a commercial project.

2. What were the most important decisions and essential choices you have made since you launched your startup, and which choices and decisions do you regret?

Max: - *I spent more than a month in California, in Silicon Valley, looking for investments, and also looking for advisors and support from the community. That was one of the most important decisions for us as a team, because first of all, I got to visit a school for deaf children in the US, I saw the kind of care and education they were getting, and I received a really good feedback on our product, on how we expand the opportunities for people suffering from those conditions. But there were some negative decisions. For example, due to disagreement between co-founders, we declined to cooperate with one of the defence contractors, which saw a potential military application for our project. It was not the goal that we had in mind when we started the project, though it could have been a good source of financing for it, which could also help develop civilian applications for that. But due to our internal disagreements, we failed to follow that offer. And I think in a long term it impacted out project very negatively, unfortunately.*

Mark: - *We managed to engage in the city municipal industry without considerable efforts. The success story cannot be written without people. The most important decisions were to involve the right people to play the right roles. It is not as easy as it may seem to be. Nevertheless, things cannot be perfect. Sometimes communication breakdown happens, and you cannot influence some decisions.*

3. Which decisions influenced your company expansion?

Max: - *Unfortunately, we had to close down the project because we failed to secure any additional investment for further development, and our prototype was not ready to go to market. The main factor why that happened is that, first of all, we failed to get the recognition rate to a sufficient level. There was lots of confusion between the gestures, and some of them were not easy to tell apart, like a classic example that we would give is the gesture for a farther and a gesture for a grandfather. They are basically the same gesture as far as the hand itself goes, and we only have the glove, right? But we needed a way to tell apart – which part of the body that gesture was being applied to, which was not possible with the existing sensory instrumentation. And also the sensors that we used on the glove did not have enough precision and were getting worse over time. For example, after three months, the sensors would become less responsive and would give many false positives. So those were some issues, and as a result, we failed to improve the recognition rate, which was definitely a problem for us. But also we received a lot of feedback that the technologies we were using would become obsolete really quickly. A lot of people, especially in the investment community, had the opinion that video recognition would become much better, much faster, and we would not need any gloves or other sensors. We could have, for example, a video camera on the necklace, and that camera would capture the gestures and basically recognise them in real time. This has failed to happen so far, after seven years, so obviously some people were really wrong about that. But since we were new to this, and it was out first project, it was hard for us to ignore this feedback from the investors' community. And after basically everyone told us this was going to happen, it was hard to say "no, we are right, this is going to work much better, much faster and we are going to do it". So those were, I would say, the main issues that affected out operations in the first two years. And after two years we failed to secure investment and had to close down the project.*

Mark: - *The right people on the right places. Here is the explanation of creating the team: always look for guys with creative imagination. Frankly speaking, choice of the team is the fundamental goal. Let us not forget about public presentations and participation in different IT meetings. You never know where you can meet the inspiration and business partners. And of course, international relationships: for us the only way to be really successful is to launch sales of our product abroad. But your business side and presentation quality must be ready for that.*

4. Could you say any words of support to young entrepreneurs?

Max: - *From our experience, I would say: you have to start thinking about raising money early on. Because when you start running out of money, it is too late to start raising it. You have to have at least 6-month worth of your expenses before you start raising another round. This is not a fast process, it is unlikely that you will meet someone who will like your presentation tomorrow and give you money in two weeks. It does take time to set up meetings with investors to give them your presentation, to hear and agree to some conditions. For example, the process of receiving the grant took us 8 months. So you have to think about money early on and plan for that, otherwise you will not have enough resources to sustain in your product development. Also you have to start working with your users as soon as possible. We tried to do this as much as it was feasible, we engaged our local community – the Ukrainian Association of the Deaf, and we tried to recruit users to use our devices and give us feedback. But unfortunately in our local conditions it was somewhat difficult because not a lot of people were technologically adapted, and that was back in 2012 when even smartphones were not as wide-spread. It also required some capital investment on our part.*

So, planning for raising money, and working with the users – these are the most important issues that we overlooked, and I wish you would not.

Mark: - *Soft skills, first of all communication skills, are playing a huge role. People are different by their nature, and you should understand it and take it into account. Work for a big company helps me a lot, because project management along with technical skills taught me to find a balance in communication. I prefer to connect this topic with emotional intelligence and business motivation. And, of course, never be afraid to lose a game, this is quite important.*

Personal development and openness to others is very important. After all, when you create a product that you do not have yet, you will hear: "There is no such thing because no one needs it" or "It already exists, so why are you doing it?" So you need to understand why you are doing this, and use this as the main direction: move on and never stop!

5. Conclusion

In this chapter, entrepreneurs are presented as a driving force for economic, social, public and cultural progress and as those who:

- pay **attention** to the challenges facing humanity, see critical situations and imagines how everything could ideally be, given the same resources are used and the minimal impact on nature is made;

- identify (**actualisation**) the need of a selected target group and find a systemic (innovative and comprehensive) solution, which provides benefits that this target group has not yet received;

- develop a business model (for driving a solution onto the market) as an innovation and competitive advantage and makes their mission **attractive** to themselves and to clients, partners, and investors;

- create ventures **(action)** that provide the market with products, services, jobs, capital and profit, enabling high, sustained, inclusive and equitable economic growth.

A new concept of *Entrepreneuring* is introduced (which means acting as an entrepreneur) and defined as the art of making practical application of marketing principles and human-centred design thinking, research and innovation, requirements and limitations to solve problems, create new values and design innovative & sustainable business models, and as the process of creating a venture and its sustainable growth. We offer entrepreneurs the **4A** approach **(attention, actualisation, attraction** and **action)**, which serves to some extent an algorithm for transform a problem into an opportunity, success in a dream, construct their future, and create the momentum for take-off. This approach has been successfully utilised by start-up founders who share their experiences in this chapter of how they performed during their first 18 months. Factors ensuring sustainable growth are:

- young people, even when they lack enough experience but have a strong desire to change the world for the better, have more chances to succeed in their initiatives, since they are not afraid to "lose a game";

- it is necessary to explore the problems our potential customers face, the pain they live with, the needs they have, get feedback on our initiative and understand the benefits they can have from the product we are going to introduce to the market;

- it is necessary to create a prototype or a platform for demonstration and to establish communication with both potential clients and investors as soon as possible;

- one of the key success factors is trust among the founders who share common values, have a vision and understanding of why they are in this business; another success factor is involving the right people to play the right roles in the team, since the choice of the team is the fundamental objective;

- when developing a value proposition, it is necessary to use various creative methods, involve in the team specialists with a good imagination, systematic and human-centred design thinking;

- in technology-based business, it is important to determine the technological feasibility and take into account all the technology trends that are evolving rapidly and may affect our business;

- active communications, public product presentations and participation in various events – this is a chance to get partners and customers who cannot be ignored, so we must always be ready for a high-quality pitch;

- the fundraising process should be divided into several steps, instead of concentrating all our efforts to raise big amounts of investment in one step. At the same time, each fundraising step should be made at least six months before the time we need to spend these funds in order to ensure sustainable development.

You have reached the end of this chapter, and we offer to reflect on what you have read. Now you know more about who entrepreneurs are, which approaches they use to create their ventures for sustainable growth, and what practice of such startups in the early stage exists. So now we encourage you to stop for a while and imagine your future. *Write your letter from the future you have created, starting with:* "Today I am a successful entrepreneur. How have I achieved it? Why am I proud of it? Why is the next generation thankful for my effort? Here is my exciting story: …".

Author details

Ihor Katernyak* and Viktoriya Loboda
Ivan Franko National University of Lviv, Lviv, Ukraine

*Address all correspondence to: ikaternyak@udl.org.ua

References

[1] Filser M., Kraus S., Roig-Tierno N., Kailer N., Fischer U., (2019) Entrepreneurship as Catalyst for Sustainable Development: Opening the Black Box, Sustainability, 11 (16), 4503, 1-18.

[2] Katernyak I., Loboda V., Kulya M., (2018) eLearning within the community of practice for sustainable development, Higher Education, Skills and Work-based Learning, 8 (3), 312-322.

[3] Bruton, Garry D., Ketchen, David J., Ireland, R. Duane, (2013) Entrepreneurship as a solution to poverty, Journal of Business Venturing, Elsevier, 28 (6), 683-689.

[4] Larson A. L., (2011) Sustainability, Innovation, and Entrepreneurship, Flat World Knowledge, Inc., 312.

[5] Wiklund J., Davidsson P., Audretsch D. B., Karlsson C., (2010) The Future of Entrepreneurship Research, Baylor University, 1-9.

[6] Greco A., Jong G. de, (2017) Sustainable entrepreneurship: definitions, themes and research gaps, Working Paper Series, Centre for Sustainable Entrepreneurship, Entrepreneurial University of Groningen/Campus Fryslan.

[7] Katre, Salipante Jr P. F., (2012) Start-Up Social Ventures: Blending Fine-Grained Behaviors: From Two Institutions for Entrepreneurial Success, Entrepreneurship: Theory and Practice, 36 (5).

[8] Schumpeter J. A., (1934) The Theory of Economic Development, Harvard University Press, Cambridge, MA.

[9] Whitelaw L., Garcia-Lorenzo L., (2017) Creative Disruption: The Everyday Innovation Practices of Intrapreneurs at a Technology Company, Academy of Management Annual Meeting Proceedings.

[10] Drucker P., (1985) Innovation and Entrepreneurship, Harper.

[11] Onuoha G., (2007) Entrepreneurship, AIST International Journal 10, 20-32.

[12] Ries E., (2011) The Lean Startup: How Today's Entrepreneurs Use Continuous Innovation to Create Radically Successful Businesses, Crown Publishing, 103.

[13] Blank S., (2013) Why the Lean Start-Up Changes Everything, Harvard business review.

[14] Katernyak I., Ekman S., Ekman A., Sheremet M., Loboda V., (2009) eLearning: from Social Presence to Co-creation in Virtual Education Community, Interactive Technology and Smart Education, 6 (4), 215-222.

Chapter 4

Organizational Support and Sustainable Entrepreneurship Performance of SMEs, the Moderating Role of Strategic Sustainability Orientation

Muhammad Auwal Abdullahi, Zainalabidin Mohamed, Mad Nasir Shamsudin, Juwaidah Sharifuddin and Fazlin Ali

Abstract

Small and medium sized enterprises' (SMEs) activities have contributed significantly to environmental degradation that causes a disastrous effect on us and our future generation. Considering this, sustainable entrepreneurship has been promoted as a resolution of ecological problems capable of addressing climate change issues, public health, and safety concerns, and has become critical for competing in international markets. SMEs activities increased pollution exclusively causing environmental degradation. In response, the world is focusing on ensuring that SMEs produce products through safe and environmentally friendly practices. Literature suggests that organizational support provide SMEs with the impetus to achieve competitive advantage regarding turnover, customer attraction and market share opportunities to achieve business performance. Nonetheless, the implementation of sustainable entrepreneurship among them is still low due to numerous challenges. This paper intends to investigate the influence of organizational support on sustainable entrepreneurship towards performance among SMEs. A case study involving 300 herbal-based SMEs were surveyed using structured questionnaire. Data was analyzed using descriptive statistics, exploratory factor analysis, confirmatory factor analysis, and structural equation model. The results show that organizational support have a positive effect on sustainable entrepreneurship and performance among the SMEs, accounting for 52% and 47% variance respectively. This finding reveals that organizational support is significantly related to entrepreneurship performance, thus substantiates previous findings on the crucial roles of organizational support in enabling organizations to achieve sustainable entrepreneurship performance. This study contributes to triple bottom line literature based on incorporation of strategic choice theory, strategic sustainability orientation and resource-based view theory in entrepreneurship framework.

Keywords: entrepreneurship, organizational support, performance, SMEs, strategic sustainability orientation

1. Introduction

Entrepreneurship is a vague concept. There are a number of perspectives the term 'entrepreneurship' meant; while it focus on business development aspects on one part, the other part focuses on entrepreneurial behavior – possibly linked to activities of those in the commercial and non-commercial sectors. For instance, 'new firms' and/or existing 'small, and medium-sized enterprises' (SMEs) are often considered synonymous with entrepreneurship, and owner-managers, or in some cases 'dynamic' or fast growing new firms. Elsewhere, it takes a view of: providing certain functions in the economy, particularly in innovation and resource allocation (innovative entrepreneurs); or as a form of behavior characterized with systematic utilization of opportunities; or as a set of personal traits, cognitive styles, attributes or motivations (such as risk taking or being a 'great leader') of entrepreneurs [1].

In the eighteenth century, Richard Cantillon used the French term entrepreneur to describe a 'go-between' or a 'between-taker' who bought goods at certain prices and sold at uncertain prices (as the goods were purchased at a given price, there wasn't any clue on what price to sell them for). So the entrepreneur bore the risk and uncertainty of a venture but kept the surplus after the contractual payments had been made. Later, the concept was widened to include planning, supervising, organizing, and even owning the factors of production by the French philosopher, Jean-Baptiste Say and others. During the nineteenth century, entrepreneurial activity became fruitful due to technological advances during the Industrial Revolution; this further provided the drive for continued inventions and innovations.

The activities of entrepreneurs have contributed greatly to environmental degradation overtime [2]. However, the essence of every enterprise lies on sound entrepreneurship [3]. It has since been linked to wealth generation and economic growth for decades and in the modern society [4] aside market failure. Such degradation has caused a devastating effect to us and to our future generations. As such, linking entrepreneurship to sustainability development has been stimulated as a resolution of environmental problems [5]. Nowadays business operators' balance between economic gains and environmental concerns [6] as a matter of utmost importance, and the new business paradigm urges leaders to substantially focus on it [7].

In recent years, entrepreneurship has attracted wide interest following global developments which emphasizes sustainability in addressing various environmental and social issues. Currently, entrepreneurship has new business hype; where every self-respecting company portrays itself as a sustainable entrepreneur. Because of its increased importance, Business schools and employers' organizations devote whole conferences to the topic [8]; different themes were used to describe it (corporate social responsibility, ethical funds, and eco-efficiency, etc). Although these words reflect different concepts, they all point at various aspects of sustainable development. They mentioned that there is also a flourishing business in (expensive) sustainable entrepreneurship certifications; exclusively for big companies that publish sustainability reports yearly. This raises the question whether SMEs can afford to be sustainable entrepreneurs?

In 2004, [8] defines sustainable entrepreneurship as "the continuing commitment by businesses to behave ethically and contribute to economic development while improving the quality of life of the workforce, their families, the local and global community as well as future generations". Therefore, from an entrepreneurship perspective, an enterprise is not only a nexus of responsibilities towards the shareholders, but also towards nature, society and future generations. When the enterprise's interest is all-encompassing, its decision making process changes, and then we can genuinely speak about a whole new enterprise with a unique operational management. For the fact that an enterprise does not operate on a deserted island, rather is entrenched in an economic, social, cultural and ecological environment that offers possibilities and poses threats and obligations which the theory and concepts of entrepreneurship try to find the right balance.

This chapter attempts to define sustainable entrepreneurship by synthesizing works from previous researchers with focus on sustainable drivers, sustainable orientation, and sustainable performance outcomes. Sustainable entrepreneurship stems from sustainable development and organizations brand themselves as sustainable entrepreneurs these days for noticeable development [9]. Indeed, integrating sustainability management into business practices have significantly contributed to sustainable development [4, 10]. Per the aforementioned, sustainable entrepreneurship refers to a firm's intra-organizational and inter-organizational practices for managing upstream suppliers, internal operations, and downstream customers to simultaneously achieve firm performance.

The SMEs form an important unit that should not be neglected when developing sustainable entrepreneurs in the society, because they contribute significantly to the economic development of a country. They significantly contribute to economic growth and employment globally (Organization for Economic Co-operation and Development) [11]. Though they exert relatively small impact individually, collectively their impact is substantial. In most nations, SMEs typically comprises about 95% of all private sector firms, thus forming a major portion of all economic activity [12]. Furthermore, they account for 35% of exports from Asia and approximately 26% of exports from developed countries including the United States [11]. For instance, SME accounted for 90% of all businesses and has employed 60% of workforce in the Asia-Pacific Economic Cooperation (APEC) region [13]. Also, they contribute up to 60% of the total national exports in countries like Italy, South Korea and China, [14].

1.1 The essence of sustainable entrepreneurship

Based on a well-known marketing principle, sustainable development is said to deal with the Triple-Bottom-Line; environmental quality, economic prosperity and social justice [15]. Additionally, some scholars [8, 16, 17] described sustainable entrepreneurship using a 3Ps formulation which includes people, profit, and the planet. They mentioned that all three aspects must be satisfied before any entrepreneurial activity can become sustainable.

In their work, [8] viewed sustainable entrepreneurship principally from the Triple-Bottom-Line; people, planet, and profit perspective. The first P (people) narrates the firm behavior concerning social and ethical dimensions, employee treatment and promotion of social cohesion – human right protection and gender relationship. The second P (planet) reviews the firm's disposition on the environment while the third P (profit) tells the enterprise's financial returns, allocation, and gains distribution between relevant stakeholders. They further opined that the sustainability of entrepreneurial activity is consistent with satisfying and maintaining balance among the components of the Triple-Bottom-Line.

Previous studies on the acceptance of environmental criterion on entrepreneurship activities have yielded economic benefits [2], innovation [18], competitive advantage [19–21], motivation [22], loyalty and customer satisfaction [23, 24] for the industry despite a reduction in levels of contamination and pollution [25]. In 2001 [26] stated that novel business opportunities and competition, value-addition measures, activities and processes were born out of environmental conservation efforts. Moreover, various involuntary factors have coerced the business entities to adopt sustainable practices [27]. For instance, the literature shows that legal compliance is the main reason for accepting environmental practices [27, 28], profit orientation and obeying the law [29–32]. It is somewhat difficult for SMEs to see the link between environmental management systems (EMS) implementation and its benefits [33]. However, to encourage the adoption of sustainable activities within an industry, it is ideal to eradicate all the obstacles surrounding it and provide incentives [32, 34, 35]. In 2008 [36] opines that the burdens and expenses related to environmental technologies execution, and their productivity vary with the stakeholders circumstances and interests. Still, nowadays customers prefer paying more to purchase environmentally friendly products. Customers prioritize environmental issues when making their purchases, for example, collectivism is a good predictor of consumers' intention to pay more for green wine packaging [37].

A possible general gain of implementing sustainable entrepreneurship among SMEs is the internal dynamics that sustainable approaches introduced in both the production process and human resource management. It is possible to lead to a bolder investment policy in both technology and personnel that will produce results in the long run. Another argument covers the concentration trend of big global companies; SMEs obviously cannot compete with these international players, so they are therefore better off when they focus on their surroundings. The other benefits can be summarized as follows: A positive image and repute; Lesser reliance on depleted resources; Higher employee motivation and new employee appeal; Efficient production due to superior technologies and better skilled staff; Superior market preferences and opportunities insight; Risk control (environmental accidents, scandals, bad publicity, etc.); Lower burden from changes in (environmental and social) legislation; Corporate social responsibility; Internal business dynamics; Business partnerships with other sustainable entrepreneurs; and Business partnerships with global players.

Sustainable entrepreneurship requires an on-going discourse between shareholders and stakeholders. Since a healthy financial basis remains essential, not only will shareholders have to live up to their social and environmental responsibility, but - especially in the case of SMEs - will stakeholders have to understand that sound financial results are essential for the survival of the enterprise. If not, there is no enterprise, let alone a sustainable one. After itemizing the possible gains of sustainable entrepreneurship for SME, a critical unsolved question remains: can SMEs afford it?

The size of a firm (SME) influences its entrepreneurship practices. SMEs could maintain a meaningful balance between profit, the environment, and social causes despite their limited business experience and financial resources, and still develop their companies successfully [18]. Yet, their involvement in sustainable entrepreneurship is still low. This low participation results from low knowledge and awareness for desired sustainability drivers, strategic sustainability orientation and sustainability practices leading to high-performance on the producers' part, while there also exist slight customer knowledge, awareness, and demand for environmentally friendly products.

1.2 Literature review

1.2.1 Sustainable entrepreneurship

The adoption of sustainable entrepreneurship in the context of SMEs has been receiving much attention recently because of the environmental issues related to their activities [22]. This is the current trend across the globe, hence; the most important direct drivers of environmental degradation are the activities involving the production, distribution, storage and other logistics along the value chain.

Thus, these activities tend to correlate to various environmental issues like the impact on the environment, rivers, natural resources, and the well-being of the people around. There also is the need for a more sustainable level of management of natural resources as this source will significantly reduce if there is no proper monitoring.

Some literature related to the drivers for environmental initiatives revealed that numerous sustainability initiative drivers exist. **Table 1** provides a summary of studies that empirically investigate the drivers for sustainability initiatives. Highlighting the eleven basic categories of drivers: Economic factors, Consumer pressure, Government encouragement [28, 42], Standard and regulation [42], Supplier participation specifically for SMEs [41], Internal and External pressure/impediments [22, 38, 39], Social corporate responsibility, Environmental concerns and profit balancing [18], Benefits to the company [40], Quality management and production and Competitive advantage [32].

Generally, SMEs attribute their difficulties to constraints such as low capital investment, low-profit margins, the small and variable scale of operation, and low productivity. Previous studies show that most SMEs produce and market low value products locally. Hence their engagement in unsustainable entrepreneurial practices causing environmental degradation, increased waste generation, severe hazards and environmental pollution (both air and water). This in turn affects business activities economically via increase waste disposal costs, inefficient production and consumption of products and materials, and decreasing business opportunities.

Relevant literature	Driver	SME field of business
[38]	Perception and Cognition (internal and external) concerns.	Malaysia Herbal-based SME Entrepreneur
[22]	Perceived relative advantage, complexity, attitude, subjective norms, perceived behavioral control and intention.	Malaysia Traditional & complimentary herbal-based entrepreneurs
[39]	External and internal impediments to expanding operations by SMEs.	Entrepreneurship management strategy by SMEs
[40]	Transformational leadership and Perceived organizational support have a relationship with Innovation Performance.	Malaysian SMEs
[32]	Continuous improvement (CI), supplier management (SM), and environmental management (EM).	Chinese and Taiwan Manufacturing Firms
[28]	Economic factors, Ethical considerations (that is, government policy has triggered the environmental initiatives among the respondents).	Service accommodation
[41]	Buyer, Supplier participation, Government encouragement. Profit balancing, Environmental issues, Social concerns.	SME supplier
[18]	Government laws and regulations, Companies responsibility towards local communities (local, national and global communities), Customers (international buyers).	Sustainable entrepreneurs in different business background.
[42]	Top management leadership, Regulations, Customer pressure, Expected business benefits, Firm ownership	Leading frozen seafood processor

Table 1.
Empirical studies on drivers towards sustainable practices and performance among SMEs.

At the same time increasing negative environmental impact through the emission of pollutants to the environment, raising the GHG emissions, subsequently leading to global warming.

In addition, it leads to the contamination of water sources posing a threat for the world to sustain its potable water sources. Lastly, human health is affected by adulterated products produced with microbial and heavy metals presence, and subsequently causes social issues (like negative company image and reputation, low employee motivation, and shunning of corporate social responsibilities). Therefore, to overcome these challenges, SMEs needs to develop an organizational culture through strategic sustainability orientation capable of enabling them to implement sustainable entrepreneurship. However, sustainability drivers and sustainability strategy factors have become crucial factors that could drive the success of SMEs in the future.

1.2.2 Organizational support

Organizational support is a prerequisite for a successful transformation of an organization. It denotes how top management guide and influence its employees towards achieving organizational goals. Effective leaders are essential in contributing to the success or failure of a group, organization, or even a whole country [43]. Previous studies show that a good leader is capable of enhancing firm performance [44–46], increasing employees' satisfaction, and improving employees' motivation [47]. Organizational support provides a sound strategic direction and encourages employee motivation [48].

Organizational support is essential for enhancing sustainable entrepreneurship because, leaders are expected to create the best possible products and services through optimum utilization of available resources [49]. Since a substantial change realization requires substantial time and energy, a possible decline in the initial motivation may occur, consequently, those leaders uninterested in sustainable entrepreneurship may fail to provide motivational support, and active participation in the change initiatives. Scholars [50–52] argued that the successful launching and implementation of changes hinges on the product of organizational support from the top leadership. An effort by the organization to shift towards sustainability is considered a vital change initiative that requires cultural change throughout the entire organization [53]. As such, the top leadership provides that support which becomes a firm's vital resource to successfully implement sustainability initiatives [50].

Based on the arguments by [38, 54] that organizational support by top management allows entrepreneurship development and continuous performance improvement among SMEs in Malaysia, the contribution of this study is to support these findings through evaluating the influence of organizational support on sustainable entrepreneurship practices towards performance among Malaysian herbal-based SMEs. Therefore, it is imperative to investigate the potential impact of organizational support in guidance and maintenance of entrepreneurship operations among the Malaysian herbal-based SMEs towards sustainable business performance [55].

1.2.3 Performance

As the global economic order unfolds, organizations are becoming increasingly aware about performance measurement. Performance is multifaceted. This chapter will dwell on only three dimensions: economic, environmental, and social performance. Also, [56] suggested that performance measurement may likely become more complex as stakeholder expectations about companies' economic, environmental, and social responsibilities are constantly shifting.

Performance is one of the most important motives for implementing sustainable entrepreneurship. In 2001, [57] suggested that initial implementation of sustainable entrepreneurship might not positively affect profitability and sales performance in the short-term due to its initial upfront costs. It will however prepare them for a greater long-term performance; through improved capacity for managing environmental risks and effecting continuous environmental and social improvement [58]. The appropriate implementation of improved practices about internal operations is positively associated with firm sustainability performance.

1.3 Theoretical framework

Researchers argued that firms that often implement sustainable entrepreneurship achieve higher performance through lower costs, higher product quality, faster and more reliable delivery, and process flexibility [32, 59, 60]. Also, the practice will help in reducing pollutants and waste to improve environmental performance [32]. Therefore, based on these premise, this chapter assumes that those SME managers that support their employees in implementing sustainable entrepreneurship would achieve business performance.

This study intends to explore the existing interrelationships among and between sustainability antecedents, business strategy, sustainable entrepreneurship implementation, and performance through four different theories, thus; Triple-Bottom-Line (TBL), Strategic Choice Theory (SCT), Strategic Orientation Theory (SOT), and the Resource-Based View Theory (RBV).

1.3.1 Triple-bottom-line (TBL)

Triple-Bottom-Line (TBL or 3BL) is a concept coined by [15] in 1997 with the sole aim of searching for a new lens to view the sustainable values in business practices. He reported that sustainable business conduct has three main value creating aspects, namely: (i) Economic prosperity; (ii) Environmental quality and; (iii) Social justice. His concept was further developed into the "3P formulation" which consists of "people, planet and profit" [16]. Nevertheless, he [16] never illustrated any diagram for TBL; as such, several researchers developed various graphical illustrations on their own to represent TBL with inspiration from him [15, 16]. Currently, there is an increasing use of TBL as a tool or device for sustainable reporting under the headings of environmental quality, social justice and economic prosperity by organizations; due to its ease in monitoring the effects of business activities on the three dimensions in TBL [61, 62].

1.3.2 Strategic choice theory

Strategic Choice Theory [63] suggests the significant role that managerial discretion, understanding, and perspective play towards making crucial choice when taking organizational actions. He further explained that the theory suggests that organizations formulate and implement strategies using freedom of choice while responding to environmental issues to ensure efficient outcomes. Strategic Choice Theory assumes that there is a need for organizations to adapt its internal abilities to external opportunities [64]. This assertion however lends support to the earlier view of [65–67] that organizational structure should follow a strategy; and the choice of the strategy of interest depends on the adjustments made in the organizational structure. Other scholars [68, 69] argue that the theory assumes that there is no specific, unique, or universal management style that can suit any type of organization in different contexts, therefore proposed that organizations should adapt their internal structures to the contingencies perceived in the surrounding environment in which they operate.

1.3.3 Strategic sustainability orientation

Strategic sustainability orientation refers to the strategy-making processes that provide firms with the basis of entrepreneurial decisions and actions [70, 71]. It refers to the strategic entrepreneurial posture that characterizes the behaviors which SMEs engages to discover and exploit entrepreneurial opportunities [71]. Basically, it refers to a firm's strategy, capturing the specific entrepreneurial aspect of decision making styles, methods, and practices [72]. In 2009, [73] defines it as the extent to which an organization is proactive and committed to economic, environmental, and social priorities in its decision-making.

1.3.4 Resource-based view

The resource-based view of the firm theory posits that when a firm have rare, valuable, and non-substitutable resources, it becomes its primary predictors of sustained competitive advantage [74, 75]. Therefore, the study emphasizes on SMEs' unique resources (which include all its assets and capabilities, its attributes, information, and the knowledge it controls) that will enable them to implement sustainable entrepreneurship towards attaining business performance [76].

The study framework examine how SMEs transform their cultural norms and organizational structure to gain social legitimacy among external stakeholders such as competitors, governmental regulators, supply chain members, and NGOs [77]. Also, it examines how SMEs management, using freedom of choice (discretion, interpretation, and perspective) changes the firms' orientation towards implementing sustainability initiatives through creating a sustainability culture [78] via business strategy formulation (that is, the relationship between drivers and strategic orientation), and finding specific ways of efficiently implementing the formulated plan to create favorable performance (that is, the relationships between strategic sustainability orientation, and performance). In essence, the study examines how organizational support trigger SMEs' strategic sustainability orientation. Moreover, using the theoretical perspective of obtaining social legitimacy, clarify on the differentiation in SMEs sustainability orientation under different pressures [79–81]. Furthermore, strategic sustainability orientation acts as a dynamic organization-wide orientation that allows SMEs to invest different types of resources in sustainable entrepreneurship. Finally, using the logic of the TBL and RBV, this study explores how sustainable entrepreneurship implementation gives firms a competitive advantage.

The role of SME entrepreneurs, managers, and employees is critical in building external relations; in this vein, the larger the firm OS, the more intense the reactiveness on SE commitment [22]. In this study, the construct of OS includes the managerial attitude and perspectives, top management support and employee motivation. To sum up, SME managers can influence firm SE adoption rate and be directly related to the degree of involvement via the use of OS and SSO. Based on the above arguments, this paper hypothesized that:

H1 SMEs' OS is positively related to their SSO.

H2 SSO is positively related to SE implementation.

H3 There is a positive relationship between SMEs' OS and SE.

H4 There is a positive relationship between SMEs' SE implementation and performance (economic, environmental, and social).

2. Methodology

2.1 Population and sample

The study used a population of the herbal-based SMEs registered with the National Pharmaceutical Regulatory Agency (NPRA) in Malaysia, because they produce herbal products. There are 532 herbal-based SMEs registered under the traditional and complementary medicine with different categories [82]. Consistent with the suggestions of [83], a total of 300 samples are sufficient for this study; census sampling was employed because of its usability under specific constraints such as budget, time frame and small size population [84].

2.2 Instrument of research

The study employed data collection survey method. A structured questionnaire was designed to elicit information about firm profile characteristics, organizational support, sustainable entrepreneurship, and performance of the herbal-based SMEs in Malaysia. All the items were designed in a five-point Likert scale to generate statistical measurements among the herbal-based SMEs' perception and opinions [85]; based on 'strongly disagree' (one) to 'strongly agree' (five) in respect of their OS and SSO respectively. For SE, the respondents were asked to choose based on 'not at all' (one) to 'to a great extent' (five). For Performance the measure includes: economic performance, based on 'strongly deteriorated (>20%)' (one) to 'strongly improved (>20%)' (five), while for both environmental and social performance, based on 'significant decrease' (one) to 'significant increase' (five) respectively. All items were adapted from previous established studies to ensure their reliability and validity. **Table 2** presents a summary of the questionnaire used for the study.

2.3 Biases controlling techniques

Some techniques were employed in the study to ensure the absence of bias in the data; for nonresponse bias, a comparison made regarding annual revenue and number of employees between early and late respondents revealed no significant difference between the two groups [86, 87]. This result suggests the absence of response bias. For common method bias Harman one-factor test was employed [88, 89].

Variable	No of Items	α
Section A Firm Profile Characteristics	5	N/A
Section B Organizational Support	4	0.931
Sustainable Entrepreneurship	7	0.915
Performance	18:	0.859
Economic	5	0.866
Environmental	7	0.820
Social	6	

Table 2.
A summary of the questionnaire used for the study.

The fundamental assumption of this technique is to detect the presence of common method variance, leading to a single factor emergence from the factor analysis or most concentration of the covariance in one of the factors [90]. As expected, the results yielded four factors which accounted for 71.049% of the total variance. Therefore, neither a single factor emerged from the Harman one-factor test nor did any factor accounted for most of the variance. These results revealed less serious concern regarding common method biases and provided support for the validity of the measurement.

3. Results and discussion

3.1 Firm profile characteristics

The summary of the firm profile characteristics of the herbal-based SMEs is presented in **Table 3**; majority of the firms were owned by sole proprietor (51%), partnership (33%) followed, then corporations (16%). More than two-third of the herbal-based SMEs were established less than 10 years (74%). Also about half of the herbal-based SMEs have staff strength of less than five employees (53.4%) and were in the market less than 10 years (88.4%). For annual revenue, majority of the

Firm profile characteristics	N = 300	
	F	%
Firm type Sole Proprietorship	153	51.0
Partnership	99	33.0
Corporation	48	16.0
Firm age <10 years	222	74.0
> 10 years	78	26.0
Firm size		
<5 people	160	53.4
5–75 people	88	29.3
>75 people	52	17.3
Annual revenue (RM)		
<0.3 Million	181	60.4
0.3–15 Million	94	31.3
>15 Million	25	8.3
Market experience		
<10 years	265	88.4
>10 years	35	11.6
Firm scope		
Local	231	77.0
International	69	23.0

Table 3.
A summary of the firm profile characteristics of the SMEs.

herbal-based SMEs were having less than RM300,000 (60.4%), and market their products locally (77%).

3.2 The structural model evaluation

This multivariate statistical model extends the possibility of relationships among the latent variables. A structural model displays the interrelations among latent constructs and observable variables in the proposed model as a succession of structural equations. **Figure 1** illustrates the research model. The model-fit indices justifies that the overall adjustment is precise (see **Table 4**). The chi-square statistic measures the distance between the original data matrix and the matrix estimated by the model, so it shows a value of 745.589 ($p < 0.001$). It also shows an agreeable $\chi 2/df$ with an index of 2.032, which is below 3.0 threshold value referred by [56]. Additionally, the comparative fit index (CFI) with a value close to one (0.932) indicates an acceptable fit. Root Mean Square of Error Approximation (RMSEA) (0.059) achieved an excellent value, which indicates that the structural model falls within the agreeable range (between 0.030 and 0.080). While Standardized Root Mean Square Residual (SRMR) of (0.065) is within the range of accepted value which indicates a close fit of the proposed model concerning degrees of freedom and the sample variances and covariance, respectively. Therefore, it can be concluded that the data fit the model well considering the entire fit indices [91]. The estimated and evaluated full structural equation model indicated acceptable measurement properties for all latent constructs and their observed indicators. In evaluating the structural model, fit indices examination is the initial step; a scenario of an adequate goodness-of-fit, therefore, demonstrates the soundness of the posited linkages.

The measurement and structural model were assessed by structural equation modeling (SEM) using Amos Graphics because of its good explanatory nature via combining CFA and multiple regression analysis in a transparent manner [84]. **Table 5** presents the psychometric properties of the constructs tested in the model. As [83] suggested, the required measurements refer to the investigation of convergent validity, individual item reliability, composite reliability, and discriminant validity of the measurement model. All AVE values were higher than 0.50. However, since composite reliability is more accurate than Cronbach alpha, we used it to overcome potential deficiencies in the different indicator loadings. All composite

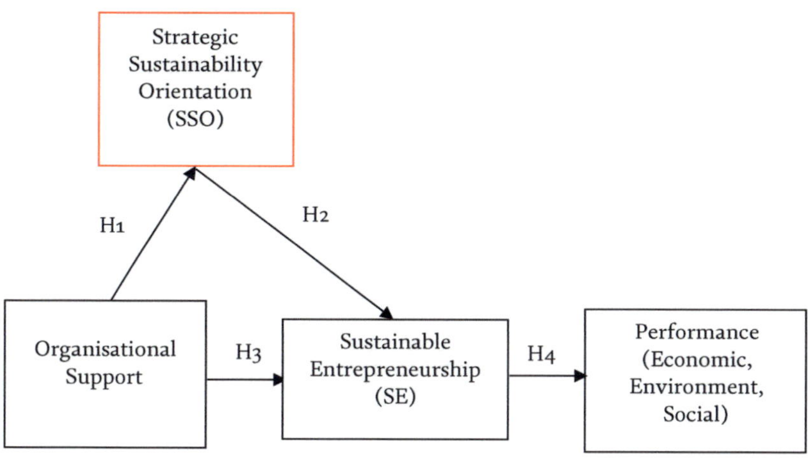

Figure 1.
Proposed model and relationships among OS, SSO, SE, and performance. Source: Author's own.

Measure	Estimate	Threshold	Interpretation
CMIN	745.589	—	—
DF	367	—	—
CMIN/DF	2.032	Between 1 and 3	Excellent
CFI	0.932	>0.95	Acceptable
SRMR	0.065	<0.08	Excellent
RMSEA	0.059	<0.06	Excellent

Table 4.
Goodness of fit (GOF) result.

Dimension	No of items	*CR*	*AVE*
Performance	Three	0.757	0.522
SEP	Seven	0.934	0.671
OS	Four	0.859	0.545
SSO	Three	0.868	0.693

Table 5.
Psychometric properties of the constructs in the model.

reliability values were above the recommended threshold of 0.70, complying with the guidelines provided by [92]. In the present research, AVE values ranged from 0.522 to 0.693 while CR values ranged from 0.757 to 0.934.

3.3 Empirical findings

All the hypotheses were tested via SEM using Amos Graphics. This multivariate statistical model extends the possibility of relationships among the latent variables. The analysis of the hypotheses presents significant values and confirms all the relationships in the proposed model. The finding shows that OS directly contributed to SE implementation and indirectly through SSO among the herbal-based SMEs. **Table 6** shows the detail of the hypothesized relationships; H1 proposed that there is a positive relationship between OS by herbal-based SMEs and their SSO. However, the result shows that the magnitude of the relationship between OS and SSO was significant (β: 0.451, $p < .001$). Meaning that, considering the standardized regression weights, when OS goes up by 1 standard deviation, SSO goes up by 0.451 standard deviations. As such, H1 was supported. However, H2 proposed that herbal-based SMEs' SSO is positively related to their SE implementation. The result shows that the magnitude of the relationship between SSO and SE implementation was strong and shows support for a significant positive relationship (β: 0.545, $p < .001$). Considering the standardized regression weights, this means that, when SSO goes up by 1 standard deviation, SE implementation goes up by 0.545 standard deviations. As such, supports H2. The relationship between herbal-based SMEs OS, and their SE implementation was significant (β: 0.289, $p < .001$). This result indicates that, based on the standardized regression weights, when OS goes up by 1 standard deviation, SEP implementation goes up by 0.289 standard deviations respectively, thus, supporting H3. H4 proposed that higher level of SE implementation is positively related to Performance. However, the result shows that the magnitude of the relationship between a higher level of SE implementation and Performance was significant (β: 0.683, $p < .001$). Considering the standardized regression weights, when

Construct Path	Estimate	Std estimate	S.E.	CR	P	Result
H1 confirmed: OS ⟶ SSO	0.562	0.451	0.074	7.630	***	Significant
H2 confirmed: SSO ⟶ SE	0.848	0.545	0.087	9.738	***	Significant
H3 confirmed: OS ⟶ SE	0.560	0.289	0.100	5.577	***	Significant
H4 confirmed: SE ⟶ Per	0.180	0.683	0.027	6.690	***	Significant

***Note: Significant at* p *< 0.001 (t > ± 2.58); R^2 = 0.52 and 0.47; SE = standard error; and CR = critical ratio.*

Table 6.
Summarized results for hypotheses in the structural model analysis.

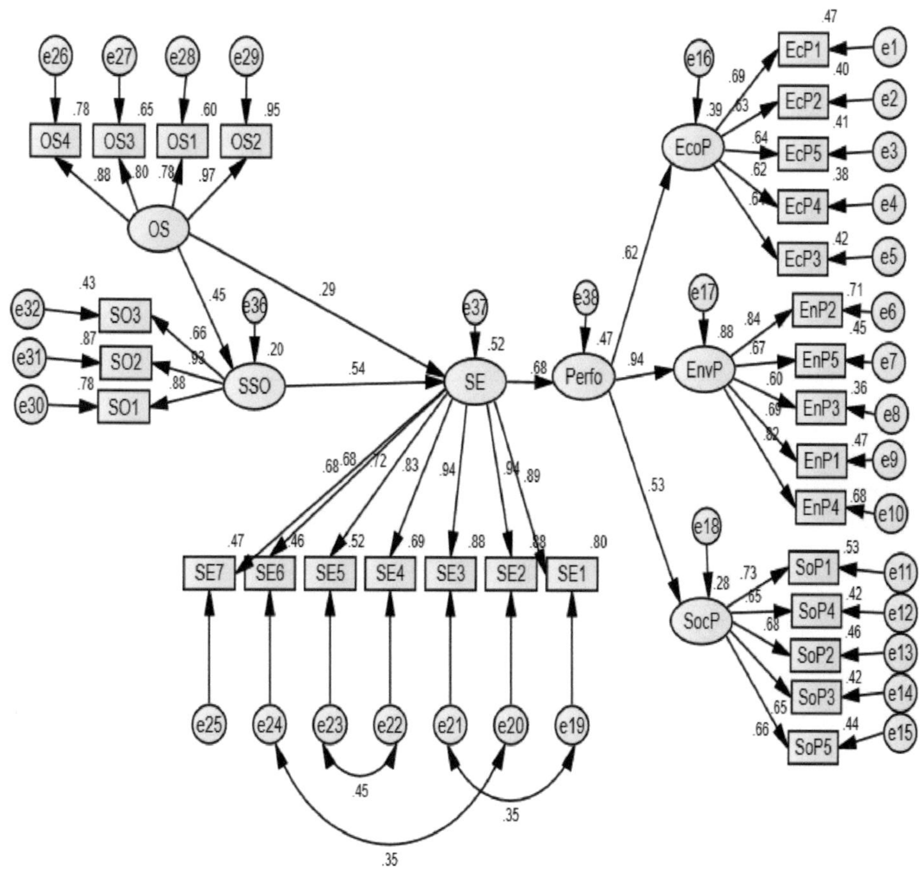

Figure 2.
AMOS test of the structural model.

the higher level of SE implementation goes up by 1 standard deviation, Performance goes up by 0.683 standard deviations. As such, H4 was supported (**Table 6**).

The results show that OS and SSO explained 52% variation in SE implementation, while implementation of SE explains 47% variation of performance among the herbal-based SMEs. The SE implementation to performance path was the most influential predictor (β = 0.683), followed by SSO to SE implementation path (β = 0.545). The least relative path was the direct OS to SE implementation (β = 0.289). Conclusively, the SSO was the main predictor of SE implementation that leads to favorable performance among the Malaysian herbal-based SMEs. **Figure 2** presents the diagram and results of the structural model.

4. Concluding remarks

Findings of this study show that OS construct have positive effects on SE implementation towards performance. As indicated in the SEM results, OS influences SE both directly and indirectly through SSO. However, the indirect influence was stronger. Hence, supports the first three hypotheses (H1, H2, and H3) which postulated that; OS has a significant direct effect on herbal-based SMEs SSO; SSO has a significant direct effect on herbal-based SMEs SE, and OS has significant direct effect on herbal-based SMEs' SE. The results have shown that the top management of the herbal-based SMEs made some commitment to sustainable business development through sustainability attitude and perspective, employee motivation, and

Sustainable entrepreneurship	
SE1	Our firm assesses the quality standard of stakeholders through ISO 9000 series certification
SE2	Our firm evaluates stakeholders' environmental commitment through ISO 14000 series certification
SE3	Our products are made from reduced hazardous materials
SE4	Our firm orders in small lot sizes from our suppliers
SE5	Our firm engages in remanufacturing of products
SE6	Our firm is committed to safe work environment
SE7	Our firm donates to community organizations
Performance:	
Environmental performance	
EnP1	Reduction of emissions
EnP2	Reduction of solid waste
EnP3	Recycling of waste materials
EnP4	Reduction of energy consumption
EnP5	Frequency for environmental accidents
Social performance	
SoP1	Social commitment
SoP2	Engagement with government officials
SoP3	The relationship with local communities
SoP4	Corporate reputation/image
SoP5	The relationship with NGOs
Economic performance	
EcP1	Conformance quality
EcP2	Ability to rapidly change production volumes
EcP3	Market share
EcP4	Return on investment (ROI)
EcP5	Profit margin on sales
Strategic sustainability orientation	
SSO1	Our firm is committed to improving market share
SSO2	Our firm is committed to pollution control
SSO3	Our firm is committed to enhancing social responsibility

Sustainable entrepreneurship	
Organizational support	
OS1	Our firm leadership believes that we will likely gain by implementing initiatives for productivity enhancements
OS2	Our firm leadership considers environmental preservation to be important
OS3	Our firm leadership considers improving the quality of life in respective local communities to be important
OS4	Our firm leadership encourages employees' efforts to reduce harmful environmental wastes

Table 7.
Operationalization of the constructs and their item.

employee support towards implementing SE in their business activities (**Table 7**). The provision of an enabling working environment for employees by SMEs (where top leadership is mindful and considerate of its employees' needs) will enhance continual improvement in performance of the organization, and encourage sustainable business development [50, 52, 93]. Therefore, it is imperative for all SMEs to concentrate on developing an organizational culture characterized by strategic sustainability orientation, positive attitude, employee motivation, and support. Though SME size and scale of production imposes a barrier to their success, nonetheless their chance to effectively achieve sustainable development lies on how their top management is committed to sustainability strategy. This study suggests that SMEs seeking for sustainable business performance should develop a sound organizational culture through sustainability orientation, which provides an enabling environment for SE implementation.

Author details

Muhammad Auwal Abdullahi[1,2]*, Zainalabidin Mohamed[1], Mad Nasir Shamsudin[1], Juwaidah Sharifuddin[1] and Fazlin Ali[1]

1 Department of Agribusiness and Bioresource Economics, Faculty of Agriculture, Universiti Putra Malaysia, 43400 UPM, Serdang, Malaysia

2 Department of Agricultural Economics and Extension, Faculty of Agriculture, Federal University Dutse, P.M.B. 7156, Jigawa State, Nigeria

*Address all correspondence to: muhammad.auwal@fud.edu.ng

References

[1] Ann GE, Zailani S, Abd Wahid N. A study on the impact of environmental management system (EMS) certification towards firms' performance in Malaysia. Management of Environmental Quality: An International Journal. 2006.

[2] Chow IH. The relationship between entrepreneurial orientation and firm performance in China. SAM Advanced Management Journal. 2006 Jul 1;71(3):11.

[3] Lubin DA, Esty DC. The sustainability imperative. Harvard business review. 2010 May 1;88(5):42-50.

[4] Tajasom A, Hung DK, Nikbin D, Hyun SS. The role of transformational leadership in innovation performance of Malaysian SMEs. Asian Journal of Technology Innovation. 2015 May 4;23(2):172-88.

[5] Crane LC. The greening of organizational culture: Management views on the depth, degree and diffusion of change. Change. 2002;15(3):214-34.

[6] OECD, Organization for Economic Cooperation & Development, Organisation de coopération et de développement économiques, Development (OECD) Staff. Environmental indicators for agriculture. Organisation for Economic Co-operation and Development; 1997.

[7] Rhee J, Park T, Lee DH. Drivers of innovativeness and performance for innovative SMEs in South Korea: Mediation of learning orientation. Technovation. 2010 Jan 1;30(1):65-75.

[8] Corbett LM, Claridge GS. Key manufacturing capability elements and business performance. International Journal of Production Research. 2002 Jan 1;40(1):109-31.

[9] Lambert DM, Harrington TC. Measuring nonresponse bias in customer service mail surveys. Journal of Business Logistics. 1990 Jul 1;11(2):5-25.

[10] Pagell M, Wu Z. Building a more complete theory of sustainable supply chain management using case studies of 10 exemplars. Journal of supply chain management. 2009 Apr;45(2):37-56.

[11] Mitchell M, Curtis A, Davidson P. Can the 'triple bottom line'concept help organisations respond to sustainability issues?. InConference proceedings in 5th Australian Stream Management Conference 2007 May 21 (pp. 21-25).

[12] Rogers KW, Purdy L, Safayeni F, Duimering PR. A supplier development program: rational process or institutional image construction?. Journal of Operations Management. 2007 Mar 1;25(2):556-72.

[13] Koe WL, Majid IA. A model for predicting intention towards sustainable entrepreneurship. International Journal of Information, Business and Management. 2014 May 1;6(2):256.

[14] Knight P, Jenkins JO. Adopting and applying eco-design techniques: a practitioners perspective. Journal of cleaner production. 2009 Mar 1;17(5):549-58.

[15] Donaldson L. Teoria da contingência estrutural. Handbook de estudos organizacionais. 1999;1:105-33.

[16] Elkington J. Enter the triple bottom line in Henriques, A. and Richardson, J.(Eds); The Triple Bottom Line: Does It All Add up. Earth scan, UK. 2004.

[17] MacGuire JW. Business and society. Ardent Media; 1963.

[18] Child J. Organization structure and strategies of control: A replication of the Aston study. Administrative science quarterly. 1972 Jun 1:163-77.

[19] Dean TJ, McMullen JS. Toward a theory of sustainable entrepreneurship: Reducing environmental degradation through entrepreneurial action. Journal of business venturing. 2007 Jan 1;22(1):50-76.

[20] Goodman A. Implementing sustainability in service operations at Scandic hotels. Interfaces. 2000 Jun;30(3):202-14.

[21] Hair J, Black W, Babin B, Anderson R. Multivariate Data Analysis 7th Edition Pearson Prentice Hall: JOUR.

[22] Shah R, Ward PT. Lean manufacturing: context, practice bundles, and performance. Journal of operations management. 2003 Mar 1;21(2):129-49.

[23] Kassinis GI, Soteriou AC. Greening the service profit chain: The impact of environmental management practices. Production and operations Management. 2003 Sep;12(3):386-403.

[24] Yi MY, Davis FD. Developing and validating an observational learning model of computer software training and skill acquisition. Information systems research. 2003 Jun;14(2):146-69.

[25] Crals E, Vereeck L. Sustainable entrepreneurship in SMEs: theory and practice. In3rd Global Conference in Environmental Justice and Global Citizenship, Copenhagen, Denmark 2004 Feb 12.

[26] Hashim MK, Zakaria M. A study on leadership styles in SMEs.

[27] Carroll AB. Corporate social responsibility: Evolution of a definitional construct. Business & society. 1999 Sep;38(3):268-95.

[28] Tarabishy A, Solomon G, Fernald LW, Sashkin M. The entrepreneurial leader's impact on the organization's performance in dynamic markets. The Journal of private equity. 2005 Aug 31;8(4):20-9.

[29] Bowen FE, Cousins PD, Lamming RC, Farukt AC. The role of supply management capabilities in green supply. Production and operations management. 2001 Jun;10(2):174-89.

[30] Hu LT, Bentler PM. Cutoff criteria for fit indexes in covariance structure analysis: Conventional criteria versus new alternatives. Structural equation modeling: a multidisciplinary journal. 1999 Jan 1;6(1):1-55.

[31] Magala S, Dixon SE, Clifford A. Ecopreneurship–a new approach to managing the triple bottom line. Journal of Organizational Change Management. 2007 May 29.

[32] Tzschentke NA, Kirk D, Lynch PA. Going green: Decisional factors in small hospitality operations. International Journal of Hospitality Management. 2008 Mar 1;27(1):126-33.

[33] Gul S, Ahmad B, Rehman SU, Shabir N, Razzaq N. Leadership styles, turnover intentions and the mediating role of organizational commitment. InInformation and Knowledge Management 2012 (Vol. 2, No. 7, pp. 44-51).

[34] Awang Z. SEM made simple: A gentle approach to learning Structural Equation Modeling. MPWS Rich Publication; 2015 Aug 1.

[35] Barney J. Firm resources and sustained competitive advantage. Journal of management. 1991 Mar;17(1):99-120.

[36] Kotter JP, Cohen DS. The heart of change: Real-life stories of how people change their organizations. Harvard Business Press; 2012 Oct 23.

[37] Baines A, Langfield-Smith K. Antecedents to management accounting change: a structural equation approach. Accounting, organizations and society. 2003 Oct 1;28(7-8):675-98.

[38] Parrish BD. Sustainability-driven entrepreneurship: Principles of organization design. Journal of business Venturing. 2010 Sep 1;25(5):510-23.

[39] Fiedler FE. Research on leadership selection and training: One view of the future. Administrative science quarterly. 1996 Jun 1:241-50.

[40] Sharma S. Managerial interpretations and organizational context as predictors of corporate choice of environmental strategy. Academy of Management journal. 2000 Aug 1;43(4):681-97.

[41] Lawrence PR, Lorsch JW. As empresas eo ambiente: diferenciação e integração administrativas. Vozes; 1973.

[42] Schaltegger S, Synnestvedt T. The forgotten link between" Green" and economic success: Environmental management as the crucial trigger between environmental and economic performance. CSM; 2001.

[43] Gladwin TN, Kennelly JJ, Krause TS. Shifting paradigms for sustainable development: Implications for management theory and research. Academy of management Review. 1995 Oct 1;20(4):874-907.

[44] Mintzberg H, Ahlstrand B, Lampel J. Safári da estratégia. Bookman Editora; 2009 Mar 31.

[45] Sumin V, Rezai G, Mohamed Z. Factors affecting the implementation of green practices among traditional and complementary herbal-based entrepreneurs in Malaysia. Borneo Akademika. 2016;1(1):79-87.

[46] Tilley F, Young W. Sustainability Entrepreneurs. Greener Management International. 2009 Feb 1(55).

[47] Ogbonna E, Harris LC. Leadership style, organizational culture and performance: empirical evidence from UK companies. international Journal of human resource management. 2000 Jan 1;11(4):766-88.

[48] Heugens PP, Lander MW. Structure! Agency!(and other quarrels): A meta-analysis of institutional theories of organization. Academy of management journal. 2009 Feb;52(1):61-85.

[49] Hansmann KW, Kroeger C. Proactive environmental management of manufacturing companies. InEnvironmentally Conscious Manufacturing 2001 Feb 9 (Vol. 4193, pp. 135-144). International Society for Optics and Photonics.

[50] Crust L, Keegan R. Mental toughness and attitudes to risk-taking. Personality and Individual Differences. 2010 Aug 1;49(3):164-8.

[51] Koe WL, Majid IA. Sustainable entrepreneurship among small and medium enterprises (SMEs) in Malaysia. International Journal. 2013 Jun;2(4):286-90.

[52] Kotter J. Leading change: Why transformation efforts fail. Harvard business review. 2007;86:97-103.

[53] Hay R, Gray E. Social responsibilities of business managers. Academy of management journal. 1974 Mar 1;17(1):135-43.

[54] Ahmed A, McQuaid RW. Entrepreneurship, management, and

sustainable development. World Review of Entrepreneurship, Management and Sustainable Development. 2005 Jan 1;1(1):6-30.

[55] Arham A, Muenjohn N, Boucher C. The role of entrepreneurial orientation in the leadership-Organisational performance relationship: A Malaysian SMEs perspectives. In24th Annual SEAANZ Conference 2011 (pp. 4-26). The Small Enterprise Association of Australia and New Zealand.

[56] Kline RB. Principles and practice of structural equation modeling. Guilford publications; 2015 Nov 3.

[57] Bohdanowicz P. Theory and practice of environmental management and monitoring in hotel chains. Sustainable tourism futures: Perspectives on systems, restructuring and innovations. 2009 Jan 13:102-30.

[58] Zhu Q, Sarkis J. Relationships between operational practices and performance among early adopters of green supply chain management practices in Chinese manufacturing enterprises. Journal of operations management. 2004 Jun 1;22(3):265-89.

[59] Schaper M. The essence of ecopreneurship. Greener management international. 2002 Jun 22:26-30.

[60] Setthasakko W. Determinants of corporate sustainability: Thai frozen seafood processors. British food journal. 2007 Feb 20.

[61] Lumpkin GT, Dess GG. Clarifying the entrepreneurial orientation construct and linking it to performance. Academy of management Review. 1996 Jan 1;21(1):135-72.

[62] McDonald, M. F. Sustainability - Understanding the Triple-bottom-line: People, Planet and Profit: Which Comes First? Retrieved 26th Feb 2015 from http://www.qualitydigest.com/inside/quality-insider-column/sustainability-understandingtriple-bottom-line.html#.

[63] Chandler AD. Strategy and structure: Chapters inthe history of the American industrial enterprise. Cambridge: MIT Press. ChandlerStrategy and structure: Chapters in the history of the American industrial enterprise1962. 1962.

[64] Kassim ZA, Sulaiman M. Market orientation and leadership styles of managers in Malaysia. International Journal of Leadership Studies. 2011;6(2):230-45.

[65] Ayuso S. Comparing voluntary policy instruments for sustainable tourism: The experience of the Spanish hotel sector. Journal of Sustainable Tourism. 2007 Mar 15;15(2):144-59.

[66] Chan WW, Wong KK, Lo JY. Environmental quality index for the Hong Kong hotel sector. Tourism economics. 2008 Dec;14(4):857-70.

[67] McCartney J, Rouse P. A framework for sustainability, strategy and management control. InFourth Asia Pacific Interdisciplinary Research in Accounting Conference, Singapore 2004 (Vol. 4).

[68] DiMaggio PJ, Powell WW. The iron cage revisited: Institutional isomorphism and collective rationality in organizational fields. American sociological review. 1983 Apr 1:147-60.

[69] Lawal FA, Worlu RE, Ayoade OE. Critical success factors for sustainable entrepreneurship in SMEs: Nigerian perspective. Mediterranean Journal of Social Sciences. 2016 May 8;7(3 S1):338.

[70] Cohen B, Winn MI. Market imperfections, opportunity and sustainable entrepreneurship. Journal

of business venturing. 2007 Jan 1;22(1):29-49.

[71] Lindgreen A, Swaen V, Maon F, Defee CC, Esper T, Mollenkopf D. Leveraging closed-loop orientation and leadership for environmental sustainability. Supply Chain Management: An International Journal. 2009 Mar 13.

[72] Choi DY, Gray ER. The venture development processes of "sustainable" entrepreneurs. Management Research News. 2008 Jun 20.

[73] National Pharmaceutical Regulatory Agency. The total number of companies registered under herbal-based categories for the year 2015. http://npra.moh.gov.my/index.php/recent-updates/quest-list-of-manufacturers-wholesales-importers. (Accessed 10 June 2016).

[74] Barber N. "Green" wine packaging: targeting environmental consumers. International Journal of Wine Business Research. 2010 Nov 9.

[75] Chung-Wen Y. The relationships among leadership styles, entrepreneurial orientation, and business performance. Managing Global Transitions. 2008 Jul 1;6(3):257.

[76] Barney J, Wright M, Ketchen Jr DJ. The resource-based view of the firm: Ten years after 1991. Journal of management. 2001 Dec;27(6):625-41.

[77] Rezai G, Sumin V, Mohamed Z, Shamsudin MN, Sharifuddin J. Implementing green practices as sustainable innovation among herbal-based SME entrepreneurs. Journal of food products marketing. 2016 Jan 2;22(1):1-8.

[78] Shah R, Ward PT. Defining and developing measures of lean production. Journal of operations management. 2007 Jun 1;25(4):785-805.

[79] Davies AR, Mullin SJ. Greening the economy: interrogating sustainability innovations beyond the mainstream. Journal of Economic Geography. 2011 Sep 1;11(5):793-816.

[80] John E. Cannibals with forks: the triple bottom line of 21st century business. New Society: Stony Creek, CT. 1997.

[81] Lee SY. Drivers for the participation of small and medium-sized suppliers in green supply chain initiatives. Supply chain management: an international journal. 2008 May 2.

[82] Meade AW, Watson AM, Kroustalis CM. Assessing common methods bias in organizational research. In22nd annual meeting of the society for industrial and organizational psychology, New York 2007 Apr 19 (pp. 1-10).

[83] Hashim F. SMEs' impediments and developments in the internationalization process. World Journal of Entrepreneurship, Management and Sustainable Development. 2015 May 11.

[84] Yoon E, Tello S. Corporate social responsibility as a driver of sustainable innovation: greening initiatives of leading global brands. In: Competition Forum 2009 Jul 1 (Vol. 7, No. 2, p. 290). American Society for Competitiveness.

[85] Covin JG, Slevin DP. Strategic management of small firms in hostile and benign environments. Strategic management journal. 1989 Jan;10(1):75-87.

[86] Armstrong JS, Overton TS. Estimating nonresponse bias in mail surveys. Journal of marketing research. 1977 Aug;14(3):396-402.

[87] Krozer Y. Innovations and the Environment. Springer Science & Business Media; 2008 May 6.

[88] Majid IA, Koe WL. Sustainable entrepreneurship (SE): A revised model based on triple bottom line (TBL). International Journal of Academic Research in Business and Social Sciences. 2012 Jun 1;2(6):293.

[89] Podsakoff PM, MacKenzie SB, Lee JY, Podsakoff NP. Common method biases in behavioral research: a critical review of the literature and recommended remedies. Journal of applied psychology. 2003 Oct;88(5):879.

[90] Papalexandris N, Galanaki E. Leadership's impact on employee engagement. Leadership & Organization Development Journal. 2009 Jun 12.

[91] Junqueira E, Dutra EV, Zanquetto Filho H, Gonzaga RP. The effect of strategic choices and management control systems on organizational performance. Revista Contabilidade & Finanças. 2016 Dec;27(72):334-48.

[92] Yang MG, Hong P, Modi SB. Impact of lean manufacturing and environmental management on business performance: An empirical study of manufacturing firms. International Journal of Production Economics. 2011 Feb 1;129(2):251-61.

[93] Epstein MJ. Making Sustainability Work: Best Practices in Managing and Measuring Corporate Social. Environmental and Economic Impacts, Greenleaf, Sheffield. 2008.

Chapter 5

Institutional Structures and Women Sustainability in the Labour Market for Developing Economies

Oluwabunmi O. Adejumo

Abstract

The peculiarity of women in developing economies, through changing status (marriage, widowhood, divorce, separation) and in some cases occasioned by locational vicissitudes, have continually challenged the sustainability of women in the labour market. Again, some of these challenges women face via social structures such as patriarchy, customs and traditions and unpaid household chores have particularly resulted in labour somersault, underemployment and forced unemployment which in certain cases could be temporary or of a permanent nature. Owing to this growing vulnerability of women, this chapter examine models and structures that have shaped (promoted or otherwise) women's' participation in the labour market. In turn, this chapter advances alternative institutional and organizational structures that can check some bewilderment of women in participating in the labour market, as well as foster the sustainability of women in the labour market.

Keywords: women, sustainability, labour market, institutions, inequality

1. Introduction

The economic inequality and social segregation faced by women in the labour market have racial, religious, cultural and residential dimensions. For instance, by examining the differences in employment and economic activity among women in Israel (Muslim-Arabs, Christian-Arabs and Druze-Arabs), Khattab [1] observed that ethnic differences affected the outcomes of women activities in the labour market.

Despite these differences, the participation of women in the labour force has been growing over the years. The *World Employment Social Outlook* [2][1], noted that on the global scene, as at 2018, women's participation rates in developed countries hit 52.4 percent, and are gradually closed in on men with 15.6 percentage points; while the case of developing economies is even more with a female labour participation (FLP) rate of 69 percent and a gender gap rate closing in at 11.8 percentage points. Of this statistics, sub-Saharan African countries recorded a FLP rate of 64.7 percent and a record low gender gap of 9.3 percentage points. According to the report of the

[1] https://www.ilo.org/wcmsp5/groups/public/---dgreports/---dcomm/---publ/documents/publication/wcms_619577.pdf

International Labour Organization [3], while the rising trend of female participation and reduction in gender gaps in developed economies can be largely attributed to increases in human capital; the experience of developing economies are as a result of socio-economic necessities to include poverty and lack of social protection. This implies that the drive towards women labour participation in developed economies is more of *pull* factors as against developing economies which tilt towards *push* factors[2]. For instance, Chaykowski & Powell [5] noted that the participation of women in the labour market is increasing and even closing in on the men; and this is largely explained by educational attainment of these women; whereas, Keck and Saraceno [6] using *motherhood penalty hypothesis* argues that education has no bearing with women's employment. Therefore, the flexibility in workplace or upheavals from work stress vis-a-vis domestic chores goes along way to determine the continual involvement of women within the labour market.

Meanwhile, in an era where the quest for sustainable development is focal, and in consonance with global goals on women empowerment, the concern of this chapter mediates beyond the participation of women in labour markets to how well women are sustained in these markets. In addressing sustainability in labour market, pertinent issues of concern include the sector of employment (formal or informal), nature of employments (skilled or unskilled), the type of wages (discriminatory or non-discriminatory), as well as work-life balance. Therefore, by examining different models of fostering women participation, this chapter takes a clue to suggest adaptive institutions for women sustainability in the labour market.

This chapter is further reviews studies that have examined women participation in the labour market. Sequel to this, is the section that identifies and infer suitable models that can foster the women sustainability in the labour market. The last section concludes this chapter.

2. Review of women participation in the labour market

Reflections on the flexibility of women experiences via their participation in labour market have been lopsided vis-à-vis their family life. For instance, human capital which is a major input to production has been continuously affected in terms of human health, especially with regard to black African women [7–9]. The World Bank Report in 2006 revealed that women have more likelihood of contacting ailments compared to men [10]. This is because of the certain demographic impacts and congenital peculiarities; thus, making women more vulnerable.

Women engagement in economic activities in sub-Saharan Africa have been shaped by certain socio-economic phenomena like culture, discrimination, crude methods or approaches to production, herculean means of sourcing finance, exposure to harassment both at family and societal levels and marketing strategies [11]. Koopmans [12] utilized the Eurislam' survey of four immigrant ethnic groups of predominantly Muslim belief—Turks, Moroccans, former Yugoslav Muslims and Pakistani—and native ethnics. Koopman noted that once socio-economic variables such as language proficiency, interethnic social ties and gender values are accounted for between natives and immigrants, the differences in the rates of labour market participation and unemployment between native ethnics and immigrants reduce and become insignificant statistically. In the meantime, Anxo *et al.* [13] examines the patterns of labour market integration in the course of life of men and women in seven European countries. By utilizing certain household characteristics such

[2] see Akinyemi and Adejumo [4]

as parenting and non-parenting, married or cohabiting as well as retired workers across different phases in life's course- Nordic '*universal breadwinner* ' model, the '*modified breadwinner*' model, the *Mediterranean* '*exit or full-time*' model and the '*Maternal part-time work*'- Anxo et al. [13] noted that the Nordic model offers important insights for EU employment policy. This is because it offers opportunities for life-long employment is a gendered-friendly model which not only reduces inequality in time allocation to employment but is also designed to encourage the participation of aging workers.

The case of migrant women workers appears more challenging. Koopmans [12] notes that most foreign-born immigrants and their successors or offspring are worse off on the labour market than natives within European immigration countries. This is because the rate of labour force participation of these migrants are lower as they are either unemployed, underemployed, discriminated against, or poorly paid. Similarly, in an assessment, Haberfeld, Semyonov and Cohen [14] utilizes the immigrants' assimilation hypothesis and ethnic-based stratification to examine the economic performance of immigrants of the former Soviet Union in Israel. They found that gender and ethnicity are crucial in integrating immigrants within the labour market in their country of destination. Assimilation into the Israeli labour market. Unlike men, this goes a long way to affect women wage bargaining powers, earnings and available opportunities. They also noted that European women prefer to participate in the labour force than Asian women in high-status occupations and to earn more than withdrawing totally from the labour market.

3. Models explaining the participation of women in the labour market

3.1 State-based vs. liberal feminism model

The state-based model encourages the participation of women in the labour market based on equal opportunities, individualism and freedom of choice. The liberals opine that the state cannot suffice to actualize the desired equality for men and women in the labour market; therefore, the point of convergence between the liberals and the state will be to institute policies that can promote equal playing field for men and women alike; as well as still enact state policies and interventions that addresses the peculiarities of women [15]. Also, Langley and Mellor [16] added that given certain structural constraints of the neoliberal ideologies, nascent global systems have begun to embrace transformative sites and spaces via state institutions and global civil society as complements or alternatives to existing structures for actualizing women sustainability in market. Meanwhile, the neoliberal feminism model added the need to promote the benefits of labour flexibility, entrepreneurship and empowerment opportunities among women, which represents market-based solutions to women in the labour market [17].

3.2 Individualist vs. collectivist model

As against the individual approach to seeking redress or advocacy within organizations or in the labour market, the collectivist approach is such that interest or homogeneous groups (such as women) within the labour market can integrate in order to tackle common challenges or advance positive courses of actions. For instance, Whitehouse [15] noted that thriving industrial relations network, high level of public employment and sustained expenditure on active labour programmes have greater prospects of yielding outputs for women.

3.3 Formal and informal models

Unlike informal systems, Ramani et al. [18] argued that formal systems are largely characterized by rigidities such that emerging and even existing women entrepreneurs often require training and re-training to master certain business capabilities. As laudable as the formal systems appear, the informal systems have their place of suitability in the labour markets in creating jobs especially for less-skilled persons as well as complementing jobs within the formal systems. As a result, hinging on the principle of social justice and equitycc, intermediary institutions such as non-governmental organizations (NGOs) and women -centered institutions relevant to women in the informal systems could gradually capture the women in the informal markets to re-establish themselves in what is referred to as the Base of Pyramid (BoP) markets especially in developing countries.

3.4 Cultural vs. enclave model

Cultural Model: used to describe the behavior of women in different set-ups such as politics, family life, labour market, etc. Basically, the model explains how socio-cultural phenomena shapes individuals. Khattab [1] noted that the patriarchal system in developing societies limit or outrightly prevent women from participating in activities other than martial duties. For instance, institutional mechanisms within the Arab communities are structured to engage women more in domestic chores rather than participate in public activities; which also hold sway for Pakistan and Bangladesh.

These are economies that evolve as a result of marginalization of certain groups or persons. The enclave model is a response of a homogenous group (persons with similar conditions) such as immigrants, intra-ethnic segregants, and war-torn persons to segregation structures or activities within the labour market. By carving a niche for themselves, they evolve measures to participate in the labour market irrespective of their seeming limitations. Through their peculiar crafting or skills, the enclave model evolves a process where minority groups find their place and contribute to the labour market. Khattab [1] noted the occupational success of the Arab enclave economy which grew because of the discrimination of the Arabs within the Israeli community. However, the enclave system is limited in opportunities and expansion owing to the specialization phenomenon. As a result, people attempt to get jobs outside the enclave community and this which easier for the men than women due to social and structural barriers [1].

3.5 Dual-earner vs. dual-carer model

This is a model that evolved in Sweden in the early 1990s as a response to negative economic growth, budget deficits and unemployment [19]. Therefore, as part of policy instruments, the Swedish government reduced public expenditures and fostered policies that encouraged the integration of men and women alike in the labour market. Through instruments such as parental leave and allowances, both men and women were opportune to work as well take leave at varying times, and still be entitled to allowances especially when it comes to catering for the home front. This pattern encouraged planning for women and men to take their turns in deciding work times and when to take leave to cater for their homes.

3.6 Nordic vs. modified Nordic model

The Nordic model is also known as the universal bread winner's model. It is a lifelong form of employment sector. Apart from the continuity or long-term nature of this form of employment, it also accommodates a high number of the labour force

[13]. The Nordic model presents high employment sustainability possibilities in the course of a workers' life as well as a very high incidence of earning opportunities for both men and women alike; apparently indicating low gender disparities in labour market integration. This model is typical of the Nordic economies such as Sweden. Some of the characteristics of the Nordic model exemplified with the Swedish economy include female part-time work, discouragement of dual-earners with either excessive work hours, low wage differentials between men and women, marginal tax system, insurance, and unemployment benefits. Anxo et al. [13] equally noted several opportunities to balance work time over the life course for periods of extended leave with employment protection. This leave could include maternity leave, leave to cater for sick children, dependents and relatives as well as flexible retirement options. For example, in cases of maternity leave, there are options for a period of full-time absence or reduced working hours reinforced with high-earnings replacement ratio. Thus, owing to the wholistic approach of the Nordic model, it has been passed as being an efficient tool for the integration and sustainability of women in the labour market.

The Modified Nordic model is linked with complete or partial (negotiated/reduced work hours) withdrawal of women from the labour market usually to gain time to cater for their children. This model is exemplified in France where mothers have access to low public child care facilities and a high coverage from the government. However, unlike the Nordic model, unemployment rate within the French economy is still high among women compared to men; also, the feasibility of being in through one's life is very low for women as well as the aged [13].

Following these models within the European economies, whether the Nordic or modified Nordic model, according to Anxo et al. [13], building families and parenting are baseline causes of women withdrawal from the labour market. Therefore, developing economies may have to still have to factor the peculiarity of women in their economies to come up with suitable and functional policies that will sustain women in the labour market.

3.7 Mediterranean vs. maternal part-time model

The mediterranean labour market model is a classic case of a rigid labour system that disorient and disintegrate women from the labour market. It is typified by an exit of women/mothers from the labour market. In economies where the Mediterranean model holds sway, female employment is at its lowest ebb, while the rate of male workers are higher. The Mediterranean model is prevalent in Italy and Spain. It appears less flexible with restricted leave opportunities for women; and where women are seen to be employed, they usually work full-time and there are little or no provisions for child-care and pre-school facilities. As a result, women in these economies defy motherhood until they can gin grounds in career paths or employments. Meanwhile, the maternal part-time model is slightly different from the mediterranean model because the exit of women from the labour market offer mothers opportunities for part-time work, hourly pay and limited child-care facilities; thereby, causing withdrawal of women from the labour market less pronounced. These models are common sights in the United Kingdom, the Netherlands and Germany. According to Anxo et al. [13], the maternal part-time model includes financial options such as transfers and tax splitting, in order to encourage short-work periods.

4. Institutions for women sustainability in the labour market: posers for developing economies

Following the reviews conducted, several models and hypothesis have advanced courses to foster the participation and integration of women in the labour market.

Following some of these tenets, a course for the sustainability of women in the labour market is advanced via institutional mechanisms for developing economies.

There are myriads of institutions that could cater or ensure the sustainability of women within the labour market in developing economies. The identified institutions in **Figure 1** above are suggestive but not exhaustive. For instance, educational institutions such as child care centers or preschool facilities can help women to plan their work-life and still participate in gainful employment. The conduct of corporate organizations and financing institutions has a great deal with stimulating women participation in the labour market. For instance, Grosser [20] noted that a corporate social responsibility targeted at women can be a policy instrument to check gender equality as well as foster women. Also, Barea & Cesana [21] added that social protection for women via health provisions and other dimensions as another instrument for extending and sustaining women in the labour market.

Meanwhile, the role government institutions that are women-focused in shaping and channeling mediations for women sustainability in the labour markets remains cardinal. As noted earlier, some women may decide to work formal or informal systems. Therefore, owing to the thriving market systems prevalent in organizations, the role of government in mediating and mainstreaming organizational policies to foster women participation and sustainability cannot be overemphasized. Again, owing to the prevalence of informal systems that permeates developing economies [18], women-centered government institutions that seeks to integrate women for sustainable participation in the labour market is equally critical in the process of development. Although, Ramani *et al* [18] cautioned against the existing labour

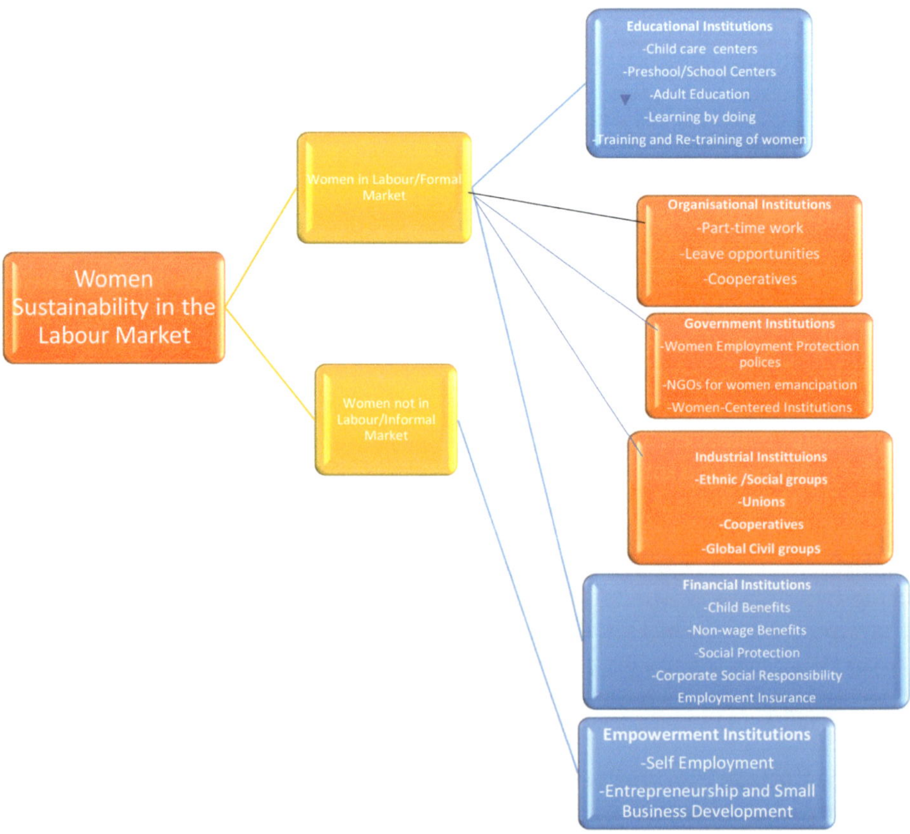

Figure 1.
Institutional framework for women sustainability in the labour market. Source: Author.

recommendations of *formalizing the informal economies* as the viable or best course for the sustainability of women in the labour market; rather, they propose that the sustainability of women within the informal sector depends on forms of agreements with other persons in business as well as the availability of women-centered mediators in different market arrangements.

In all, some other institutions could be in form of industrial relations such as cooperatives and unions; as well private and public empowerment institutions where the peculiarities of women especially as dual earners and carers are considered for sustainable labour outcomes.

Author details

Oluwabunmi O. Adejumo
Institute for Entrepreneurship and Development Studies, Obafemi Awolowo University, Ile-Ife, Nigeria

*Address all correspondence to: jumobum@gmail.com; adejumobum@oauife.edu.ng

References

[1] Khattab, N. (2002). Ethnicity and Female Labour Market Participation: a New Look at the Palestinian Enclave in Israel. *Work, Employment and Society*, *16*(1), 91-110. https://doi.org/10.1177/09500170222119263

[2] Kuhn S, Milasi S, Yoon S. World Employment Social Outlook: Trends 2018. Geneva: ILO; 2018

[3] International Labour Office. World employment and social outlook: trends for women 2017. International Labour Office; 2017

[4] Akinyemi F, Adejumo O. Entrepreneurial motives and challenges of SMEs owners in emerging economies: Nigeria & South Africa. Small. 2017;**10**:50. DOI: 10.13189/aeb.2017.051105

[5] Chaykowski, R. P., & Powell, L. M. (1999). Women and the labour market: Recent trends and policy issues. *Canadian Public Policy/Analyse de Politiques*, S1-S25.

[6] Keck, W., & Saraceno, C. (2013). The impact of different social-policy frameworks on social inequalities among women in the European Union: The labour-market participation of mothers. *Social Politics*, *20*(3), 297-328.

[7] Asongu, S. A., & Odhiambo, N. M., (2018). "ICT, Financial Access and Gender Inclusion in the Formal Economic Sector: Evidence from Africa", *African Finance Journal*, 20(2), pp. 45-65.

[8] Asongu, S. A., & Odhiambo, N. M., (2019a). "Inequality and the Economic Participation of Women in Sub-Saharan Africa: An Empirical Investigation", *African Journal of Economic and Managment Studies*. DOI: 10.1108/AJEMS-01-2019-0016.

[9] Asongu, S. A., & Odhiambo, N. M., (2019b). "Inequality thresholds, governance and gender economic inclusion in sub-Saharan Africa", *International Review of Applied Economics*, DOI: 10.1080/02692171.2019.1645817

[10] Dunga, S. H. (2019). Analysis of the Demand for Private Healthcare in South Africa. *Studia Universitatis Babes Bolyai-Oeconomica*, *64*(1), 59-70.

[11] Eboiyehi FA, Adeyemi MO, Adejumo OO. Barriers and Constraints to Women Entrepreneurship in Ile-Ife of South-Western Nigeria. Ife Journal of Entrepreneurship and Business Management, Maiden Issue Vol. **1**(1); 2015

[12] Koopmans, R. (2016). Does assimilation work? Sociocultural determinants of labour market participation of European Muslims. Journal of Ethnic and Migration Studies, 42(2), 197-216.

[13] Anxo Dominique, Colette Fagan, Inmaculada Cebrian, Gloria Moreno (2007). Patterns of labour market integration in Europe—a life course perspective on time policies, *Socio-Economic Review*, Volume 5, Issue 2, Pages 233-260, https://doi.org/10.1093/ser/mwl019

[14] Haberfeld, Y., Semyonov, M., & Cohen, Y. (2000). Ethnicity and labour market performance among recent immigrants from the former Soviet Union to Israel. *European Sociological Review*, *16*(3), 287-299.

[15] Whitehouse, G. (1992). Legislation and labour market gender inequality: an analysis of OECD countries. *Work, employment and society*, *6*(1), 65-86.

[16] Langley, P., & Mellor, M. (2002). 'Economy', sustainability and sites of

transformative space. *New Political Economy*, *7*(1), 49-65.

[17] Shade, L. R. (2018). Hop to it in the gig economy: The sharing economy and neo-liberal feminism. *International Journal of Media & Cultural Politics*, *14*(1), 35-54.

[18] Ramani, S. V., Thutupalli, A., Medovarszki, T., Chattopadhyay, S., & Ravichandran, V. (2013). Women entrepreneurs in the informal economy: Is formalization the only solution for business sustainability?.

[19] Nyberg, A. (2003). Economic Crisis and the Sustainability of the Dual Earner, Dual Carer Model: Working Paper, ESRC seminar series 'Work, Life and Time in the New Economy.

[20] Grosser, K. (2009). Corporate social responsibility and gender equality: women as stakeholders and the European Union sustainability strategy. *Business Ethics: A European Review*, *18*(3), 290-307.

[21] Barea, M., & Cesana, G. (2006). Social protection sustainability, prolongation of working life and greater participation of women in the labour market. *La Medicina del lavoro*, *97*(2), 148.

Chapter 6

Protection of Craft Products Embodied in Cultural and Creative Industries in South Africa

Abisuga Oluwayemisi Adebola

Abstract

The Culture and Creative industries are commonly recognised as one of the strategic sectors. This sector has the potential for innovation and development which may lead to economic growth of a nation. Even though the culture and creative industries (CCIs) is the focus of several studies, precise consideration has not been given to the craft sectors as an essential component of the South African industrial development. The objective of this research is to identify the problems faced by crafts sectors, and to address those issues by providing policy intervention towards protection and sustainability of the sector. Also, the position of craft has been widely acknowledged, but the research regarding the protection of craft products is scarce. This gives rise to the research question: how can the crafts sectors be protected towards the sustainability and development of these sectors? This study provides an overview of the concept of craft and the CCIs focusing on the craft production and marketing activities. For this study, a qualitative research was conducted using a secondary data, and conducting an in-depth interview with crafters in the city of Durban South Africa. The results established some basic issues that need an urgent intervention towards the preservation of the craft sector in South Africa.

Keywords: craft, cultural industries, creative industries, entrepreneur, sustainability

1. Introduction

The craft sector's potential for job creation is one of the main attractions of this sector. Buschfeld Dilger and Heb [1] also has shown that craft business is a significant creator of jobs and the improve livelihood in all Sub-Saharan African countries including South Africa. It does not only generate income for groups or individual which have access to resources, but also offers employment opportunities to the underprivileged people in South Africa. Many South African rural areas have a low literacy rate, and low level of education, but have artistic skills [2]. These underprivileged people could survive through artistic or natural crafting skills, if the industry is well established. Hence, the craft sector is one of the few entry opportunities available to South Africans currently exempted from the formal economy. Alexander [3] has shown that promoting the craft sector is a key strategy of alleviating poverty in communities that need liberation from economic deprivation.

Even though, the position of craft sector has been known long before, but in Africa this sector has experienced many challenges such as innovation, globalisation and industrialisation [4], therefore, the artisans were unable to compete with well-ordered industrial division and had to market their products at lower cost [5]. Consequently, the craft product is threatened, and this sector requires attention to protect the knowledge, heritage, and inherited skills. Nevertheless, it is very important to intensely understand and discuss the challenges confronted by the craft sectors, so as to protect traditions and heritage, failure to do this can make heritage disappear in the near future.

The position crafts represented in cultural and creative products are of a different nature, that cut-across all the components in the classifications of CCIs. Therefore, the strategic agenda to facilitate the crafts entrepreneurs needs to be set down, so that this sector can effectively function as a national CCI, enhancing the import, export and local trade of craft products [6]. This research argued that an inclusive intervention and approach should be engaged to support craft entrepreneurs through the entire CCIs, so as to strengthen both producers and marketers, and improving their products to protect the sector. The research is qualitative using a secondary data and structured interviews to better provide an answer to the question; how can the crafts sectors be protected towards the sustainability and development of these sectors? This study specially focuses on the craft sectors to quantify the trade activities of the sectors within the statistical core of the culture and creative industries as defined by the United Nations for Conference on Trade and Development (UNCTAD). The study comprehends the exact depth of the craft industry in the cultural and creative industry trade activities of South Africa with selected countries. The results and policy intervention provided in this study will be helpful to the researchers, policy and decision makers in the government or other interested stakeholders to improve, infrastructure, support measures and policies towards the protection and sustainability of the craft sectors.

2. The concept of cultural and creative industries

The concept of creative Industry is a term that was initiated in the 1990s. Today, many ideas have been provided as to what the Creative Industries consist of. Nevertheless, there has been no specific definition as many debates surrounding this term. The diversity in definitions of creative industry is linked to the associated terms such as Cultural Economics, Creative Economy, and Cultural Industries which are most difficult to define. However, the scope of the creative economy is determined by the level of the creative industries [6]. "Creative Industry" is a term initiated in the early 1990s. Today, the definition is broadened encompassing many ideas and definitions. Nevertheless, there has been no single definition as there are many debates surrounding this term. Many a time's creative industries are linked or associated with the terms such as 'Cultural Economics', 'Creative Economy', and 'Cultural Industries'. Sometimes these terms are used interchangeably. Moreover, the scope of the creative economy is determined by the level of the creative industries.

2.1 Cultural industries

Jodhpur initiatives [7], provided the following framework for cultural industries, from a long-term interagency support programme for the promotion of cultural industries in the Asia-Pacific region, as a means of strategy for poverty reduction and community regeneration:

> *"Those industries which produce tangible or intangible artistic and creative outputs, and which have a potential for wealth creation and income generation through the exploitation of cultural assets and the production of knowledge-based goods and services (both traditional and contemporary). Cultural industries have in common their application of creativity, cultural knowledge and intellectual property to manufacture products and provide services with social and cultural meaning."*

The European Parliament according to its resolution [2002/2127 (INI)], described the Cultural Industries as one in which emphasis is given to the active relationship between culture and the production of cultural goods and services, national economic development, and employment and training rendered at the national, regional and local levels.

2.2 Creative industries

According to the Department of Culture, Media and Sport UK., Creative Industries are defined as; those industries which have their origin in individual creativity, skill and talent with the potential for wealth and job creation via the generation and exploitation of intellectual property.

Although, there are many models and definitions have been presented to the logical understanding of the important characteristics of the Creative Industries. This study adopts the UNCTAD classification of Creative Industries. The Creative Industries is divided into four categories: *Heritage, arts*, *media*, and *functional creations*. These groups are further divided into nine sub-groups, as presented in the **Table 1** below.

2.3 Craft

The term craft covers a wide collection of artefacts. The International Labour Organisation (ILO) [8] define this type of informal sector as "… .segment of economic activity characterised by certain attributes like dependence on local accessible resources and skills, small scale businesses, traditional technology, unregulated and competitive markets skills commonly attained outside the formal school system, family business, and labour intensity". Abisuga-Oyekunle and Fillis [9] gives one of paramount definition of crafts as: craft products are those created by artisans, neither fully in hand, by mechanical means or even with the assistance of simple hand tools, provided the direct contribution of manual dexterity of the artisan is retained as the most significant element of the finished product. The Department for Culture, Media and Sport mapping document (1998) describes the craft as comprising the groups in the **Table 2** below.

3. Groupings craft producers in South Africa

The South African Department of Sports, Arts, Recreation and Culture grouped craft producers as hand-manufacturing enterprises and small-batch producers. The small-batch producers comprise of craft artist, start-up, and emerging enterprises, these are informal enterprises that are survivalist in existence [10]. The established and exporter enterprises give more consideration to the marketing than the small-batch craft producers. They have a marketing strategy, product brand, improve brochures, develop a website, and creates a catalogue, and also produced a package for their products. The case of with the craft artist, small or emerging producers, and micro-enterprises. Evidence shows that craft producers also use various types

Heritage		Media				Functional	Arts	
Arts crafts	**Cultural**	**Audio visuals**	**Publishing**	**Design**	**New media**	**Creative services**	**Performing arts**	**Visual Arts**
Carpets	Archaeology sites	Film	Books	Architectural drawings	Recorded media	Architecture	Musical instruments	Antiques
Celebration	Museum	CDs, DVDs, tapes	Newspaper	Fashion and fashion accessories	Video games	Cultural and recreation	Live music	Painting
Other art crafts	Libraries		Other printed matter	Glassware	Soft wares	Creative R&D	Theatre	Photography
Paperware	Festivals			Interior design		Advertising	Dance	Sculpture
Wickerware	Celebrations			Jewellery				
Yarn and fabrics				Toys				

Table 1.
Categories of creative industries goods and services.

Core activities	Related activities	Related industries
Textiles	Raw materials	Design
Ceramics	• Clay Fashion	Fashion
Jewellery/silver	• Timber Art	Art
Metal	• Tools & machinery	Antiques
Glass	Craft fairs	
	Craft magazines	
	Books	
	Magazines	

Table 2.
Description of craft.

of distribution channels [11]. The craft artist is open to both the local and international market, selling through galleries and top retailers while the small-batch and emerging craft producers sell within their own communities through direct sales. The established and exporter enterprises have permanent premises for their business activities, while the start-up and emerging manufacturers still undertake production from home. According to Frazer [12], the craft-artist carried out production from a private studio. Also, only the established and exporter, manufacturers produce a quality product that meets the export requirements at ease, while the start-up manufacturers and emerging producers do not meet the required product quality [10]. This study targets all types of craft enterprises with the aim to discover their structures how they behave in terms of their operation, the economic prospect of crafts products and their development requirements.

3.1 The craft production and marketing

In South Africa, the craft producers and marketers are largely black women. Mostly, they are middle-aged women and are the main economic providers in the family. The men involved in craft control in the woodcarving, painting etc. sub-sector of the industry, whereas women dominate in the production of clay pottery, quilting and sewing, embroidery, woven baskets and grass products, mural painting etc., this is as a result of substantial differences in education levels amongst the producers (UNIDO [13]). However, Yang et al. [14] in their study on preservation of cultural heritage and traditional crafts reveals that there are signs that increasing numbers of men are starting to participate in the production of traditional craft as a result of few employment opportunities available to them. Also, several workers are returning from city centres as they are retrenched and cannot get new employment, this could prove to be a source, securing more producers of craft products [15].

In many African nations, the local markets are being oversupplied with mass-produced and cheap goods from the East, which most times end up substituting locally produced goods. This is contrary to the creation of job opportunities and to the sustainability of local traditional production. This has an extremely negative effect on some producers of such items, which directly affects the tourist revenue that is encouraging and developing local production [16]. Nevertheless, product development must be an uninterrupted exercise that makes sure that innovation and creativity are the first concern. As a result of the variety of craft products, craft producers should understand and note the trends affecting different types of

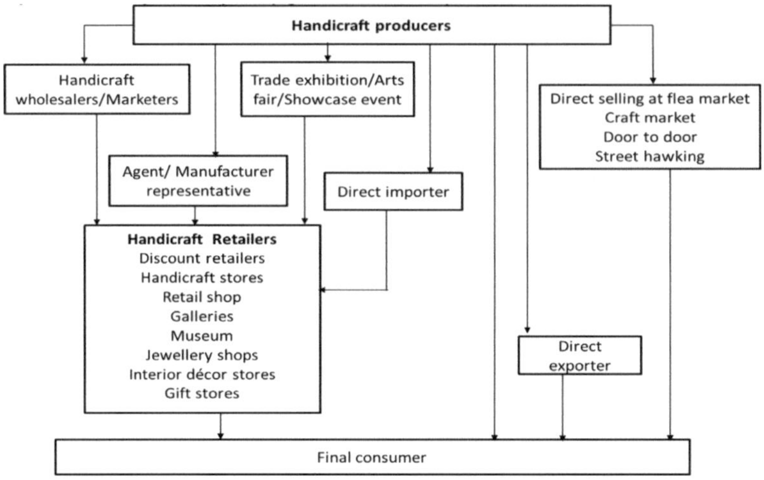

Figure 1.
Marketing channels for craft producers in South Africa. Source: Adapted from [17, 21].

products they produce [17]. For instance, retail markets like the decoration and fashion that are markets were driven that need continuous change.

According to Hay [18] retailers are the market creators, able to source for new products and likewise developers of new products. The retailers communicate with the craft producers to guarantee quality control measures and make sure that product development and innovation is up to standard (Urban-Economic [19]). A study conducted by Department of Sports, Arts, Recreation and Culture [10] amongst the craft producers in Gauteng, discovered that the producers go through difficulties selling to craft retailers because they only purchase 36% crafts produced in South Africa. The Wesgro [20] also confirmed in its study that craft producers only have little access to craft retail markets as a result of competition from imported craft products which are more superior to the locally produced ones.

Figure 1 below (by Frost & Sullivan and Makhitha [17, 21]), shows a summary of three major chains of which products move from the producers to the final consumer.

1. The producer → final consumer (the major actor in this type of distribution is the producer as he is the only actor).

2. The producer → marketing organisation → craft dealer →end customer (The major actor here is the marketing organisation, because they source for markets for the products).

3. The producer (in rural areas) → intermediary trader/distributor/wholesaler (distributors to towns) → craft trader →final consumer (The major actor is the retailer because he is the one who knows the customers' needs, therefore, guarantee that the products are made in accordance with the customers' demand).

4. Methodology

4.1 Designs

The design of this research is descriptive using a qualitative method of data collection and analyses. The sampling frame is handicraft entrepreneurs operating in the city of Durban of KwaZulu-Natal Province. The gateway to Zulu Kingdom is Durban, an active, cultured cosmopolitan port city and top holiday destination well-known for its beaches and wide-ranging mix of cultures which form a unique assortment of western, eastern, and African influences. The City of Durban is historically and economically quite significant as it has been the port of entry of tourist and traders for thousands of years. Handicrafts reflect the city region's cultural mix. Many markets in the city have regular open-air markets where the arts and handicrafts are displayed for sale. Several art and handicraft routes are widely known around Durban i.e. Durban North Beach, Durban South Beach, Victoria Street Markets and Durban station. These four locations in Durban were used for the present study. The respondents were divided into 3 groups, group 1 concentrated on craft producers and marketers, group 2 concentrated on craft producers only, while the group 3 concentrated on craft marketers only. A tape recorder was used in conducting an in-depth structured interview. Tallying, coding, text analysis, content analysis is used for performing qualitative data analysis [22]. Also, this study used secondary data, from UNCTAD statistics to conduct a situational analysis of the place of the crafts in the cultural and creative industries nexus.

4.2 Methods

To unravel the problems faced by crafts sectors, and to get a deeper understanding of what policy intervention is required towards the protection and sustainability of the sector, a qualitative research was employed using a both primary and secondary data sources to satisfy the data requirements of the study, and make findings more robust. For this study, the secondary data is sourced from the United Nations for Conference on Trade and Development (UNCTADSTAT) data center. The UNCTAD data was used because it analyses the trade in creative goods using the Harmonised System (HS) and BPM6 (International Investment Position Manual and Balance of Payments) respectively. It provides annual data of value and shares, growth rates and concentration index of creative goods exports and imports, from 1995 to 2015. The secondary data is used because it is inexpensive, less demanding, and faster means of obtaining information compared to primary data. Primary data collection was conducted by using in-depth face-to-face interviews with 15 craft enterprises in Durban, KwaZulu-Natal Province of South Africa. A structured, pretested, and validated interview question of study were used for collecting data as part of the qualitative aspect of study. The primary data is rather expensive, and the delays and cost of primary data was being minimised by complementing it with secondary data. However, only enterprises that are established in the production and marketing of purely handicrafts products were purposively selected for this study. Also, participants were purposively selected to include only three races (Black, White, and Indian) based on availability and readiness to partake in the interview. The coloured race was not included due to non-availability to fit into the purpose of the present study. The interview was conducted by verbally delivering the questionnaires with the help of a Zulu interpreter for those who are more comfortable with local language.

5. Results and discussions

5.1 Secondary data

Regarding the cultural and creative Goods there is need to break the data down to a sub-sector level across the various categories, differentiating between trade with South Africa and the rest of the world, respectively. The data connected to South African export trade with the rest of the world show that the decline in exports to this world region has been driven by a marked downward trend in the export of design products, with only visual arts and new media showing. The cultural and Creative Good data has been broken down into sub-sector level across the groupings differentiating between trade with South Africa and the rest of the world respectively. **Figure 2** shows the data of South African creative goods export as a percentage of the total world trade between the period of 2002–2015.

Table 3 shows that South African trade of creative goods has increased considerably up to 69%, of exports, which goes to the African market in 2015, relative to just 33% in 2006. By 2015, trade with the United States and the Europe had reduced, and the top five export partners for creative goods were Namibia, the United States, Lesotho, and Botswana.

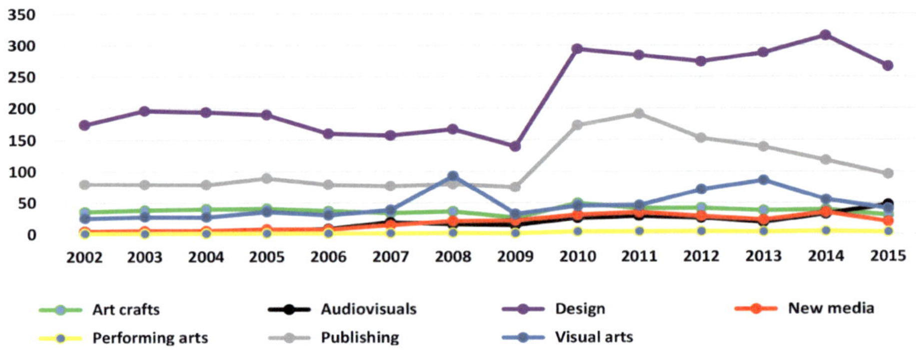

Figure 2.
Values and shares of creative goods exports, annual, 2002–2015. Source: UNCTAD statistics [23].

	2006				2015			
Economy	Values in Million US $				Values in Million US $			
Ranking	Partner	Export	Import	Balance	Partner	Export	Import	Balance
1	United States	14,79	1,45	13,34	Namibia	5,68	0,01	5,67
2	United Kingdom	4,06	1,39	2,68	United states	2,55	1,98	0,57
3	Italy	1,83	2,58	−0,75	Lesotho	2,53	0,06	2,48
4	Germany	0,95	3,18	−2,23	Bostwana	2,27	4,64	−2,37
5	Mozambique	0,61	0,01	0,60	Germany	2,01	1,33	0,68
6	Zambia	0,54	0,00	0,54	Zambia	1,93	0,099	1,93
7	Netherlands	0,22	0,55	−0,33	United Kingdom	1,12	0,55	0,57
8	United States of Tanzania	0,21	0,02	0,19	Zimbabwe	0,49	0,68	−0,19
9	Nigeria	0,18	0,01	0,18	Nigeria	0,32	0,029	0,32
10	Angola	0,49	0,00	0,49	Eswatini	2,81	1,23	1,58

Source: UNCTAD Statistics [23].

Table 3.
Top 10 export Partners for Craft Products Only.

South Africa creative goods exports increased from $370 million in 2005 to $629 million in 2011. The values decrease gradually by 2% between 2012 and 2015. However, the total value of South African exports to the rest of the world between 2002 and 2015 is $6.3 billion. Design goods have the highest export category generating values of $3.1 billion of the total export between 2002 and 2015; this is followed by publishing which total $1.5 billion; Visual arts $653 million. Crafts at $528 million; and new media at $257 million. Nevertheless, South Africa was a net importer of creative goods. Regardless of having a growing creative economy, by 2015, the creative goods trade deficit was $1.4 billion.

Figure 3 illustrates the Key creative goods imports for South Africa between, 2002–2015 were Design (46%); Audio Visuals (15%), Publishing (14%); and new media (13%); respectively of the total import. The design shows the highest rate of import between these years. Meanwhile, total imports stood at $20.8 billion, three times higher than the total export values. Despite having a growing creative economy, between 2002 to 2015 the creative goods trade deficit was $979 million in 2015. Design goods were the strongest import category generating total values of South African import with the rest of the world from 2002 to 2015 as $9.4 billion; followed by audio visual $2.9 billion; new media as $2.6 billion; and arts crafts at $1.5 billion.

5.2 Research interview

Table 4 shows that eleven of the interviewees were male and ten were female. There was no division between male and female regarding the type of craft they market or produce. About seventeen different categories of craft are being produced and marketed by the respondents. This is comparable to the South African pocket guide to Arts and Culture (2011), which puts forward that South Africans

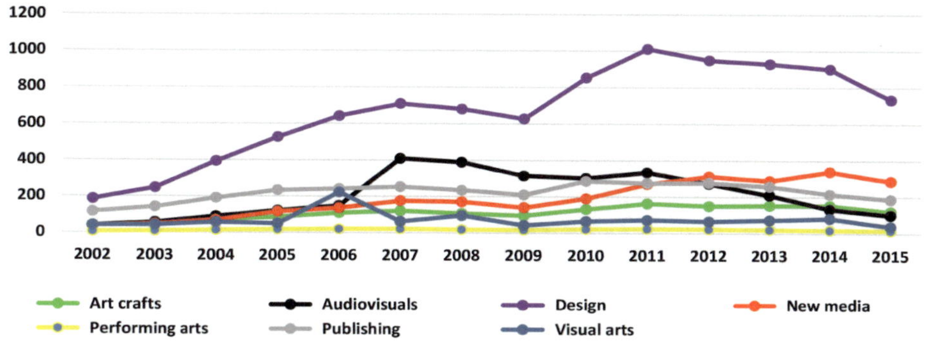

Figure 3.
Values and shares of creative goods imports, annual, 2002–2015. Source: UNCTAD statistics [23].

Locations of interviews	Number and percentage
Queen Victoria Market	6(40%)
South Beach Front	4(26.7%)
North Beach Front	3(20%)
Durban Station	2(13.3%)
Total	15(100%)

Table 4.
Sites used for data collection (n = 15).

produce an outstanding collection of arts and crafts comprising various types of traditional artwork. Regarding the type of enterprise activities, 5 interviewees were producers/marketers of craft products, 5 were producers only and 5 were marketers only. The locations of data collection and percentage of enterprises interviewed are described in the **Table 4** below. The Queen Victoria Market has the highest number of interviewees i.e. 40% of the participants, while the participants from Durban station amounts to only 13.3%. The following gives the description of each respondents personal profile as displayed in the **Table 5** below: a – 'Sex'; B – 'Age'; C – 'Race'; D – 'Education'; E – 'Artisan Training'; F – 'Years of experience'.

However, in addition to other business activities, the monthly income made by interviewees from crafts varied substantially as shown in **Table 6**. As illustrated in the table, bigger portion of the 9 (60%) of the interviewee reported a low sales performance of below R10, 000 monthly, while a minority of 6 (40%) of the respondents experiences a high sale monthly performance of above R10, 000. Only 2 of interviewees earn the highest amount higher than R20, 000 monthly income on craft sales totaled only 13.3% of all the respondents. There are many active enterprise factors that determine how much can be earned monthly from craft products. The non-financial factors are based on measures that are individually determined by the business owner. These non-financial factors assume that there is a given level of financial security already established, which maybe that, the business is not the primary source of income for the owner [24]. Out the total number of interviewees 9 were black, while there are 3 Indians and 3 whites, respectively. Likewise, the total number of females is 6 blacks, 1 Indian and 2 whites. **Figure 4** shows that a total number of 6 (40%) of the interviewees are between the age brackets (41–50), and 4 (26.7%) are between the age range of (31–40), while 2 (13.3%) of total interviewed are between ages (21–30), and only 3 (13.3%) is between the age range (51–60), meanwhile there is no representative with the age below 21 amongst the respondents. The Cultural Industries Growth Strategy (CIGS) (1998) reports that the craft producers are predominantly black women, and they are mostly middle-aged women who are the primary economic providers within the family.

5.3 The business activity engagement

Even though only 15 interviewees were in the sample and no statistical significance can be drawn, it is important to cross-compare the status, and sales performance of the interviewees. **Table 5** summarises the data.

To present the sales performance of interviewees', they are categorised according to their business status as either involved in production, marketers, and production/marketing based on the performance on their monthly enterprise activities. The limit level of R10, 000 is based on average gross household incomes in South Africa as reported by the Statistics South Africa (2010). For this study, interviewee with a monthly gross household income of less than R9, 990 per month (approximately R120, 000 per year) are considered "poor" or "low income". As with estimation, **Table 6** shows that the lowest sales obtained amongst all interviewees were experienced by those engage in craft production. The results show that only one (#10 – R20,200) of the 'producers' obtained a monthly gross income above the average gross household income of R10, 000 for the South African standard. The interviewees who are involved as marketers of craft product obtained the highest monthly sales in their business. A total number of three out of the five interviewed in this category experienced gross monthly earnings above the limit level, such as R12,000, another of which R15,500, the highest of R16,000, respectively. This indicates that the craft producers do not earn a reasonable amount from their productions. Kaiser and Associates [25] evidence that majority of craft

Production/Marketing											
Number	Personal profile	Technology required	Other source of income	Types of handicraft produced	Staff employed for the business	Handicraft no longer in production. When and why?	Problems with raw materials	External support/ assistance	Types of support	Average monthly sales	Notes on product innovation and development
1	a. Male b. 31–40 c. Black d. Grade 12 e. Dress making f. 8 years	Sewing and bead machine	None	Traditional attires Beads	Self	None	None	None	None	R8,000	Creating business website for easy trade
2	a. Male b. 21–30 c. India d. Degree e. No training f. 6 years	Wood craft machines	Self-employed	Wooden products (photo frames, chairs coffee table)	1 employee	Wooden masks	Stock is slowly disappearing	Friends Family		R8,800	Youths need to be trained in design of traditional crafts instead of importing
3	a. Female b. 51–60 c. Black d. Postgraduate e. No artisan training e. 30 years	Knitting equipment', Chizzol, Rasper	None	Wooden masks, Sculptures, and hat knitting	Family and 3 employees	Beaded shirts (Isigege) 2013 Mother Partial blindness	Getting materials, which I usually get from Thuthuka and Mpumalanga	Bank loan	None	R25,500	Exposure, advertising, networking and training with other African crafters
4	a. Female b. 41–50 c. Black d. No education e. Artisan training f. 12 years	None	Self-employed	Grass picnic baskets, Grass sun hats, Grass mats	Self and family	Leather shoes, bags, and interior decorations 2005 Materials not available	It takes killing animals to get original raw material	Family	Production equipment's/ tools, Raw materials	R5,000	Introduction of more new craft and teaching more youth on our own heritage and how to create wealth using our natural resources
5	a. Female b. 41–50 c. White d. Diploma e. No artisan training f. 20 years	Thread runners, Beads making machine	Part-time salary work	Beaded shoes, Beaded products for decoration, Beaded necklaces	Family and 5 employees	Attires, Beaded skirts (Isigege) 2013 Mother Blind	Its seasonal and cannot be produced anytime	SETA	None	R19,800	Opportunities to travel to other places to showcase product

Production											
Number	**Personal profile**	**Technology required**	**Other source of income**	**Types of handicraft produced**	**Staff employed for the business**	**Handicraft no longer marketed. When and why?**	**Problems with raw materials**	**External support/ assistance**	**Types of support**	**Average monthly sales**	**Notes on product innovation and development**
6	a. Female b. White c. 41–50 d. Diploma e. Artisan training f. 15 years	Yes	Part-time salary work	Ceramics, Sculptures, paintings	1 Employees	Clay pot 2010 Time consuming	Some raw materials are usually imported from other countries	None	Raw materials, Production space, Sales/ marketing	R9,500	Education is priority. More training and exposure
7	a. Female b. 21–30 c. Black d. Grade 12 e. No artisan training f. 3 years	Embroidery and knitting machines	Permanent salary work	Knitting, Tapestry, Embroidery	None	None	None	Family	Raw materials, Sales/ marketing	R5,800	Funding, Advertising, and publicity
8	a. Male b. 51–60 c. Black d. Grade 12 e. No artisan training f. 10 years	Camera Printing machine Laptop	None	Painting, Coffee drawing (painting), Print making (wood cut)	None	None	Materials are expensive and not making enough profits to buy materials	Family	Technical skills	R8,000	We need to study how to do things ourselves and how to market them
9	a. Female b. 41–50 c. Black d. Degree e. Training fine arts f. 28 years	Goldsmith Jewellery Making equipment	None	Jewelries, Beaded necklace, beaded shoes	Family	None	The beads used are scarce cannot found them anymore	Friends Family	Raw materials, Sales/ advertising	R9,800	More raw materials to be always made available
10	a. Male b. 51–60 c. India d. Grade 12 f. No training f. 27 years	Industrial sewing machines.	Self-employed	Beaded shoes, Beaded bags, and wire works	5 employees	Yes	A lot of products we have stop producing because the sales dropped badly	None	None	R20,200	Need for a proper shop and exhibition for exposure

Marketers											
Number	**Personal profile**	**Technology required**	**Other source of income**	**Types of handicraft marketing**	**Staff employed**	**Handicraft no longer in marketing. When and why?**	**Problems with marketing**	**External support/ assistance**	**Types of support**	**Average monthly sales**	**Notes on product innovation and development**
11	a. Female b. 31–40 c. Black d. Grade 12 e. No training f. years	None	Self-employed	Woven blankets, Carved wood sculptures	None	None	None	Family	Sales and marketing	R12,000	Government should help with exporting
12	a. Male b. 41–50 c. Black d. Degree e. Training f. 5 years	None	None	Beaded shoes, Neck wear, Calabash drum	Self	None	None	DTI	Production equipment, Raw materials, Sales/ marketing	R8,000	Funding, Advertising, and publicity
13	a. Male b.31–40 c. White d. Grade 12 e. No training f. 7 years	Computers	None	Bead works, Ceramics, Sculptures	none	None	None	None	None	R16,000	Finance and support from the government
14	a. Female b. 41–50 c. India d. Grade 11 e. No artisan training f. 15 years	None	Self-employed	Flower container with beads, Wire bowls, Wire baskets	Family	None	Yes	Friend Family	Raw materials	R9,000	Provide the youth with resources and funding for growth. Visit to other countries to learn how they produce
15	a. Female b. 31–40 c. Black d. Grade 12 e. No training f. 12 years	None	Self-employed	Wooden drums, Side tables, Animal skin shields	2 Employees	Clay pots 2013 Grandmother Scarcity of clay	Clay for crafts is scarce and sometimes not available		Raw materials Sales and marketing	R15,500	Business owners needs website and training to advertise their work

Table 5.
Interviewees' profiles (n = 15).

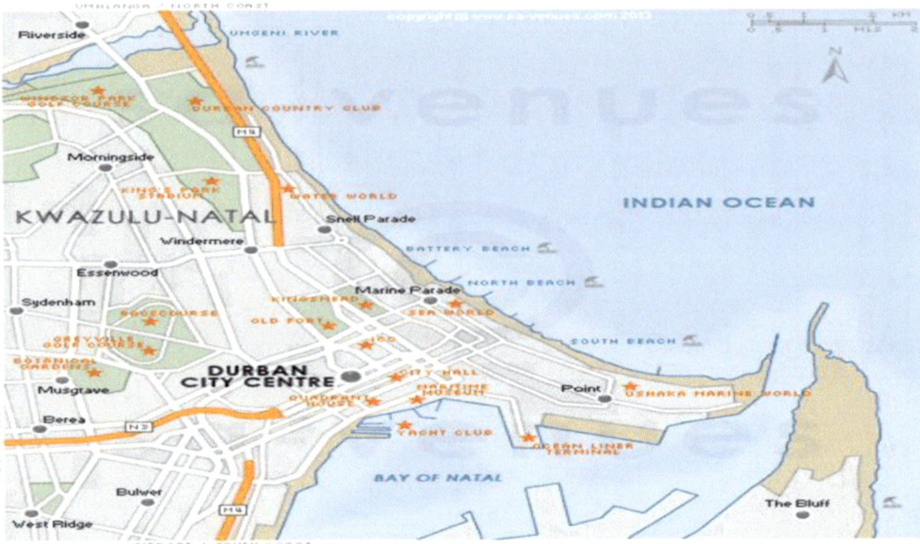

Figure 4.
Map showing the City of Durban and nearby beach fronts. Source: sa-venues.com (2018) https://www.sa-venues.com/maps/kwazulunatal/durban-central.php.

Interviewees' business status	**Sales performance (Average monthly sales)**	
	≤R10,000 (n = 9)	**>R10,000 (n = 6)**
Production/Marketing (n = 5)	#1(R8,000) α #2(R8,800) α #4(R5,000) β	#3(R25,500) β #5(19,800) β
Production (n = 5)	#6(R9,500) β #7(R5,800) β #8(R8,000) α #9(R9,800) β	#10(R20,200) α
Marketers (n = 5)	#12(R8,000) α #14(R9,000) β	#11(R12,000) β #13(R16,000) α #15(R15,500) β

β = Female; α = Male; # = Number.

Table 6.
The business status, and performance levels of the interviewees (n = 15).

producers are small enterprises operating in an informal economy. Hence, how will craft producers sustain their livelihood, or decide on the future sustainability of their business?

6. Discussions

6.1 Issues relating to crafts protection

Crafts are a huge attraction to local and international tourists. Based on a study conducted in Algeria by Asma, Diabate and Othman [26] they presented that craft business is worthy of support by national governments and tourist operators in terms of attracting visitors and earn foreign currency. Oyekunle and Sirayi [27] revealed that craft entrepreneurs in most African countries are adversely affected by lack of specialised skills, training opportunities, support of national governments and support of non-governmental organisations (NGOs). According to Aigbavboa and Thwala [28], national government is less attentive for this sector as seen from the lower support for the craft sector. According to Wood [29], the contribution of government to craft practitioners in South Africa is insufficient because, they are still facing many challenges which make it difficult for them to thrive and be profitable businesses. Thus, identifying and addressing enterprise factors that affect the craft enterprises makes a significant contribution to the literature of cultural and creative industries as a whole. However, the increasing need for the development of the craft sector in South Africa, accompanied by the growth of design, has caused a rise in exhibition projects in the country, including the annual Design Expo at the South Africa Handmade Collection in Johannesburg and the Design Indaba Conference in Cape Town [30]. The results of these are shown in **Figure 2** above with subsequent growth each year report resulting in increase of international tourist and export orders. The figure also shows the arts craft export reaching its peak in 2010 as a result of the world cup activities and events and declined gradually by 2015.

Also, craft sectors are confronted by several marketing problems (see, [31–33]). Taking into account lack of financial resources and their small scale of enterprises, publicity and advertising activities is not possible for artisans [34]. The South African Presidential Review Committee recommends that in the future the government will intensify publicity and advertisement for all craft sectors. However, to adequately promote and conserve the African cultural heritage, artisans need to be provided an effective marketing support and several advertising and marketing strategies [35]. Benson further point that the promotion of African cultural heritage is not to be the responsibility of crafters who sell these products, but likewise the government ministries should intervene. Therefore, it is required for South African government to perform an important role in solving the marketing problems confronted by artisans. This is highlighted by the two respondents (#9 and #10):

> *Sometimes the whole day I do not sell anything. I want to be exporting my craft products because the local market is too slow, also I cannot import production materials because they are too expensive to buy from South Africa. Most of us crafters need capital to help us import, equipment and materials together. I applied for bank loan but did not get it. (#9, α black).*

> *Sales are always very high at the period when we have a lot of tourist around. The tourist mostly pays dollars for the crafts and I make most profit through them [...]. Durban is also known for tourism [...], so we rely on sales from both local and international tourists and visitors more that the local buyers. (#10, α Indian).*

6.2 Issues on product sustainability

According to the result gathered from this research, the South African craft products are fading away, considered as weak, and insufficiently targeted for growth. These are for following main reasons:

a. *Problem of clarity in target market.*

   Overwhelmingly, craft producers have created products without adequate planning vis-à-vis for the target customers. Not only do they not know what their target market is, they lack information on who exactly are their target customer.

b. *Products produced stagnation.*

Few products have had designers help in product development, there is no investment in continuation of design efforts or investment in fostering artisans to be creative themselves.

c. *Lack of vision for a sustainable strategy for the product.*

Overwhelmingly, the government institutions and other organisations assisting producers and marketers group lack medium to long-term strategies for success. This has translated into the following scenarios:

- Products being produced, but not sold, or sold at very low prices.
- Lack of money to hire qualified, skilled workers.
- No funds allocated to marketing or business planning.

d. *Inadequate business capacity.*

Neither the associated agencies that are sponsoring the craft products, nor the producers themselves understand the business. Most importantly, this is seen in their lack of ability to price products according to real costs plus a realistic profit margin. Profit is not paramount in their thinking [36].

e. *Lack of a sufficient funding to see products through preservation.*

None of the products are sustainable functioning as businesses, and so funding received is used for immediate needs, due to the inability of the business to sustain the owners.

f. *Deficiency in coordination of vertical and horizontal levels.*

There is virtually no coordination of efforts at either a vertical or horizontal level amongst stakeholders. This has translated into craft products that have failed; poor investments, unmotivated workers, products sitting on shelves, and an overall inability to take advantage of the money spent by the influx of tourists in South Africa.

g. *Insufficient creativity and innovation in product development.*

Most products have relied on local community old men and women to do product development. This has resulted in products that are not saleable in the tourist market and only marginally saleable to the local markets. Producers are taught to produce, not to innovate or be creative.

h. *Competition of crafts from other African countries as well as those being imported.*

The few products produced in South Africa still must compete in price, style, and aesthetics, with those from other areas of Africa, as well as imports found throughout the souvenir stores in South Africa. This has raised the competitive bar of imported crafts over the locally made, but yet has not resulted in innovation in the South African products.

i. *Craft business is not treated as an important sub-sector of the growing cultural and creative industry in South Africa.*

   There has been no treatment of the craft sector as an important sub-sector within the growing CCIs in South Africa. Few, if any, vertical or horizontal linkages have been made to build success for the entire industry, including the local community.

j. *Need for critical thinking and design skills amongst producers.*

   Producers are not taught to be critical thinkers in product development or design, but rather they do exactly same as the olden days, repeating steps and processes. While not everyone is a designer, this limits innovation and product development potential.

6.3 Issues on policy intervention

The policy interventions provided in this study are developed from the qualitative research carried out by the author to identify problems faced by crafts entrepreneurs in South Africa and to discourse those issues in order to contribute to the preservation of craft sector. These recommendations concentrate on those policy interventions, which act to propose to the craft industries and government, the ultimate benefits from the development of the sectors. The research evidently shows the importance of strategy implementation towards expanding the craft sectors. This research also evident from international illustrations and in South Africa, that the sustainability and development of the craft sector should be set aside for the advantage of those economic disadvantage segments of the society such as women, disabled, homeless people, and the unemployed [17]. Though, there are key gaps in the development of the craft sector identified by this research. Lots of these gaps could be secure through developing more logical synchronisation between this research and existing literatures. Relevant craft sector initiatives that need urgent interventions are identified by the respondents and concisely presented below with the list of possible policy interventions.

1. *Government Obligation*

Rather than demoting craft entrepreneur to the municipalities only, this study strongly recommends that craft support actions should be integrated into the operation of all local government departments, provincial and national government agenda. Through this, the craft sector in South Africa can gradually change into an important employment generating sector, low investment, and enthusiastically being part of the social-economic development strategy for the country [30]. This was emphasised by the following respondents:

> *I have received a support from SETA for raw materials before but have not been able to receive any from the NGOs. I have approached some NGOs before, for funding to support my business in the last two years ago, but no success yet. I started this business when I could not get a job after school, but I will need a loan or funding to sustain it. (#9, β black).*

> *I applied for a funding support at the DTI for machines to help with production, but it was not approved. I had to stop production of some products because working with hand tools wastes a lot of energy and time. The government also needs to build a craft market for us, where the whole world will know, and tourists will visit. We*

do not have a craft market, except those sitting together in a temporary shelter by the beach front. (#13, α white).

2. *Education and training*

Crafting skills are acquired in a several ways, such as high school or primary school; general education; through observation; inherited cultural or family traditions; formal art education; informal courses and training programmes; as well as apprenticeship. Chan [37] believes the informal sectors of the rural and urban economy in South Africa rely on the support of artisans, and the induction of apprentices either from within the family in the rural areas or from drop-outs of the formal educational system in the urban areas, but all of which has not been properly studied or documented.

I learnt the production from my grandmother. I need more training on the production, but it will be good if the government can organise training and workshop to assist me. I have some apprentice who are learning and assisting with the business. Many people in the handicraft business need training but could not afford it [… .]. (#6, β white).

I always make sure to attend workshops and training for crafters. But I have only attended the ones organised by NGOs, I have not attended any one by the government. The Queen Victoria Market committees have organised a workshop for us before through the government agencies, but people refused to attend, because they felt they are being neglected by the government. I have applied to a school to get more education in sales and marketing. (#1, β India).

The committee of Queen Victoria Markets has organised a training for us before through the Small Enterprise Finance Agency (SEFA). Through the training I was able to get a fund to support my business, and this funding has really helped in sustaining my business. I was able to rent another shop and could stock better. (#3, β white).

3. *Preserving Cultural heritage*

In South African promotion of culture and cultural product is an important element in enhancing knowledge of the craft both international and domestic markets [6]. Black South Africans were set apart from their cultural heritage through the time of apartheid. The fine arts and craft, such as – painting, sculpture, traditional attire, indigenous knowledge, showcases the traditional worth and gives a better understanding of the cultural value of people and community [15]. The craft sector needs to be seen locally and internationally as a cultural expression through which African heritage is promoted.

I have worked as a permanent employee before I quit after 15 years. This business has been a family business and my mother wants me to continue in order to preserve the business. [… .] I love creativity and creating my own design, so I decided to go into handicraft production […]. The business is very lucrative is helping to preserve and build an African culture and tourism. (#2, α India)

I believe the South African craft business are for the blacks because it tells so much about our heritage and history. Almost all my family are doing the business […]. My grandfather does weave and painting, likewise my uncle does wooden craft and wire works. I also have two of my siblings in the business. We do export SA crafts to other Southern African countries because we share almost same culture. (#15, β black).

I did not have any training or formal education to doing this business. I love traditional music and dance and do a lot within the community. The arts and culture are my number one priority, because a lot of people are leaving the business. I make a lot of money from selling craft and will like to learn more about the production. (#4, β black).

4. *Market Identification*

This research asserted that the market for the craft products must be initially recognised before any thoughtful promotion of new craft product. Mostly, this occurs in rural craft schemes that production come first before the conception of adequate market demand for a specific type of the craft products. Thus, if the craft products have no demand or buyers, there will be no cash to pay for the materials of production or cost of the labour. It is important here that all rural craft development projects should start with a cautious assessment of market demand or consumer preference, then move into the promotion, training, and new phases of enterprise development. In order to provide basic information about craft sector operations in South Africa, a series of catalogues, articles, publications (e.g., weekly magazines), and brochures need to be circulated to craft producers and marketers. The stakeholders (for instance, the DAC) could assist to encourage others such as home choice, sheet streets and the major retail outlets to create a system that will allow small producers to produce a product that is sold through their channels.

I learn the craft marketing trade from my mother. I do not like the production because it takes a lot of time, and the buyers will not want to pay good price. This affects the production with low quality items, thereby more difficult to sell. Marketing of crafts is very difficult because people do not appreciate the value and wants to pay cheaply, only the tourist pays good price. Some products are also seasonal and […] the demand falls. (#13, α white).

Crafts products need promotion and advertisement. In most African homes you will hardly see craft or traditional items. The government need to help create the awareness and promoting of this industry. Everything is changing now, and crafters too need to improve what they produce and how the market it. Otherwise a lot of people will be out of business. (#12, α black).

The producers do not understand the market, they keep producing the same product. The same product design I have been selling for more than 10 years. There is not new design and innovation. In order to fight competition, I have to stock imported crafts sometimes. The customers are tired of buying the same products, especially the locals. The producers do not have the ability to identify the customers need and satisfy them. (#14, β Indian).

7. Delivery systems and sustainability

Market accessibility to import, export, and local markets is a big problem for craft sectors. However, this study has identified that the more difficult the solution, the more expected failure. The best way is to use the existing infrastructure which involves the smallest possible external intervention is the best approach that delivers well for craft producers. Therefore, appropriate publications informing craft marketers and producers about demand and supply for craft products, infrastructures and technologies should be provided to crafters. For instance, inclusion of craft sectors in SMEs programmes by DAC and DTI; Encyclopaedia of the craft sector in South Africa, similar to the fashion magazines; Business desks which acknowledge the craft industry as a group to organise themselves into associations of craft producer and marketer.

With the purpose to make marketing of craft products grow to the best the following were suggested for implementation:

a. *Organising craft marketing network:* Lack of organised marketing networks has been a hindering import in the sector. The Kaiser and Associates [38] proposed that the artisans must structure themselves by forming a co-operative system for marketing their craft products by themselves. This can develop into more associations with external partners towards good export and import trade, especially with other African countries.

b. *Uniformity in price:* There has been critics that craft prices are very much inconsistent and not uniform, even with items purchased from two shops or two places. This circumstance makes customers feel exploited, which might have a negative consequence of the demand for the products. Therefore, craft should be classified and priced by a team of experts according to the skill displayed and quality of raw materials used [25].

c. *Creating awareness:* Most artisans are not aware of new schemes (for instance, loan and rates, raw materials, free tools). It is the responsibility of the promotional organisations to create awareness for artisans about the different welfare schemes and to device same warfare.

d. *Reluctance of youth to practice the profession:* The youth finds it difficult to endure time-consuming and complex process of craft production, instead they prefer to market the end product. Therefore, they normally do not aim to choose this profession. This has caused culture and heritage vulnerability (UNESCO, undated).

e. *Engaged in more craft research and development:* In order to improve the quality of the products, there is a need for research and development. Oyekunle [39] believe this will aid the development of many new items and new designs.

f. *Collaboration with foreign artisans and designers:* Foreign expert designers may be invited to render guidance and assistance to the craftsmen [39].

g. *Adding value to craft:* Specialised organisations may assist the local units in the production of different value-added items which would help to penetrate the local market and exporting of such items to foreign countries.

h. The economic impact of craft on urban and rural livelihoods has not been researched in South Africa. The government needs to oversee a large number of projects that sought to tackle poverty through craft developments, which could also bring development into rural areas where the levels of poverty were highest [18]. I argue for the impracticality of attaining rural regeneration through successful reorganisation of the rural industrial economic system.

i. *Craft publicity:* In order to attract both local and foreign buyers, marketing and promotional organisations emphasise on wide publicity of local products [40].

j. *Craft exports:* Organised effort may allow some of the selected products develop into earning major foreign exchange in the near future (Khan and Amir, 2013). But care should be taken before exporting such items on price, product identification, payment terms, quantum of production, supply arrangements, quality, delivery, etc.

k. *Display of Craft items*: All the marketing and promotional organisation must display the local items in different places like railway stations, bus stands, commercial centres and airports [27]. This will assist the local artisans to secure more orders from traders, tourists, marketing organisation etc.

l. *Strategic positioning of craft Products:* Most crafts produced with traditional skill are increasingly facing competition with machine made products. Abisuga-Oyekunle and Fillis [9] claimed that a high number of craft items are either substitute or competing for entrant into the market.

8. Conclusion

The craft production and marketing are very dynamic part of the economy in many developing countries. In the literature, the position of craft practise has been broadly acknowledged for development in Africa, hence it becomes essential to give consideration regarding suitable policy measures to protect the craft practise [9]. Most research has shown that craft entrepreneurs in most African countries are adversely affected by lack of specialised skills, training opportunities, support of national governments and support from non-governmental organisations (NGOs). Consequently, the question of transferring craft knowledge and skills from generation to generation is real. This study identified various issues faced by crafts entrepreneurs with the purpose of preserving the cultural heritage and contributing to the sustainability.

This study pointed several issues and limitations that craft sectors in South Africa faced with the position of crafts products within the cultural and creative industries, such as low youth participation, lack of basic materials, lack of innovation, limited financial resources and skills/training facilities [41]. These problems are declining the importance of the craft sectors. This study shows that these sectors are slowly misplacing their existence and require urgent intervention to preserve the business and cultural values.

With the intention to make available empirical evidences to back the assumptions of this study, it examined the case of South African craft sector. The case of South Africa demonstrated the assumptions of the study providing evidence of problems faced by craft businesses and the need for developing the sector. Also, this study indicates that the government needs to implement several policies because export and employment in craft sector are declining compared to other sectors (e.g., design, visual arts and publishing) within the CCIs [41]. Even though several measures to support craft products were introduced before, but due to many challenges as stated above, the sector is losing its import resulting from high flow of total imports into the country, this has affected the craft sectors to a great extent.

Appendix: interview guide

Biographic Data

a. Sex

b. Age

c. Race

d. Education

e. Artisan Training

f. Years of Experience

Enterprises Factors

1. What is the nature of your business?

    a. Handicraft Production only

    b. Handicraft Marketing only

    c. Marketing/production

2. What crafts do you produce/market?

3. I would like to ask you some questions about these craft products.

    a. Where is the production process taking place?

    b. Who buys the craft?

    c. Where is it sold?

4. Are there any handicrafts which you or any member of your household used to produce but are no longer producing? If yes.

    a. Mention the crafts

    b. When did they stop producing this craft (year)?

    c. Why do they stop producing this craft?

5. Do you have problems in getting raw material for production?

6. Have you added any innovation to your business/product in past three years?

7. Presently, what innovation and development do you think the handicraft sector needs?

8. What type of equipment or machine do you require to make your business more effective?

9. Do you have employee or people you work with?

10. Do you have other sources of income beside handicraft work currently?

11. What are the average monthly returns on this work? (sales/month)

12. Have you attended any social event in the past two years (e.g. workshop, seminal, exhibition)?

    a. Who organised the event?

    b. Mention where the event took place?

13. Have you received any fund/loan for the business before?

    a. State the source of the fund/loan?

14. Is the handicraft business good enough to sustain you and family?

15. Could you tell me about the problems you face with your business?

16. Have you ever participated in any of the government's programmes to assist entrepreneurs?

17. In sustaining your business, describe the types of support you have received (non-governmental organisation, government, relatives, or friends)?

18. Does your family background or history relate to your business?

19. Do you normally export your craft products?

    a. Where do you export to?

20. Do you import anything for your production process?

    a. What do you import?

21. Do you have any other business or job outside the handicraft business?

Author details

Abisuga Oluwayemisi Adebola
Department of Industrial Engineering, Tshwane University of Technology, Private Bag X680, Pretoria, 0001, South Africa

*Address all correspondence to: yemisuga@yahoo.com; oyekunleoa@tut.ac.za

References

[1] Buschfeld D, Dilger B, Heb LS. Identification of Future Skills Needs in Micro and Craft (–Type) Enterprises up to 2020. Final Report. Wilke, Maack und Partner: Germany; 2011

[2] Oyekunle OA. Building the creative industries for sustainable economic development in South Africa. International Journal of Sustainable Development. 2015;**7**(12):47-72

[3] Alexander P. Rebellion of the poor: South Africa's service delivery protests–a preliminary analysis. Review of African Political Economy. 2010;**37**(123):25-40

[4] Barber TMK. Global market assessment for handicrafts. USAID. 2006;**1**:1-78

[5] Jena PK. Indian handicrafts in globalization times: an analysis of global-local dynamics Pradeep. Interdisciplinary Description of Complex Systems, 8(2). Dec. 2010: 119-137

[6] Oyekunle OA, Sirayi M. The role of creative industries as a driver for a sustainable economy: A case of South Africa. Creative Industries Journal. 2018b;**11**(3):225-244

[7] UNESCO. 2007. Intersectoral Programme on the Cross-Cutting Theme. United Nations: France. "Poverty Eradication, Especially Extreme Poverty".

[8] International Labour Organization. The informal economy: enabling transition to formalization. ISIE/2007/1. Geneva: ILO. In: 1 v. 2007

[9] Abisuga-Oyekunle OA, Fillis IR. The role of handicraft micro-enterprises as a catalyst for youth employment. Creative Industries Journal. 2016;**10**(1):59-74

[10] Department of Sports, Arts, Recreation and Culture. Gauteng Craft Development Strategy: 2007–2012, October 2007. South Africa: Gauteng; 2007

[11] Makhitha, K.M. 2016. Marketing strategies of small craft producers in South Africa: Practices and challenges. The Journal of Applied Business Research, 32(3), June: 663–680.

[12] Frazer TA. The Nature of the Studio: An Artist's Method of Inquiry. PhD thesis. Australia: University of Melbourne; 2016

[13] United Nations Industrial Development Organisation. Creative Industries and Micro & Small-Scale Enterprise Development A Contribution to Poverty Alleviation. Project XP/RAS/05/002. UNIDO: Austria; 2009

[14] Yang Y, Shafi M, Song X, Yang R. Preservation of cultural heritage embodied in traditional crafts in the developing countries. A case study of Pakistani handicraft industry. Sustainability. 2018;**10**(1336):1-18

[15] DACST. Department of Arts, Culture, Science and Technology, South Africa. 1998. Cultural Industries Growth Strategy (CIGS). The South African Craft Industry Report. Pretoria: DACST.

[16] Ardahaey FT. Economic impacts of Tourism industry. International Journal of Business and Management. 2011;**6**(8):206-215

[17] Makhitha KM. An Investigation into Buyer Behaviour of Craft Retailers in South Africa. PhD Thesis. Faculty of Economic Management. University of Pretoria; 2013

[18] Hay, D. 2008. The business of craft and crafting the business: Strategies for success in the rural craft sectors, 1–60.

[19] Urban-Economic Tourism. 2010. Feasibility Study for Umbumbulu Arts and Crafts Trade Centre. Quotation 38DED/2008.

[20] Wesgro. Wesgro Background on the Craft Industry in the Western Cape. August. South Africa; 2000

[21] Frost & Sullivan. Market Feasibility Study and Business Development Plan for the Handicrafts Sector. Indian: Export Promotion Council for Handicrafts; 2005

[22] Ritchie J, Lewis J, Nicholls MC, Ormston R. *Qualitative Research Practice: A Guide for Social Science Students and Researchers*. New York: SAGE; 2013

[23] United Nations. UNCTAD Global Database on Creative Economy. UN COMTRADE: UN DESA Statistics Division; 2016 Retrieved from http://unctadstat.unctad.org/EN/Index.html

[24] Walker E, Brown A. What success factors are important to small business owners? International Small Business Journal. 2004;**22**(6):577-594

[25] Kaiser and Associates. Western Cape Microeconomic Development Strategy. Crafts study. First report: Crafts profile. Revised draft. In: 28 April. (2005b)

[26] Asma BB, Diabate A, Othman A. Establishing the factors affecting the growth of small and medium- sized Enterprises in Algeria. American International Journal of Social Science. 2015;**4**(2):101-115

[27] Oyekunle OA, Sirayi M. The role of design in sustainable development of handicraft industries. African Journal of Science, Technology, Innovation and Development. 2018a;**10**(4):381-388

[28] Aigbavboa CO, Thwala WD. Challenges facing black owned small and medium handicraft companies: A case study of Nelspruit- Mbombela municipality, South Africa. Journal of Economics and Behavioural Studies. 2014;**6**(10):771-778

[29] Wood S. Sustaining crafts and livelihoods: Handmade in India. Craft +design enquiry. 2011;**3**:1-16

[30] Rhodes, S. 2011. Beyond 'Nourishing the Soul of a Nation': Craft in the Context of South Africa. Making Futures: The Crafts as Change Maker in Sustainably Aware Cultures 2.

[31] Khurana C, Paliwal V. An analysis of problems faced by handicraft sector in Jaipur, Rajasthan. International Journal of Research Science & Management. 2014;***1***(*4*) *Sep:1-6*

[32] Makyao RI. Challenges Facing Handicraft Businesses in Implementing Promotion Strategies for their Products. Masters dissertation. The Open University of Tanzania; 2013

[33] Mohapatra, S. & Dash, M. 2011. Problems associated with artisans in making of handicrafts in Orissa, India. Management Review: An International Journal, 6(1), May: 56–81.

[34] Richard, N. 2007. Handicrafts and Employment Generation for the Poorest Youth and Women. UNESCO Policy Paper No. 17.

[35] Benson W. The Benefits of Tourism Handicraft Sales at Nwenge Handicrafts Centre in Dar es Salaam. Tanzania. Bachelor thesis: Tampere University of Applied Sciences; 2014

[36] Mcauley A. Lost or just at a crossroads: Is entrepreneurship the way forward for marketing? Journal of Research in Marketing and Entrepreneurship. 2011;**13**(2):161-166

[37] Chan S. "Belonging, Becoming and Being First-Year Apprentices" Experiences in the Workplace.

Wellington: National Project Fund. Ako Aotearoa; 2011

[38] Kaiser and Associates. Western Cape microeconomic development strategy: Craft sector study. Overall executive summary. In: 27 May. (2005a)

[39] Oyekunle OA. The contribution of creative industries to sustainable urban development in South Africa. African Journal of Science, Technology, Innovation and Development. 2017;**9** (5):607-616

[40] Khan WA, Amir Z. Study of Handicraft Marketing Strategies of Artisans in Uttar Pradesh and Its Implications. Research Journal of Management Sciences, 2(2). Feb. 2013: 23-26

[41] Oyekunle, O. A. 2014. Developing creative education in South Africa: a case of Western Cape Province. Cultural Entrepreneurship in theory, pedagogy, and practice. Editors: Olaf Kuhlke, Schramme and Kooyman Rene. Eburon Publishers: Delft.

Chapter 7

Sustainable Business Practices by Nigerian Organizations

Nkemdilim Iheanachor

Abstract

Sustainability is the lifeline of any organization and it begins with its people. This paper investigates the sustainable business practices of Nigerian organizations. The pillars of sustainability, economic, social and environmental, have been linked to improve business performance when entrenched into long term strategies of a business. To address the challenges of power supply, multiple taxation, pollution and waste management faced in the business environment, it is imperative to develop solutions that will not compromise future needs yet meeting the needs of the present. Recycling, recovery and reuse, safe work initiatives, continuous learning are strategies businesses can adopt to reduce environmental waste, social and economic issues. For this purpose, this chapter examines sustainability practices of businesses from selected industries; construction, manufacturing, banking and hospitality industries were selected based on availability of sustainability reports of industry leaders. This research is expected to help business managers and policy makers understand sustainable business practices and its implications on business performance.

Keywords: business practices, economic, environment, recycling, sustainability, Nigeria

1. Introduction

Sustainability is meeting the needs of the present without compromising the ability of future generations to meet their own needs it is an approach to creating true and real value to systems. Nigeria is the largest economy in Africa, home to a lot of businesses and investments from around the globe with real GDP growth rate expected to rise by 3.3% in 2021 [1, 2].

The sole aim of every business is to continue to make profit and continue in perpetuity while meeting the expectations of all stakeholders. Management of organizations must engage in practices and corporate strategies that would aid the accomplishment of going concern objective. Organizations and companies are seeking to belong to the universal space; conforming to the requirements of stakeholders and global organizations by carrying out operations to reflect transparency and sustainability in reports and activities.

Nigerian organizations are a subset of the international space with the economy being driven by the manufacturing and service sectors, and the incorporation of sustainability ethics to business approach and processes are gradually taking over higher positions on the itinerary of policy makers, market regulators, companies and shareholders alike [3].

2. Sustainability in Nigeria

Business sustainability ensures management of resources needed to thrive as an organization and profitable in the long run, has hedged its risks and take shocks as they may occur [4]. Business sustainability focuses on two categories; its effect on the environment and the society focusing on the long term [5]. With roots in social justice and other movements, it is a rounded approach that considers conservation, social and financial dimensions, knowing that all must be considered together to find lasting wealth with history rooted in post industrial revolution [6].

Sustainability can be explored through resource optimization via recycle, re-use and reduce' strategies in business processes and supply chains, protecting brand value through stakeholder engagement and support including fulfilling regulatory requirements and selling to a niche market of green consumers ready to buy products and services at a premium.

Environmental, social and governance (ESG) themes remains priority for shareholders; it is imperative for businesses to build ESG considerations into continuing strategy, measure with the right metrics, disclosures and transparency bringing it up during meetings and using investor proposals to force companies to take action [7]. Expertise and education of the board of a company has solid impact on the sustainability disclosure of a company; however, many directors and non-executive directors have low experience in environmental issuer resulting in an insignificant on the disclosure of the sustainability reporting [8].

ESG business implementation are faced with barriers- shortage of financial resources; a lack of time; a dearth of information; risks associated with executing a new sustainable practice; current policies and regulations; and existing organizational culture [9]. To ensure success of successful sustainable business practice, cohesive processes, endless upgrading, investor meetings streamlining processes are important.

National Environmental Standards and Regulations Enforcement Agency, a federal parastatal established in 2007 enforces compliance with law guidelines, policies and standards on environmental matters, enforce compliance with policies, standards, legislation and guidelines on water quality, eco-friendly health and sanitation, including reduction in pollution and enforce through compliance monitoring, the environmental regulations and standards on noise, air, land, seas, oceans and other water bodies other than in the oil and gas sector among other functions [10].

2.1 Challenges of Nigerian business environment

2.1.1 Power supply

Nigeria suffers from insufficient energy generation. As it's the life wire of all businesses, businesses source alternative ways of generating power, especially large scale companies which increases overhead cost and reduction of net profits [11]. This problem is as old as the nation and has made companies relocate to other countries where there is relatively supply, with over 800 shutting down operations in the past decade.

2.1.2 Waste management

Waste generation rate in Nigeria is estimated at 0.65–0.95 kg/capita per day which gives an average of 42 million tons of wastes generated in a year. The poor condition of refuse management is attributable to an inefficiently articulated and below par implemented environmental policy, among other factors [12, 13].

Intensified in Nigeria by rapid development, economic growth and population density, government environmental agencies are faced an increasing amount of waste to handle.

2.1.3 Multiple taxation

Business owners in Nigeria have stated multiple taxes are obstacles to ventures, erodes equity base of firms and cause failure of industries [14]. Numerous taxes particularly affect the oil and gas industry, the manufacturing and service sector, the telecommunications industry, the insurance industry as well as the micro, small and medium enterprises (MSMEs).

2.1.4 Pollution

Nigeria's pollution problems are intricately linked with some of Nigeria's most headstrong issues; crushing poverty, dysfunctional public services, and political decadence creating highest burden of fatalities from air pollution in Africa and 4th highest in the world with 150 deaths per 100,000 people [15, 16]. Sound pollution due to erratic power supply from generating plants from households and industries increases carbon emission.

2.2 Sustainable business practices in Nigerian organizations

Countries have witnessed swift urban growth globally, increased economic and technological development in the years past; increasing industrial development coupled with various forms of contamination of the physical and biological components of the earth. Nigeria accounts for more than 150,000 metric tons of plastic bottles annually, half of it from the megacity of Lagos [17].

In Nigeria, many industrialized cities still have inadequate waste management; poorly controlled open dumps and illegal roadside dumping remain a problem. These are environmental issues that destroy scenic resources, pollute soil and hydro resources and habitation. Nigeria generates more than 32 million tons of solid waste annually, out of which only 20–30% is collected [18].

Businesses have adopted sustainable practices for effective waste management. Sustainable practices techniques embraced are total quality management, recycling, bio treatment, incinerations, neutralization and secure sanitary landfill [19]. Total quality management like continuous improvement and the zero-defect call are apt solutions and guides to effective waste management. This method guarantees waste eradication, high quality and increased profitability hence is a sustainable practice for companies. Bottling companies, for example use technological facilities with high efficiencies that are automated to reduce process waste generation.

Lagos, as Nigeria's industrial and densely populated city has numerous dumpsites. With a long value chain that is highly valuable ranging from the scavenger to the middlemen who sell or are representatives of companies, recycling is a sustainable method of managing waste and reducing its impact on the environment. Waste recycling saves raw materials, costs less, generates cash, creates jobs, and sustainable living [20, 21].

[22] revealed landfilling as the most common method of waste disposal, which is closely trailed by reuse as backfill and recycling. Landfilling is a sustainable practice. Large corporations adopt incineration, burying, and flaring, while small companies adopt reuse as backfill, landfilling, open dumping, and recycling. An industry leader in carbonated drinks industry adopts 3Rs –reduce, recovery, reuse, increasing the use of recycled content and implements light-weighting techniques [23]. To reduce

environmental impact, collection, recovery and recycling are focus areas. The company set up recycling infrastructure to encourage consumers to recycle their bottles establishing a post-consumer PET Recycling Project.

2.3 Sustainability reporting in Nigerian industries

2.3.1 Construction/manufacturing industry

Sustainable practices performed throughout a project cycle positively affect the environment in three dimensions; environment, society, and economy [24]. The construction industry and manufacturing industries are major drivers of development nevertheless activities from these industries add considerably to pollution and unmaintainable ingestion of depleting natural resources. Green growth alternatively, is an innovative growth which influences businesses to adopt eco-friendly friendly activities [25].

Selecting the precise procedures for resource conservation and consideration of the client's fulfillment is a major sustainability practice professionals implement in the stage of building projects with high awareness level of sustainability as it will lead to adoption of sustainability that will lead to high performance of construction firms [26, 27].

Dangote group, Nigeria's largest manufacturing conglomerate operates a data-centric sustainability culture, collecting data via Microsoft SharePoint to protect the integrity of data input and retrieval. The industry is generally perceived to be masculine, 9% of women make up the group's workforce.

Sustainable practices of the group are full-time education study leave, a scheme that ensured training for 9915 employees across all plants and head office in 2018. The group created the safe work initiative to minimize exposure to threats and inhibit cases and near-misses; customer service week to create responsiveness and consciousness on the dire importance of exceptional customer service across various business value chains [28].

As a form of support to SME distributors, over N3 billion were used to purchase 125 trucks with a 5 year payback period at no interest to enhance efficiency in operations. The major subsidiary of the group, Dangote cement is currently using new trend of expending waste from companies processing by using the high amounts of energy from waste as fuel to heat the kiln and replacing primary mineral materials in cement with fractional mineral traces from wastes.

2.3.2 Banking industry

Sustainable banking infers carrying out banking operational and business activities, with conscious consideration for the environmental and social impacts of those activities. By including sustainability principles into corporate strategy funding decisions and product/service definition processes, banks can be influential in supporting and promoting environmentally and/or socially responsible projects and enterprises. Innovative products and services that target certain populations (e.g. women) or that encourage purchase of green products (e.g. green credit cards) go a long way to promoting sustainable practices.

The Central Bank of Nigeria in 2012 directed all banks to implement principles and guidelines to develop a management approach that balances environmental and social and the economy [29]. [30] discovered 83.3% of Nigerian banks have a sustainability strategy with top priorities being energy, financial inclusion, and human and labor rights.

Banks enjoy reputational benefits, cost reduction and operational benefits, cost reduction, eventually directly linked to business growth in terms of financial and non-financial benefits to their sustainable banking activities. Principle 9 of the Nigerian Banking Sustainability Principles (NSBP) requires banks to regularly review and report on –progress in meeting the principles at the individual institution (**Table 1**).

[31] investigated sustainability report of 14 Nigerian banks with major findings being community investments than climate change disclosures and financial assistance received from the government. Fidelity Bank is guided by the international bill on human rights and keenly relies on the CBN principles of sustainable banking principles as shown in **Table 1** [32].

Sterling Bank has an effective environmental and social risks management systems to effectively manage the risks of credit fraud, reduction of carbon footprint by implementing several energy saving initiatives, adopted a sustainable waste management approach with Lagos state waste management agency and a recycling company and adopts the UN Declaration on Human rights with transportation and energy still in incubation [32]. To promote sustainable practices and environment, the bank embarked on a recycling campaign with the most innovative users of recycled materials winning the sum of one million naira each for their entrepreneurial journeys.

Sterling bank achieved success in financial, social and environmental sustainability. The bank reduced carbon footprint by switching to alternative energy at

Principle 1 | Business activities: Environmental and Social Risk Management	Incorporate environmental and social considerations into policymaking processes relating to business activities to avoid, minimize or offset negative impacts.
Principle 2 | Business Operations: Environmental and Social Footprint	Avoid, minimize or offset the negative impacts of business operations on the environment and local communities in areas of operations and where possible, promote positive impacts.
Principle 3 | Human Rights	Respect human rights in our business operations and business activities.
Principle 4 | Women's Economic Empowerment	Promote women's economic empowerment through a gender inclusive workplace culture in business operations and seek to provide products and services designed specifically for women.
Principle 5 | Financial Inclusion	Promote financial inclusion, seeking to provide financial services to individuals and communities that traditionally have had limited or no access to the formal financial sector.
Principle 6 | E&S Governance	Implement robust and transparent E&S governance practices in respective institutions and assess the E&S governance practices of our clients.
Principle 7 | Capacity Building	Develop individual institutional and sector capacity necessary to identify, assess and manage the environmental and social risks and opportunities associated with our business activities and operations.
Principle 8 | Collaborative Partnerships	Collaborate across the sector and leverage international partnerships to accelerate collective progress and move the sector as one; ensuring approach is consistent with international standards and Nigerian development needs
Principle 9 | Reporting	Regularly review and report on progress in meeting these Principles at the individual institution and sector level.

Source: Central Bank of Nigeria, 2012.

Table 1.
The Nigerian Sustainable Banking Principles.

branches and branches worldwide, completed solar projects, deployed hybrid power and renewable energy to ten branches. Investor's relations team regularly sent updates to analysts and shareholders, engaging via social media channels to drive real time engagements; also achieving 3.1% deposit market share and 12.6% capital adequacy ratio.

2.3.3 Hospitality industry

The hospitality industry is rapidly growing, with Nigeria experiencing 20% growth in 2018 consisting of food and beverage, tourism and travel, hotel lodging and recreation subsectors [33]. The industry is facing challenges accepting green practices due to insufficient information on sustainability and its advantages, government incompetence to impose guidelines on environmental health, and absence of highlighting the importance of green practice. Going green drives businesses to improve know-hows and execute groundbreaking ideas to protect the environment and improve business performance [34].

[35] discovered the industry is yet to understand the UNSDGs prevailing conditions for business undertakings in improving community wellbeing. There is dearth of information regarding sustainable practices as trainings are nonexistent for employees. Activities of these companies disrupt the serenity of the environment via waste from production, heavy noise from generating plants creating carbon emissions to residents of the areas.

Corporate social responsibility is alien to these enterprises; many do not understand its necessity with host communities and have been unsuccessful in assisting the community in reversing the rising threat of land degradation, community development and building infrastructure.

3. Conclusion

To ensure sustainable business practices, business leaders need to develop processes, structures to meet up with the requirements of green practices while still focusing on achieving the strategic goals of the business. Enterprises should evade routines that can trigger changes to the climate, hydro resources, forestry, and embrace alternative sources of energy like solar, energy saving bulbs etc.

Disclosing sustainable practices of companies helps maintain transparency about risks and opportunities faced as a business, alleviating negative ecological, social and governance impacts and improving the reputation of the brands. Conglomerates like Dangote Ltd., commercial banks, manufacturing companies disclose sustainability reports yearly; shareholders and the general public are aware of the true value, assets and practices of the organizations.

Nigerian organizations must endeavor to key into making the environment they are functioning better by proposing and enforcing the reuse and recycling of plastics especially and advance waste policies; create safe work initiatives, continuous learning, and alternative energy measures for sustainability. Using green methods and decreasing the impact of work and actions on the environment, society and economy could improve efficiency and make sure businesses remain a going concern.

Author details

Nkemdilim Iheanachor
Lagos Business School, Nigeria

*Address all correspondence to: niheanachor@lbs.edu.ng

References

[1] Available on http://www.ask-force.org/web/Sustainability/Brundtland-Our-Common-Future-1987-2008.pdf Accessed 2020-07-24

[2] Nigeria Available on https://www.afdb.org/fileadmin/uploads/afdb/Documents/Generic-Documents/country_notes/Nigeria_country_note.pdf Accessed 2020-07-28

[3] The World Bank in Nigeria Available on https://www.worldbank.org/en/country/nigeria/overview Accessed 2020-07-29

[4] Available on https://sustyvibes.com/wp-content/uploads/2016/10/AGuidetoBusinessSustainabilityinNigeria.pdf?source=ebook-page-download Accessed 2020-07-2

[5] Spiliakis, A. (2018). What does "sustainability" mean in business? https://online.hbs.edu/blog/post/what-is-sustainability-in-business Accessed 2020-07-29

[6] Available https://www.mcgill.ca/sustainability/files/sustainability/what-is-sustainability.pdf Accessed 2020-07-29

[7] Available https://assets.kpmg/content/dam/kpmg/cn/pdf/en/2020/01/integrating-esg-into-your-business.pdf Integrating ESG into your business. Accessed 2020-09-16

[8] Umukoro OE, Uwuigbe OR, Uwuigbe U, Adegboye A, Ajetunmobi O, Nwaze C. Board Expertise and Sustainability Reporting in Listed Banks in Nigeria. InIOP Conference Series: Earth and Environmental Science 2019 Sep (Vol. 331, No. 1, p. 012048). IOP Publishing.

[9] Caldera HT, Desha C, Dawes L. Evaluating the enablers and barriers for successful implementation of sustainable business practice in 'lean' SMEs. Journal of Cleaner Production. 2019 May 1;218:575-90.

[10] Available on https://www.nesrea.gov.ng/our-functions/ Accessed 2020-08-01

[11] Oyedepo SO. Energy and sustainable development in Nigeria: the way forward. Energy, Sustainability and Society. 01 December 2012;**2**(1):15

[12] Ike CC, Ezeibe CC, Anijiofor SC, Daud NN. Solid Waste Management in Nigeria: Problems, Prospects, and Policies. The Journal of Solid Waste Technology and Management. 2018 May 1;44(2):163-72.

[13] Agunwamba JC. Solid waste management in Nigeria: Problems and issues. Environmental management. 1998 Nov 1;22(6):849-56.

[14] How multiple taxes affects Nigerian companies Available on https://nairametrics.com/2019/02/20/how-multiple-taxes-affects-nigerian-companies/ Accessed 2020-08-02

[15] Amid Pollution and Political Indifference, Nigerians Struggle to Catch Their Breath Available on https://undark.org/2018/10/22/air-pollution-lagos/ Accessed 2020-08-02

[16] Nigeria: Air Pollution - Nigeria Ranks 4th Deadliest Globally Available on https://allafrica.com/stories/201809010001.html Accessed 2020-08-02

[17] Available on https://www.bloomberg.com/news/articles/2019-11-13/nigeria-enlists-big-beverage-companies-to-fight-plastic-waste Accessed 2020-08-02

[18] Solid Waste Management in Nigeria Available on https://www.

bioenergyconsult.com/solid-waste-nigeria/ Accessed 2020-08-02

[19] Taiwo A. Waste management towards sustainable development in Nigeria: A case study of Lagos State. International NGO Journal. 2009 Apr 30;4(4):173-9.

[20] Available on https://nairametrics.com/2018/03/19/waste-management-and-the-business-of-recycling-in-lagos/ Accessed 2020-08-02

[21] Edet HU, Maduabuchi, MN [] Waste Recycling as a Key to Conservation of Natural Resources in Nigeria: An Overview. Advance in Environmental Waste Management & Recycling. 2019

[22] Ogunmakinde OE, Sher W, Maund K. An Assessment of Material Waste Disposal Methods in the Nigerian Construction Industry. Recycling. 2019 Mar;4(1):13. DOI https://doi.org/10.3390/recycling4010013

[23] Available on https://ng.coca-colahellenic.com/en/sustainability/environment/environmental-overview/ Accessed 2020-08-02

[24] Pham H, Kim SY. The effects of sustainable practices and managers' leadership competences on sustainability performance of construction firms. Sustainable Production and Consumption. 2019 Oct 1;20:1-4.

[25] Tunji-Olayeni PF, Mosaku TO, Oyeyipo O, Afolabi AO. Sustainability strategies in the construction industry: implications on Green Growth in Nigeria.

[26] Oladokun, M. G., Isang, I. W., & Emuze, F. (2020). Towards sustainability practices deployment in building construction projects in Nigeria. Smart and Sustainable Built Environment.

[27] Otali M, Ujene A. Assessment of the level of awareness of sustainability practices among construction firms in Niger delta, Nigeria. Journal of Building Performance ISSN. 2020 May 1;2180:2106.

[28] 2018 Sustainability Report Championing Impact & Sustainable Development Available on http://www.dangotecement.com/wp-content/uploads/reports/2019/DangoteCementPlc_2018SustainabilityReport.pdf Accessed 2020-08-02

[29] Available on https://www.cbn.gov.ng/out/2012/ccd/circular-nsbp.pdf Accessed 2020-07-29

[30] Available on https://www2.deloitte.com/content/dam/Deloitte/ng/Documents/strategy/ng-deloitte-west-africa-sustainability-banking-survey.pdf

[31] Nwobu, O. A., Owolabi, A. A., & Iyoha, F. O. (2017). Sustainability reporting in financial institutions: a study of the Nigerian banking sector. The Journal of Internet Banking and Commerce, 1-15.

[32] Available on https://www.fidelitybank.ng/documents/Sustainable%20Banking%20Report%202018.pdf Accessed 2020-07-29

[33] Available on https://www.pwc.co.za/en/publications/hospitality-outlook.html Accessed 2020-07-29

[34] Muazu L, Rashid B, Zainol NA. Predictors of likelihood of adoption of green practices in hotels: the case of Abuja and Lagos, Nigeria. Environmental Management and Sustainable Development. 2017;6(1):72-90.

[35] Nwokorie EC, Obiora JN. Sustainable development practices for the hotel industry in Nigeria: Implications for the Ilaro area of Ogun State. Research in Hospitality Management. 2018;**8**(2):125-131

Chapter 8

Evolving a Sustainable Paradigm for Harnessing Intellectual Resources in the Nigerian Space Industry

Ngunan Monica Ikpaya, Ikpaya Ikpaya, Eseoghene Ovie, Chisom G. Nwokike, Sesugh Nongo and Godwin Ogor-Igbosuah

Abstract

Over the years, one of the ways that have been identified as pivotal in building sustainable organisations is the manpower development component of any organisation. Such manpower development through capacity building can be gained by training and retraining to retool the workforce into having the relevant and up to date skill set that spurs competitiveness and growth. For the Nigerian space industry, this human capacity development component has been embraced, encouraged and adopted into a working model for sustainability. The Nigerian Space Industry has leveraged on its potential to harness its intellectual capital through a collaborative culture with national and international partners to provide sustainable growth in attaining technological competence in Space Science and Technology (SST). In this chapter, we present a capacity building context as a model by which Nigeria's Space Industry mobilises its intellectual resources and collaborative efforts towards achieving sustainable development.

Keywords: sustainable organisations, collaboration, capacity building, sustainable development

1. Introduction

1.1 Sustainability

Sustainability is a system level property which describes the ability of a system to operate in its present state indefinitely [1]. In answer to the question "what is to be sustained - consumption, income levels or the ecosystem"? Chopra and Kadekodi, [2], state that eco-fundamentalist will solicit for resource sustainability, which will eventually force the acceptance of a level of well-being that will ensure sustainability. The ideal situation that may ensure sustainability will be a judicious balance between meeting the needs and expectations of this generation without endangering the environment or the ability to meet the needs of future generations [3]. Such an approach assumes that the society has a coping mechanism for any unforeseen challenges that may severely inhibit resource requirements. These challenges therefore ensure sustainability not just in the use of resources but of improvement in the resource base so that future challenges are tackled with ease. The capacity to achieve this depends on the ability to monitor and assess resource requirements and effectively respond without undue environmental or social restrain [3]. It lays emphasis on the long-term aspect of the concept of sustainability, introducing the ethical principle of achieving equity between the present and future generations [4].

The term sustainability is a concept that evokes diverse viewpoints that continue to be debated on. However, these different views raise a fundamental question – what is to be sustained and how can organisations implement it? To maintain a broad domain for discussion there is a necessity to describe the concept.

The concept of sustainability is therefore treated in this paper as a target or end result of a process called 'Sustainable Development'.

Luqmani [1] defines sustainable development as "a global development paradigm describing human, social and economic transformations which contribute to an enlargement of people's choices to lead a long, healthy life, are able to be maintained, supported and intensified indefinitely for current and future generations".

Diesendorf [4] proposes that a broad definition of sustainability should convey three principal components explicitly – social, ecological and economic. A socially sustainable system is one that achieves fairness in opportunity, distribution and adequate provision of social services; an ecologically sustainable system maintains a stable resource base avoiding over exploitation of renewable resource systems and depletion of non –renewable systems without investment in adequate substitutes; an economically sustainable system is one that maintains and augments its different kinds of capital for continual economic production of goods and services.

1.2 Intellectual capacity

Capital theory distinguished human capital only in the last 50 years, although there has been interest since the 17th century [5]. From 1900, knowledge as a means of production was no longer contestable, therefore predicating the statement made by Charles Hardy, "*Karl Marx would be amused. He longed for the day when the workers would own the means of production. Now they do*" [5]. According to Bontis [6], intellectual capital (IC) encompasses all intangible assets of an organisation, including its operations, innovation capability, as well as the tacit knowledge possessed by its employees and their network partners. Cavicchi [7], refers to IC as knowledge that can be transformed to value. It covers the competitive assets of creativity and innovation-based development. Serrat [5], proposes that IC has become the one indispensable asset of organisations; he defined management of the three components of IC as the essence of business; as follows:

Human Capital: the cumulative capabilities and engagement of an organisation's personnel, rooted in tacit and explicit knowledge, that can be invested to serve the joint purpose; Relationship Capital: This refers to the organisation's formal and informal relationships with suppliers, customers and partners to co-create products and services, expressed in terms of width (coverage), channels (distribution), depth (penetration), and attachment (loyalty); and Structural Capital: these are the collective capabilities of an organisation including its governance, values, culture and management.

IC embodies the imperative assets of an organisation critical for long term value creation which is necessary for sustainability, sustainable growth and competitiveness. In today's highly dynamic and competitive world, IC offers organisations and countries a sustainable competitive advantage through utilisation of technology and IC management to create value and spur innovation.

1.3 Overview of the Nigerian space industry

The National Space Research and Development Agency (NASRDA) Act, 2010 is Nigeria's primary law regulating the operation of space related activities. The Act set up the National Space Research and Development Agency and the National Space Council which is the country's highest policy-making body for space science and technology development [8].

NASRDA is a major player in Africa's space development. With a total of five (5) satellites launched between 2003 and 2012, the nation has established sustainable national growth and demonstrated peaceful utilisation of outer space by economic, educational, humanitarian and governmental applications [9]. The three remote sensing satellites; NigeriaSat-1, NigeriaSat-X and NigeriaSat-2 and two communications satellites; NIGCOMSAT-1 and NIGCOMSAT-1R highlighted the status of space operations and adhered to globally agreed practice of the peaceful use of outer space treaty [10].

As a testament to the competence of the highly trained scientists and engineers who make up the nation's space programme, NigeriaSat-1 was the first satellite to send back images of the Hurricane Katrina in the east coast of the US in 2005. Joining other nations in space operations; the Nigerian Earth Observation satellites are part of the Surrey Satellite Technology Limited (SSTL)–coordinated Disaster Monitoring Constellation (DMC). This network of satellites includes spacecrafts from Algeria, China, Spain, Turkey, and the UK, they provide rapid imagery from space when environmental disasters occur [10, 11].

NigeriaEduSat-1 is a part of BIRDS-1 constellation of five cubesats with membership of the following countries: Japan, Nigeria, Ghana, Mongolia, Bangladesh and Thailand (5). The Nanosat project was launched on June 3, 2017 aboard SpaceX rocket at Cape Canaveral, Florida, USA and deployed in orbit on July 7, 2017 at the International Space Station (ISS) [12, 13].

NIGCOMSAT-1 and NIGCOMSAT-1R have been used for tele-medicine, teleconferencing, data transfer, internet services, e-library etc. [10].

NASRDA is made up of seven (7) activity centres to implement research and development programmes and foster local and international collaboration in order to provide solutions for sustainable national socio-economic development and help achieve the Sustainable Development Goals (SDGs) [10].

One of the mandates of the Nigerian Space Agency, through its centres, is to strengthen capacity building and human resources development in the various specialisations that can be found in the entire space sector value chain. This is in line with NASRDA's 2030 road map – to develop and launch a satellite locally – encouraging capacity building and strengthening the Agency's intellectual resources [8].

Since inception, NASRDA has focused on intellectual capital, training engineers and scientists in all areas of satellite technology in Know How Transfer Training (KHTT) programmes in UK, China and Ukraine. NASRDA has also recorded training of over a hundred and twenty staff (120) at Masters Level and over seventy (70) staff at PhD level [10, 14].

Continuous research and development through capacity building and sustained funding will be a veritable asset and resource towards placing the Nigerian space journey on surer footing for sustainability. In this paper, we review and share our operational experiences and present a collaborative context as a model by which

Nigeria's Space Industry mobilises its intellectual resources and collaborative efforts towards achieving sustainable development.

2. The evolution of sustainability models

The work of the Club of Rome and The Limits to Growth in 1972 is a good starting point in the evolution of sustainability models [15]. Its central proposition is humanity's waking up to the limits of its natural environment and the negative impacts that population and its "development" have been having on it [16]. This concept missed out the dynamic potential for technology development and resource discovery which was unimaginable at the time. It is evident now however that the transformative and disruptive potential of technology is crucial to meeting our sustainability and development goals [17].

A powerful first step towards the modern concept of sustainability was the Stockholm Declaration (1972) [18]. It describes key environmental goals as connected to economic development drivers and the integrated nature of the solution path it describes. It's concept of sustainability ticked most of the boxes from a broad and holistic viewpoint but considerably underestimated the effects of technology and the associated effects of how changing economic markets, policy and culture drives beneficial technologies. A considerable part of the Stockholm Declaration's understanding of the main challenges of economic production, development and consumption to achieving sustainability, access to technology and the need to bridge gaps of cooperation and financial resources for a more global implementation of sustainable solutions is included in the framework of the Brundtland Report [19]. It roughly provided steps for transition on a large scale to a low- carbon global economy and how industries could efficiently "produce more for less" by deploying and developing new technologies.

A natural extension of the Brundtland *Report* was the Triple Bottom Line Framework. It powerfully describes sustainability's primary objectives and potential [20]. It highlighted significantly some of the key relationships between cultural, social and economic institutions in relation to environmental goals; bringing us to the realisation that we need more, not less intelligent, analytical thinking about economics and markets, if we are to achieve global sustainability.

Climate Change was the bolt from the blue that changed the focus and discussion on global sustainability. While the scientific research and evidence regarding anthropogenic climate change had been growing since the 1960s [21], the first Intergovernmental Panel on Climate Change (IPCC) [22] impact assessment report marked the beginning of a much broader and significant outlook on climate change and highlighted exactly how interdisciplinary and integrated our efforts would need to become.

In the early to mid-1990s, Michael Porter and Stephan Schmidheiny opened us up to the possibility that sustainable development was not just a cost but an opportunity for business, and therefore a necessity for modern business strategy. Schmidheiny [23] in *Changing Course*, spoke in broader strategic terms, which certainly was a precursor to Creating Shared Value (CSV), another more modern strategic sustainability paradigm [24].

A major milestone was the notion that major stakeholders could actually transform the paradigm and playing field through economic markets. It was no longer economy versus environment, but the potential that business and economic market development would no longer be a liability to sustainability, but could become one of its most powerful drivers and foundations.

A positive reaction to the Brundtland Report in the early 1990s was the creation of the World Business Council for Sustainable Development (WBCSD), and the 1992 United Nations Conference on Environment and Development (UNCED), also known as the Rio Earth Summit, which certainly changed the dynamics in favour of implementing sustainability solutions that are fully integrated, involve all stakeholders working cooperatively, engage economic markets and incentive systems, on a global scale. WBCSD's comprehensive corporate representation and membership, is as significant as the perspectives it develops and endorses. In terms of models, WBCSD's Circular Economy projects are an evolution from earlier versions of the factor approaches at the Wuppertal Institute in Germany [25]. Without dismissing the relevance of Environmental, Social and Governance (ESG) standards or Socially Responsible Investing (SRI) criteria developed and earnestly utilised in the early 2000s, these rather general guidelines have significantly repackaged the triple bottom line approach [26]. However, on the other hand, the general ideas and flexible roadmaps of the ESG's may help trigger changes in thinking and practices of the financial sector's process, which have always been somewhat conservative [18].

More recently the evolution of sustainability approaches and thinking is influenced greatly by urbanisation- rapid global urbanisation, a fact that will have major impact on how most people live, and with big implications and opportunities for sustainable economic development.

In the twenty-first century, Creating Shared Value (CSV) takes a fully modern and proactive approach with market actors and corporations creating positive, sustainability opportunities, social impacts and new green markets consistent with long-term profitability and survival strategies [24].

The UN's Sustainable Development Goals (SDGs) are a set of universal objectives developed within a process that included government, the private sector, academia, and civil society [27]. The SDGs are now without question the leading organisational and planning prototype across many sectors and projects, and one supported in a complementary manner by the more solutions-oriented focus of the three pillars of sustainability framework [18]. The three pillars of sustainability framework are based upon the key and connected roles of: technology and innovation; laws and governance; economics and financial incentives [28].

The Brundtland's Report defines sustainable development as *"development that meets the need of the present without compromising the ability of future generations to meet their own needs. It is in essence a process of change in which the exploitation of resources, the direction of investments, the orientation of technological development, and institutional change are in harmony and enhance both current and future potential to meet human needs and aspirations"* [29].

Diesendorf [4] states that the ecological and social equity are primary of the tripartite components of sustainability. He believes that any social or economic development is sustainable, if it protects and enhances the environmental and social equity. His definition is: *"Sustainable development comprises types of economic and social development which protect and enhance the natural environment and social equity"* [4].

Social equity here is used as a sense of equal opportunity for all rather than equality.

Development here may or may not involve economic growth, its focus is on 'qualitative improvement of human well-being' or 'unleashing of human potential' as opposed to quantitative growth in economic activity.

The significance of the ecological aspect of sustainability follows from the fact that the society and economy depend ultimately on the integrity of the biosphere and ecological processes within it. Unfortunately, a vast majority of humans are oblivious of their impact on their life support system. Scientists and scholars over the last four decades have written extensively about these adverse effects of human beings and their activities on the environment [11, 30, 31] and large groups of eminent scientists [32].

A synopsis of the evolutionary trends identified and discussed Club of Rome, the first documented effort to identify the need for sustainability models; Stockholm Declaration was the first real attempt at understanding the linkages between environmental goals and economic development. The Triple Bottom Line Framework clearly identified the key objectives needed for setting sound sustainability models while IPCC traced the deleterious impacts of climate change to more of anthropogenic factors and recommended an integrated and interdisciplinary effort to tackle the causes and effects of climate change. Michael Porter and Stephan Schmidheiny advocated that the environment wasn't a hindrance to economic growth and development but benefitted from new economic models which utilised technology to its advantage and preservation. The CSV unique in its total embrace of the identification of symbiotic linkages between economy and ecology was designed to lessen the possibility of disenchantment and disillusionment with economic growth and wealth distribution.

Evolutionary trends in the development of the outlined sustainability models are mostly underpinned by the need to create a world that is in harmony with the competing needs and demands of production and consumption. As with all measures to satisfy the needs of mankind, inevitable constraints and drawbacks can arise in the form of disenchantment or disillusionment occasioned by inequalities stemming from the resulting imbalances in earths' ecosystem caused by man's cultural, social and economic practices and activities. These facts have been instrumental in the search and development of sustainability models at different times and by different individuals or groups.

3. Existing sustainability models

There exist various sustainability models, developed and or adopted by organisations and institutions. In this section, we have selected an independent and two organisational sustainability models for review.

3.1 Diesendorf's model of sustainability

This model of sustainability and sustainable development explicitly sets out the underlying ethical assumptions, measurable objectives (sustainability indicators), broad goals and actions measured for implantation, integrating the ecological, social and economic aspects without requiring trade-offs. It makes the ecological aspect a constraint on economic and social development types. It offers both a comprehensive theoretical framework and a six-step implementation action plan. This action plan involves facilitating community participation and empowerment to create a vision, develop sustainability policy and implement Ecological Sustainable Development (ESD) by changing the system [33] (**Figure 1**; **Table 1**).

The model has four logical levels:

- Level 0, comprising the broad ethical principles
- Level 1, comprising broad goals arising from these principles
- Level 2, comprising measurable objectives and indicators
- Level 3, comprising the action plan for implementation of Ecological Sustainable Development (ESD)

The sustainability model illustrated below answers the fundamental question: "What is the scope of sustainability and how can we present it in a systematic way, making distinctions between ethical principles, broad goals and objectives which are measurable and actionable. This is illustrated in Levels 0–2. Level 3 is the six-step systematic implementation process itemised below.

Sustainability indicators or measurable objectives are necessary for monitoring progress and motivating action. These indicators however do not produce good policies or implementable actions in themselves. To create appropriate indicators, one must ask the question "What behaviour am I seeking?" to develop policy and then create indicators to serve the policy [33].

The Diesendorf model's systematic process of implementation and assessing progress is a six – step plan which utilises the combined approach drawing the most appropriate components from the Ottawa Charter and the Bellagio Principles [4] as follows:

- Present a guiding vision, goals and scenario
- Develop sustainability policy in all sectors, at all levels, with all types of instrument

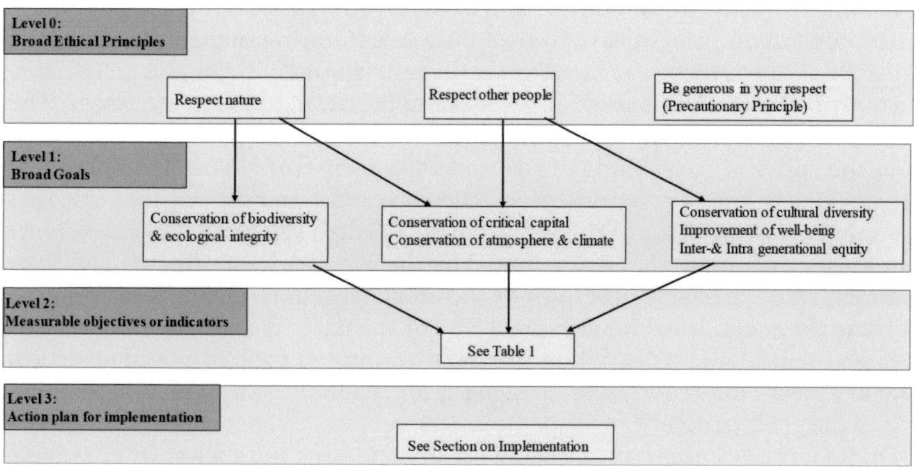

Figure 1.
Sustainability model or framework [33].

Ecological	Economic	Social
Rate of materials 'flow; Rate of energy use; Total and per capita rate of greenhouse gas emissions; Vehicle kilometres travelled per capita; Human population and growth rate; Area of land degraded and polluted; Water pollution; Air pollution.	'Genuine Progress Indicator'; Distribution of household and personal income; Percent of income needed to pay for basic 'needs' of a person; Percent of children living in households with no adult earner; Mortgage repayments and rents relative to median income in region; Employment by top five companies in the region.	Basic services within walking and cycling distances of dwellings; Availability of day care for under 5 s Levels of education, including literacy and numeracy; Life expectancies at birth and at age 20; Morbidity rates; Crime rates; Homelessness; Teaching of indigenous languages in schools.

Table 1.
Examples of some measurable objectives [4].

- Create supportive environment
- Strengthen community action
- Develop personal and organisational skills
- Reorient the system

3.2 The natural step

3.2.1 Organisation background

The Natural Step (TNS) is a non-profit, non-governmental, environmental organisation dedicated to achieving ecological, social and economic sustainability; opening and maintaining communication pathways between stakeholders; and building consensus. Founded in 1989 by Dr. Karl-Henrik Robert, a Swedish cancer physician and scientist with a keen interest in nature. In the course of his work Dr. Roberts was touched by the compassion and resources that were mobilised by families, society and caregivers in response to children with cancer at his clinic. He found their approach swift, comprehensive and co-ordinated, an absolute contrast to the commotion between government, businesses and environmental movements over our rapidly deteriorating planet. Dr. Robert soon realised that the crux of the matter was that environmental debates were focused sparingly on systemic causes of problems and more on downstream issues. The solution required a holistic approach, a new way of looking upstream to understand the underlying systemic causes and walk away from them. Dr. Roberts then decided to find a comprehensive, rigorous and concrete way to tackle these systemic causes; working with more than 50 Swedish scientists, they developed a consensus document that was adopted by the Swedish government. The document described the basic functions of the biosphere, how societies influence the natural system, how humans are a part of the natural systems, how humans threaten themselves by degrading natural systems and functions and lastly how there are great opportunities to change the situation into an attractive sustainable society [34] (**Figure 2**).

Dr. Robert has since then worked with an increasing number of international scientists to develop a framework or model for strategic decision making, enabling a systematic step by step approach towards sustainability while reducing risk and promoting design and innovative decisions in government and business. This framework is the intellectual foundation of The Natural Step. Several major Swedish companies like IKEA and Electrolux have incorporated this framework into their business practices. The TNS framework has gained grounds internationally, recognising the unique challenges businesses and governments face locally, TNS decided to licence the framework to local non for-profit partners while TNS International is steward of the framework. The organisation is established in the US, UK, New Zealand, Australia, Israel, Canada, Japan, Brazil, South Africa, France and Italy.

3.2.2 TNS sustainability model

The Natural Step sustainability model or framework is embedded in four system conditions which have slightly evolved through the 1990s. The rationale

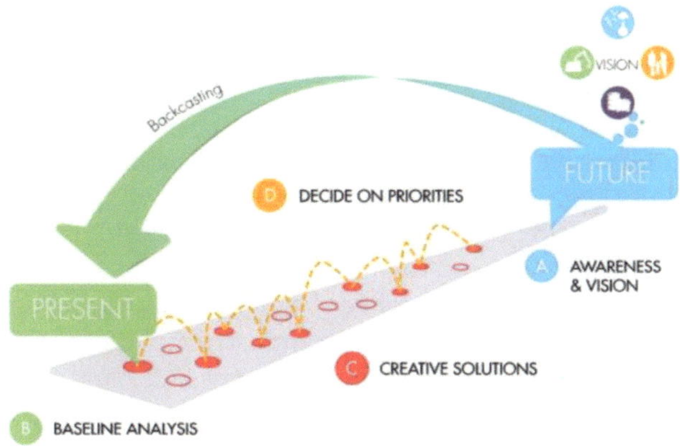

Figure 2.
The ABCD process [36].

behind the system conditions is that since the number of possible designs of sustainable societies is probably without limit, the definition must be principle based such that any sustainable society would be able to adopt such principles [4]. The system conditions are stated as not allowing the destruction of the ecosphere:

"*In order for society to be sustainable, nature's functions and diversity are not subject to systemically increasing:*

- *concentrations of substances extracted from the earth's crust*
- *concentrations of substances produced by society*
- *impoverishment by overharvesting or other forms of ecosystem manipulation*

Together these first three conditions provide a framework for ecological sustainability, implying a set of constraints within which the sustainable societal activities must be incorporated. It is on this basis that a first order principle for the society's internal turnover of resources is formulated as follows:

- *resources are used fairly and efficiently in other to meet basic human needs worldwide*" [35].

3.2.3 TNS implementation strategy

TNS Implementation Strategy enables the application of the system conditions to an organisation's daily operations and implementing sustainability through the ABCD process.

These principles are at the core of TNS sustainability framework and aim at the efficient and fair utilisation of resources; the substitution of rare and toxic materials for environmentally friendly and abundant materials; developing new technologies and protecting ecosystems. TNS model offers a strong focus on businesses and governments in the control of flow of materials released into the environment by humans and human activities, thus it establishes a structure for the creation of measurable indicators in the area of ecological sustainability for decision making; it is limiting however, in its treatment of the social and economic aspect of sustainability [4].

3.3 Interface

3.3.1 Company background

Interface, an innovative company founded in 1973 by Ray Anderson, with radical sustainability goals is a global manufacturer of modular carpet tiles with an annual revenue of approximately $1bn. Boasting a sizable employee base and expansive geographical spread and manufacturing operations in North America, Europe and Asia-Pacific; Interface has been recognised as the pioneer of sustainable business practices in the carpet and flooring industry and one of the global leaders particularly in the area of sustainability, for more than 10 years.

3.3.2 Interface sustainability oriented innovation (SOI) model

Interface SOI model posits that, innovation is critical for long term business; successful innovation promotes growth, profit and access to new markets. SOI, a term first used by Hansen *et al.* [37] to describe innovation that produces improved sustainability. *"SOI is the production, assimilation or exploitation of a product, process, service, method, structure or social institution that is novel in its application, and which improves economic, environmental and social outcomes throughout the life cycle of the application, compared to relevant alternatives"* [38]. Discussions bordering on SOI are a bit complicated in literature as it is defined in several different ways [39]. Eco-innovation is debated as a related concept. Another area of debate is intent; Kemp and Pearson [40] and Machiba [41] discuss whether improvements that are financially driven and lead to environmental and social well- being as a by-product can be considered SOI. Innovation can be classified as incremental (minor or radical) e.g. minor efficient improvements or dramatically increased performance or reduced cost [42]. Bessant and Tidd [43] suggest that radical innovations sometimes result in entirely new products or markets; these may be classified as disruptive or discontinuous. However, Machiba [41] suggests that the most radical forms of SOI lead to a fundamental change in the business model and the wider system. Hansen *et al.* [37] defined SOI as innovation with a positive net effect on the overall capital stock. A well-rounded definition of SOI should achieve several criteria - encompass new ideas, production of ideas from internal sources and assimilation of ideas from external sources [40]. It should include old ideas that have found a new purpose and describe a full range of innovation products (incremental, radical and or disruptive) [43]. To ensure sustainability, the definition of SOI should describe innovations that result in improvement of the environmental, social and financial outcome or those that reduce the negative impact on these outcomes in comparison with other options.

Interface implements SOI with its co-innovation and other related innovation processes to achieve the company's ambitious environmental goals. Co-innovation is a global process within Interface designed to accelerate and systematise innovation projects within the company towards its Mission Zero Goals [38]. Interface's environmental programme is called Mission Zero, illustrated in **Table 2** with its sub goals.

Mission Zero, a priority objective for the company and the company's reputation as a leader in sustainability are its key market differentiators that endear its customers especially the architectural and design community [44].

Interface through innovative activities between 1994 to 2014 was able to cut waste, reduce greenhouse emissions and reliance on fossil-derived energy a remarkable progress towards goals 1, 2,3 and 5 which formed the basis of their claim of a "cumulative sum of $480m savings and avoided costs since 1994" [1]. The Mission

Mission Zero Goals	Goal Description
1. Eliminate Waste	Eliminating waste in all forms- material waste, wasted time and wasted effort
2. Benign Emissions	Eliminating waste streams that have negative or toxic effects on natural systems
3. Renewable Energy	Reducing energy demand and substituting fossil fuels with renewable ones
4. Closing the Loop	Redesigning processes and products so that all resources can be recovered at the end of life and reused, closing the technical and natural loop
5. Resource Efficient Transport	Transporting people with minimal waste and emissions. This includes consideration of plant location, logistics and commuting
6. Sensitising Stakeholders	Creating a community within and around Interface that understands the functioning of natural systems and our impact on them
7. Redesign Commerce	Redesigning commerce to focus on delivery of service and value instead of material
	Encouraging external organisations to create policies and market incentives

Table 2.
Mission zero goals and Interface description [38].

zero goals 4, 6 and 7 were achieved through various standalone innovation projects and research and development activities; the use of the principle of biomimicry [45] to develop a non-directional carpet tile with good material saving properties and strong aesthetics. This design brought about an affinity towards non directional tiles in the industry [46]. The company made commendable progress with Mission goal 4 in 2013 as it launched its first product line with post-consumer recycled nylon; they partnered with Universal Fibres [47] using a novel process. Net-works, a socially-oriented recycling programme which progressed goal 7 significantly and less so goals 1, 4 and 6.

InterfaceRAISE was an attempt in 2011 to create a consultancy arm that leveraged on the company's global sustainability leadership to deliver on its promise of becoming a restorative enterprise in line with its Mission goal 7; and FairWorks, initiated by the co-innovation team in 2008 attempted to create a tangible social benefitting product that used local skilled artisans in India to weave handmade products from grass [48] providing them access to the global market through an inclusive business model. It made no market impact and failed after 4 years due to high cost, lack of scale, variable quality and poor integration into the company's core product range.

3.4 Interface net-works

Fairworks failure between 2011 and 2012 led the co-innovation team to seek the use of their existing core product range to address the social dimension of sustainability. Interface's European Sustainability Director met Hill a researcher from Imperial College who had recently completed his PhD in livelihood approaches to marine conservation at the Zoological Society of London (ZSL) at a conference and made a connection between his work and the Aquafil recycling technology (ECONYL). Aquafil, a fibre manufacturer and yarn supplier to Interface at the time launched ECONYL to convert postconsumer nylon waste mainly from the fishing industry into premium quality recycled yarn.

Interface launched Net-Works in 2013 a disruptive, cross-sector, ongoing partnership between Interface, Aquafil and ZSL. The core concept was to partner with fishing communities to recover discarded fishing nets in the Philippines through an "inclusive business" social enterprise model using ECONYL to recycle the waste into high quality nylon to be used in manufactured goods and integrate them into part of the Interface core product range such as yarn for their carpet tiles. Net-Works has had significant impact and gained unexpected global recognition for its sustainability component. Networks' prominent characteristic is its integrated and tangible approach to addressing, social, economic and environmental sustainability. Socially, Net-Works is self–supporting and integrates with the existing livelihood of the community based partners. Economically, it has been a powerful, differentiation tool that has resonated with customers; at a local level it has benefitted the partnering communities as a steady source of supplementary income. Environmentally, it has reduced pollution and improved local marine stocks and biodiversity at the partnering sites and created awareness of waste and recycling among the partnering communities [38], on a wider scale, it has lowered CO_2 emissions per kilogramme [49]. Currently, Net-works is its own organisation supported by the original project partners with the primary objective of creating a social enterprise model which could be adapted to other contexts, inspiring similar activities by other companies.

3.5 Comparison of sustainability models

This section compares and presents a process classification of the three sustainability models discussed above. Time related criterion forecasts the state of sustainability; place related criterion models the state of sustainability with respect to their spatial scale and or localisation while scale related criterion models sustainability of systems according to composition and structure [16] (**Table 3**).

Drawing inference from the three sustainability models compared above, it can be observed that the models share similar indices, therefore, the three aspects of sustainability: ecology, social and economic are adopted as specific metrics, to further analyse the various points of departure of one model from the other.

The first two models are ecologically centric, however, while Dissendorf's model proposes that social and economic development is sustainable if it protects and enhances ecological development; the TNS model seeks to address the role of businesses and governments in the control of materials from human beings and their activities into the environment and create measurable indicators for decision making in the area of ecological sustainability.

The Interface model places greater emphasis on the social aspect of sustainability through a shared network system of collaboration, assistance and biodiversity management. It creates a veritable platform of contributory efforts that lead to sustainable and inclusive outcomes for all.

In summary therefore, it has been established that all three models place particular importance to varying degrees on an aspect of sustainability. Overall, what is sought after are model types that have capacity to present the co-evolution of the global system and charge humanity to realise and fulfil its stewardship obligation as sustainability Guardians. These models can be described as "Dynamic, Global and General" [16].

Sustainability Model	*Time Related*		*Place Related*		*Scale Related*	
	Static	*Dynamic*	*Global*	*Regional*	*General*	*Specific*
Diesendorf		√	√	√	√	√
The Natural Step		√	√	√	√	√
Interface		√	√	√	√	√

Table 3.
Process classification of the reviewed sustainability models.

4. Research design

4.1 Method

This research uses a descriptive case study paradigm in order to analyse NASRDA's sustainability capacity building process and context, while being guided by literature. The case study method was adopted for its suitability to address the key questions of "How" and "Why". It has been established that a case study research methodology approach provides a rich contextual analysis of the unit of study, at a level of qualitative detail which can be obtained using quantitative or experimental methodologies [50].

In this instance, the research examines "how and why NASRDA implements its own sustainability capacity building process", in view of extenuating circumstances and peculiar environmental factors. This is done with the ultimate aim of highlighting how these all come together and intervene to form a generalised view and central idea of its core processes and systems that have kept it going for more than twenty years. The unit or analytical baseline selected is the human capacity development model that ties the individual staff skills and knowledge base with the organisational core strengths, competencies and projected or forecasted goals.

To expatiate on the peculiarities of NASRDA's model, a multi-entity study is proposed and adopted for this work. Such multi-dimensional approach is to serve as a foundation for generalisations in claims and conclusions which can be broadly adopted and further improved upon as per our recommendations and contributions by others. Overall, the human capacity building approach as a component in engendering sustainable organisations is proposed in this work drawing from the inherent experience of NASRDA as a holistic whole.

4.2 Data collection

Most of the data used for this work was drawn from literature as the case study approach earlier mentioned in Section 4.1 bears out. This work has drawn from the long and varied experiences of different governmental and non-governmental actors working at regional and global levels to present a case for the utility of a mixed CCT-RBV model that is human capacity development centric in its central theme, ethos and workings.

Strength: 1. Human capital 2. Collaboration and linkages 3. Space and ground assets 4. Service and product regulation	Weaknesses: 1. Inadequate working facilities 2. Inadequate funding 3. Low products and or service sensitization and awareness 4. Accountability and transparency
Opportunities: 1. Rising global space market 2. Space based solutions and innovation for socio-economic development 3. Private sector participation in space technology	Threats: 1. Declined Government funding 2. Public sector/ individual interest 3. Insurgency 4. Brain drain and loss of competent hands

Table 4.
SWOT analysis.

4.3 The NARSDA SWOT analysis

This section presents a SWOT analysis, a strategic tool to review and evaluate the Nigerian Space Industry's internal and external environment reflecting specifically on its organisational strengths and opportunities that reinforce the development of future strategic options and its weaknesses and threats which can be further developed for sustainability. This analysis will aid the development of an effective sustainable model by identifying critical areas to leverage on and develop within the organisation (**Table 4**).

5. The NASRDA sustainability model

Organisations adopt and implement sustainable models based on peculiarities in their operations and unique set of challenges faced. At NASRDA, we have implemented a sustainable capacity building approach with technology transfer as its starting point. As noted by [51], the best measure of development by any nation is the quality of products and services produced by its people. Therefore, capacity building through quality formal education and other capacity building mechanisms provides the needed solution for a sustained growth in our nascent space industry.

NASRDA has over the years adopted the concept of Core Competence Theory (CCT) and Resource-Based View (RBV) theory. CCT was first developed in 1990 by Garry Hamel and C. K Prahalad while RBV was developed by E.T. Penrose in 1959 [52]. Core competency can be defined as a unique capability acquired by a firm over a period of time in form of a resource, operations facility, specially skilled manpower, technology know-how or delivery of service which gives the firm sustainable competitive advantage in the future, in quality, design, production or distribution of a product/service or in cost of the product and is viewed as a relative value addition by a prospective customer"; RBV focuses on the human resources and the way they are deployed by management in the organisations, and how they contribute to the creation and development of value within the firm [52].

Being the premier space industry in Sub-Saharan Africa, it was paramount to invest heavily in capacity building to ensure sustainability of its space programme. From the design, build and launch of NigeriaSat-1 – Nigeria's first satellite in 2003; the Nigerian space programme witnessed its pioneer KHTT training programme of 15 young engineers and scientists at SSTL, UK. During this KHTT programme, we were able to deduce that technology cannot be transferred but could be acquired. This was possible through capacity building by applied research, hands on training, retraining and experimental development. Like other emerging sectors in developing economies, brain-drain poses a huge challenge to the Nigerian space industry especially when working conditions are not at par (or close) with counterparts in developed countries.

Over the years, acquisition of space technologies training has led to innovation through research and development and strengthened our indigenous capacity development and competency in satellite design, development and launch as well as ground facility management, operations and maintenance. It has also enhanced the optimal use of each satellite to fully derive its benefits and exploit its potential. Furthermore, it has promoted educational qualifications up to PhD in most areas of space science and technology and in a collaborative context, nano and small satellites for education and operational applications. The services and technologies developed for nano and small satellite programmes create opportunities for the establishment of commercial businesses [53], and this in turn promotes Public-Private Partnership (PPP).

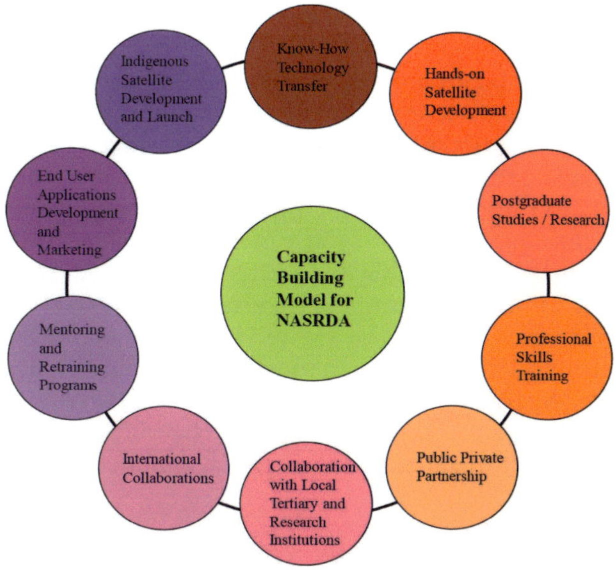

Figure 3.
NASRDA's sustainability model for capacity building development.

As the nation aims at diversification of its economy from oil and gas dependency, the space sector is strategically positioned to contribute to the economy sustainably by harnessing space technologies for innovation.

The figure below depicts NASRDA's sustainability model for capacity building development (**Figure 3**).

5.1 Know-how technology transfer (KHTT) training programme

From inception of her journey into Space Research and Development, NASRDA has adopted the Know-How Technology Transfer (KHTT) training approach for ensuring sustainability in the sector. This has been a major component for the satellite projects done so far for Nigerian capacity building in space science, engineering and technology. These satellite projects KHTT programmes included: 15 engineers and scientists for NigeriaSat-1 (2001–2003) at SSTL, UK; 55 engineers and scientists for NigComSat-1 (2005–2006) at China Great Wall Industry Corporation (CGWIC) China and 26 engineers and scientists for NigeriaSat-2/X (2006–2009) at SSTL UK. Of emphasis to the success of these programmes is the preparedness of transfer of proprietary knowledge and skills that have been protected by intellectual property rights and patents to the trainees [51]. The knowledge and specialised skills have been of tremendous impact towards a sustained space industry. Most of the efforts which have been significant in this regard include the development of spin-off projects from the various aspects of satellite technology development.

As discussed in [10], NigeriaSat-1 was indigenously operated and managed from its Mission Control Ground Station (MCGS) in Abuja, Nigeria. Similarly, NigeriaSat-2, NigeriaSat-X and NigComSat-1R (a replacement of NigComSat-1) MCGSs in Abuja were also operated and managed indigenously.

The takeaway from the foregoing therefore is that the KHTT trainees have since put their training to good use through the advancement in space research that has brought about numerous home-grown projects and innovations that have impacted positively in solving various challenges. This in turn has contributed towards the socio-economic development of Nigerians.

5.2 Hands-on satellite development

One of the successes recorded in each of the KHTT programmes was the provision of hands-on experience in satellite engineering and technology. Apart from participating in the design, build and launch of the satellites, the KHTT trainees had to design and build their own Training Model (TM). The NigeriaSat-1 TM for instance, had similar features and components like NigeriaSat-1 satellite apart from the solar panels and a substitute for the 32 m Multi-Spectral Imager Payload. This was a proto-flight model and was not intended for flight. However, during the NigeriaSat-2 programme, NigerriaSat-X – X represents eXperimental, was the TM and was designed for flight and thus, had to be space qualified. This practical hands-on experience was a giant milestone recorded by NASRDA with the capability of designing a 22 m high-resolution imager. The hands-on experiences for Nigeria Sat-1, NigeriaSat-2 and NigComSat-1 KHTT included ground-station modules, operations and maintenance.

5.3 Post-graduate studies/research

Formal education and other capacity building mechanisms are most needed in order to ensure technology acquisition and utilisation [51]. As a result, NASRDA has over the years encouraged advancement in formal education for its staff. This was one of the reasons NigeriaSat-2 satellite programme was designed to run concurrently with a Master's programme in their areas of specialisation. On completion of the program, outstanding staffs were further sponsored to pursue their PhDs. Currently; NASRDA's teeming experts are supporting various tertiary institutions across the country in teaching and research activities. NASRDA has also established an educational arm for post graduate research called the Institute of Space Science and Engineering (ISSE). It provides advance research in space science and technology and is an affiliate of the African University of Science and Technology (AUST). The lecturers of the Institute comprise mainly staff of NASRDA who specialise and have been trained in various aspects of space exploration.

5.4 Professional skills training

The routine professional skills training in NASRDA which is designed to facilitate career competencies can be regarded as value-added skills. Training areas include but are not limited to software package development, IT, space applications, administrative and project management courses have been highly beneficial to staff of the Agency.

5.5 Public-private partnership

Public-Private Partnership (PPP) is an important institutional innovation in infrastructure and public service and can be considered as a long-term partnership through contracts between members of the public and private sectors [54]. Through PPP, government and businesses cooperate to provide goods and services to the populace. This innovative initiative brings about real economic potential and sustainable development of the space industry.

There has been a consistent effort by certain key technology innovators to partner with NASRDA. To contribute towards the fight against the COVID 19 pandemic, NASRDA initiated PPPs in the area of its tele-medicine programme.

5.6 Collaborations

NASRDA has imbibed the culture of collaboration at both local and international levels in its model. This has yielded fruitful results in technological advancement. With its accomplishment in capacity building, opportunities in collaborative capacity building becomes essential as nations partner together to achieve common goals in space technology. To this end, NASRDA has signed working Memorandum of Understandings (MoUs) with several tertiary institutions, such support spans the gamut from teaching to developing high end research activities that are capable of gaining patent status and commercial traction due to the innovative component within such projects. NASRDA is also collaborating within the educational framework, through its activity Centre, the African Regional Centre for Space Science and Technology Education (ARCSSTE) in Ile Ife, and ISSE which is affiliated to the AUST, Abuja Nigeria.

Reiterating some of the collaborations already mentioned, we have the KHTT framework with SSTL UK and CGWIC China; space training collaboration with Indian Space Research Organisation (ISRO) India and Korea Aerospace Research Institute (KARI) South Korea to mention a few. Some of the products of these collaborations include Nigeria's inclusion in the Disaster Monitoring Constellation International Imaging (DMCii).

Furthermore, Nigeria through NASRDA is a member of the Committee on Peaceful Uses of Outer Space (COPUOS), the International Telecommunications Union (ITU) and several other local, regional and international bodies working in space related endeavours.

5.7 Mentoring

As one of the building blocks of capacity building for NASRDA, mentoring plays a key role. Mentoring is essential for developing skills to take on more responsibilities and guide the progress of mentees on the acquired knowledge. This could be through a formal education setting such as the ISSE, Abuja, or informal settings by supervising and coordinating departments, divisions, projects etc. All these avenues provide a platform for knowledge transfer and channelling the next generation of space scientists and engineers towards technological advancement.

5.8 End-user applications development and marketing

According to Adams, [55] the three dimensions of core mainstream of sustainability adopted by the World Conservation Union are environmental, social and economic sustainability. The effectiveness of NASRDA's sustainability model is its capacity for effective application of acquired space technologies to impact positively on the quality of lives and socio –economic development of Nigerians. This is achievable through provision of valuable information to end-users in areas of agriculture, disaster monitoring, land cover/land use change, environmental monitoring, health and wellbeing etc. The application of the space resources and data into meaningful information and services is therefore essential in making the populace and global community reap the benefits of space science and technology.

5.9 Indigenous satellite development and launch

With the accomplishment demonstrated in the design, build and launch of NigeriaSat-X, and the existing sounding rocket launch activities at NASRDA's Centre for Space Transport and Propulsion Epe. The Agency is poised to achieve one of the milestones on its roadmap which is to indigenously develop and launch a satellite; this giant milestone is achievable through the effective harnessing of its intellectual resources. Such an achievement strengthens the space Agency and the Nigerian economy, offering potential benefits such as sustainable revenue, infrastructural development, science and technology advancement, space and global competitiveness.

6. Conclusion

In summary therefore, the strategic and operational goals of the Nigerian Space Agency has followed a model and trajectory that subscribed to the hybrid concept of CCT and RBV. This has proven to be invaluable in its pursuit of space technology mastery with the inadvertent result of leaning heavily towards technology acquisition as a first step in its chosen hybrid sustainability model. On closer analysis, however, it can be seen that CCT and RBV are just two sides of the same coin, with one being unable to do without the other for effective functioning of the described model. CCT requires a critical mass of manpower resource that is well trained and up to-date in the various fields of space science and satellite technology. Conversely, the possession of such expertise in human resource creates a fertile ground for the incubation and enculturation of a technology culture that is driven by a common underlying thread of scientific method and sustainable technological model in the conceptualization and development of various space science and technology related products and services.

Drawing inspiration from the discussed sustainability models, NASRDA has adopted a little bit of each of the three principal models. While not specifically applying the underlying strategies in these models to ecology in the Dissendorf's case, natural resource exploitation and allocation in the TNS model or social responsibility (CSR) in the Interface model. The core of NASRDA's sustainability model makes the continuity and unmitigated improvement of manpower resource its raison d'etre. As has been well documented, all the sustainability model types ultimately have the benefit of mankind as the central aim of their workings. These models have also gone to sufficiently show that organisations do not have to walk a fine line between meeting their goals and balancing the needs of lives versus livelihoods. In anchoring NASRDA's sustainability thrust on its manpower, it underscores the identification of human capacity as the fundamental component of any organisation just like the upstream factor component addressed by the TNS model. This fact captures the logic that a satisfied workforce means good and efficient deliverables or products downstream that satisfies both workers and consumer's needs.

It is therefore seen that the inadvertent adoption of a hybrid, mixed, collaborative sustainability model which has underpinned NASRDA's successes so far was quite logical for fledgling organisational coming into the heavily regulated and tightly controlled space science and technology sector. Projecting its strength into the future with such applications that are targeted indigenously and driven from Nigerian technology space and the African continent remains one of the most salient ways to prove the ultimate workability of this sustainability model.

Author details

Ngunan Monica Ikpaya*, Ikpaya Ikpaya, Eseoghene Ovie, Chisom G. Nwokike, Sesugh Nongo and Godwin Ogor-Igbosuah
National Space Research and Development Agency, Abuja, Nigeria

*Address all correspondence to: ngunan.ikpaya@nasrda.gov.ng

References

[1] A. Luqmani, "Sustainability and Innovation: The Case of a Global Carpet Manufacturing Company," PhD Thesis, Centre for Environmental Strategy, University of Surrey, Guildford, Surrey, 2016.

[2] K. Chopra and G. K. Kadekoki, Operationalising Sustainable Development: Economic-Ecological Modelling for Developing Countries (Indo-Dutch Studies on Development Alternatives), vol. 22, New Delhi: SAGE Publications Pvt. Ltd, 1999, p. 301.

[3] W. Jayatilaka, "Capacity Building for Sustainable Development," Journal of National Science Foundation of Sri Lanka 2003, vol. 31, no. 1&2, pp. 81-97, 2003.

[4] M. Diesendorf, "Models of Sustainability and Sustainable Development," Int. J. Agricultural Resources, Governance and Ecology, vol. 1, no. 2, pp. 109-123, 2001.

[5] O. Serrat, "A Primer on Intellectual Capital," in Knowledge Solutions: Tools, Methods, and Approaches to Drive Organizational Performance, Singapore, Springer and Asian Development Bank, 2017, pp. 197-205.

[6] N. Bontis, "Intellectual capital: an explanatory study that develops measures and models," Management Decision, vol. 36, no. 2, pp. 63-76, 1998.

[7] C. Cavicchi, "Healthcare sustainability and the role of intellectual capital: Evidence from an Italian Regional Health Service," Journal of Intellectual Capital, vol. 18, no. 3, pp. 544-563, 2017.

[8] G. Etomi, "Overview of space exploration in Nigeria: challenges and solutions for the effective operation of the sector," 2018.

[9] R. J. Umunna and E. Ovie, "National Space Programs: Africa's Experience," Academia, 2016.

[10] I. O. Ikpaya, S. O. Onuh, C. U. Achem, B. M. Okehie and F. Y. Madalla, "Pursuit of Nigeria into Space for Sustainable Development," in Space Operations: Contributions from the Global Community, C. Cruzen, M. Schmidhuber, Y. H. Lee and B. Kim, Eds., Heidelberg, Germany, Springer International Publishing AG, 2017, pp. 233-251.

[11] J. Aron, "How Nigeria has been using its satellites. New Scientist," New Scientist, 2013.

[12] M. Samsuzzaman, M. T. Islam, S. Kibria and M. Cho, "BIRDS-1 CubeSat Constellation Using Compact UHF Patch Antenna," IEEE Access, p. 54282-54294, 2018.

[13] O. Akingboye, "Nigeria: Edusat-1 Satellite Goes Into Orbit Today," AllAfrica.Com, July 2017. [Online]. Available: https://allafrica.com/stories/201707070166.html. [Accessed 29 July 2020].

[14] F. D. Chizea, R. J. Umunna and E. O. Ovie, "NASRDA's Experience in Human Capacity Development and Capability Accumulation in Satellite Technology," Advances in Sciences and Humanities, vol. 5, no. 3, pp. 70-75, 2019.

[15] D. H. Meadows, D. L. Meadows, J. Randers and W. W. Behrens, The limits to growth—a Report for the Club of Rome's Project on the Predicament of Mankind, New York: Universe Books, 1972.

[16] V. Todorov and D. Marinova, "Models of Sustainability," in 18th World IMACS / MODSIM Congress, Cairns, Australia, 2009.

[17] UN Commission on Science and Technology for Development, "The impact of rapid technological change on sustainable development. Report of the Secretary-General," UN, 2019.

[18] W. H. Clune and A. J. B. Zehnder, "The evolution of sustainability models, from descriptive, to strategic, to the three pillars framework for applied solutions," Integrated Research System for Sustainability Science (IR3S), 2020.

[19] WCED, World commission on Environment and Development, Oxford: Oxford University Press, 1987.

[20] J. Elkington, Cannibals with forks: the triple bottom line of 21st century business, Stony Creek CT: New Society Publishers Gabriola Island BC, 1998.

[21] S. Kempe, "Carbon in the freshwater cycle," in The Global Carbon Cycle: SCOPE Report 13, B. Bolin, E. T. Degens, S. Kempe and P. Ketner, Eds., Chichester, New York, Brisbane, Toronto, John Wiley & Sons, 1979, pp. 317-342.

[22] W. J. McG. Tegart, G. W. Sheldon and D. C. Griffiths, "Climate Change: The IPCC Impacts Assessment," Australian Government Publishing Service, Canberra, 1990.

[23] S. Schmidheiny, Changing course, Cambridge: MIT Press, 1992.

[24] M. E. Porter and M. R. Kramer, "Creating Shared Value," Harvard Business Review, vol. 89, no. 1-2, pp. 62-77, January-Febuary 2011.

[25] F. Schmidt-Bleek, MIPS and factor 10 for a sustainable and profitable economy, Wuppertal: Wuppertal Institute, 1997.

[26] UNCTAD, "Investment Policy Framework for Sustainable Development," United Nations, 2015.

[27] United Nations, "Making the SDGs a Reality," [Online]. Available: https://sdgs.un.org/. [Accessed 30 July 2020].

[28] W. H. Clune and A. J. B. Zehnder, "The three pillars of sustainability framework: approaches for laws and governance," Journal of Environmental Protection, vol. 9, p. 211-240, 2018.

[29] Brundtland Commission, Our Common Future, Oxford: Oxford University Press, 1978, pp. 3-34.

[30] R. Carson, Silent Spring, Boston: Houghton Mifflin, 1962.

[31] World Resources Institute, "World Resources 1994-95: A Guide to the Global Environment, report in collaboration with the United Nations Environment Program and the United Nations Development Program," Oxford University Press, New York & Oxford, 1994.

[32] Science Summit on World Population 1993, "Joint Statement by fifty-eight of the World's Scientific Academies," 1993.

[33] M. Diesendorf, "Sustainability and sustainable Development," in Sustainability: The Corporate Challenge of the 21st Century, D. D., B. J., G. A. and S. P., Eds., Sydney, Allen & Unwin, 2000, pp. 19-37.

[34] The Natural Step, "The Natural Step Framework," 2000. [Online]. Available: https://web.stanford.edu/class/me221/readings/NaturalStepOverview.pdf. [Accessed 28 July 2020].

[35] J. Birch Holmberg and R. K-H., "Backcasting – A Framework for Strategic Planning," The International Journal of Sustainable Development and World Ecology , vol. 7, no. 4, pp. 291-308, 2000.

[36] The Natural Step, "Approach: Accelerating Change," 2020. [Online].

Available: https:// thenaturalstep.org/ approach/. [Accessed 28 July 2020].

[37] H. E.G., F. Grosse-Dunker and R. Reichwald, "Sustainability Innovation Cube - a Framework to Evaluate Sustainability-Oriented Innovations," International Journal Innovation Management, vol. 13, pp. 683-713, 2009.

[38] A. Luqmani, M. Leach and D. Jesson, "Factors behind sustainable business innovation: The case of a global carpet manufacturing company," Environmental Innovation and Societal Transitions, 2016.

[39] R. Adams, S. Jeanrenaud, J. Bessant, P. Overy and D. Denyer, "Innovating for sustainability: a systematic review of the body of knowledge," in Innovation, T. Bansal, Ed., Western University, 2012, p. 107.

[40] R. Kemp and P. Pearson, "Final Report MEI Project About Measuring Eco-innovation," Universiteit Maastricht, Netherlands, 2007.

[41] T. Machiba, "Eco-innovation for enabling resource efficiency and green growth: development of an analytical framework and preliminary analysis of industry and policy practices," International Economics and Economic Policy, vol. 7, p. 357-370, 2010.

[42] R. Leifer, C. M. McDermott, G. C. O'Connor, L. S. Peters, M. P. Rice and R. W. Veryzer, Radical Innovation: How Mature Companies can Outsmart Upstarts, Boston, Massachusetts: Harvard Business School Press, 2000.

[43] J. Bessant and J. Tidd, Innovation and Entrepreneurship, Hoboken, N.J. ; Chichester, England: John Wiley & Sons, 2007, p. 542.

[44] C. D. Hensler, "Shrinking Footprint: A Result of Design Influenced by Life Cycle Assessment," Journal of Industrial Ecology, vol. 18, no. 5, pp. 663-669, 2014.

[45] J. M. Benyus, Biomimicry, New York: William Morrow, 1997.

[46] A. Larson and J. York, "Shaw Industries: EcoWorx and Cradle-To-Cradle Innovation in Carpet Tile," Darden Business Publishing Cases, vol. 1, no. 1, pp. 1-4, 2017.

[47] E. Nelson, "How Interface innovates with suppliers to create sustainability solutions," Global Business and Organizational Exce, vol. 28, no. 6, pp. 22-30, 2009.

[48] K. M. Fritz, "Cultural Interface FairWorks: A Case Study on Sustainable Business Models," kfritzdesign, 2010. [Online]. Available: http://www.kfritzdesign.com/cultural-interface-fairworks-a-case-study-on-sustainable-business-models. [Accessed 30 July 2020].

[49] Aquafil Global, "ECONYL – Life Cycle Comparison," 2014. [Online]. Available: https://web.archive.org/web/20160612011350/http://www.aquafil.com/sustainability/the-econyl-project/. [Accessed 27 July 2020].

[50] R. K. Yin, Case Study Research Design and Methods, 4th ed., Thousand Oaks, CA: Sage Publications, 2009.

[51] T. T. Isoun and M. J. Isoun, Why Run Before Learning to Walk: Reflections on High Technology as a Strategic Tool for Development in Nigeria, Ibadan, Nigeria: BookBuilders Edition Africa, 2013.

[52] E. I. Sunday, "Intellectual Capital and Organizational Sustainability in Manufacturing Firms in Rivers State," International Journal of Advanced Academic Research, Social & Management Sciences, vol. 3, no. 4, pp. 1-17, 2017.

DOI: http://dx.doi.org/10.5772/intechopen.93905

[53] W. Balogh, "Capacity Building in Space Technology Development: A New Initiative within the United Nations Programme on Space Applications," Space Policy, vol. 27, no. 3, pp. 180-183, 2011.

[54] Z. Cheng, H. Wang, W. Xiong, D. Zhu and L. Cheng, "Public–private partnership as a driver of sustainable development: toward a conceptual framework of sustainability-oriented PPP," Environment, Development and Sustainability, 2020.

[55] W. M. Adams, "The Future of Sustainability: Re-thinking Environment and Development in the Twenty-first Century," IUCN, The World Conservation Union, Uto Kulm, Zurich, 2006.

Chapter 9

Sustainable Development and Islamic Ethical Tasks for Business-Organisations

Abul Hassan

Abstract

The paper seeks to addresses the issues of sustainable development and it would be viewed as Islamic moral duties for business. To what level should business bodies should join in the sustainable development activities? Based on the existing literature, this study assimilates conventional as well as Islamic points about environment and sustainable development and contends that whatever explanation of sustainable development one may subscribe, ultimately, each should culminate in environmental concern. This study contends that Islamic style is more friendly to environmental protection and issues touching sustainable development have moral, social and ethical responsibility. With intense commitment of the businesses in the matter of Islamic ethics to equity, justice and wellbeing of humans, it demands that business organisations in the Islamic and other countries should participate in the sustainable development endeavours. Because of ethics of environmental aspects in Islam, the value chains of suppliers through customers, many companies may be alert for the environmental characteristics and effects of their businesses.

Keywords: Islamic ethics, environmental development, sustainable development

1. Introduction

Business ethics sometimes denoted to as economic structural ethics merely restricts its edge of point to economic concerns. Concurring to Islamic perspective, the term very closely related to principles in the Qur'an is *khuluq* (means equilibrium, justice and goodness, etc).[1] Islamic business ethical policies vary from secular system and from the ethical code encouraged by diverse religions. All the way through civilization, these conventional business models assumed the ethical codes that were myopic and transient since they are grounded on the beliefs of their human initiators e.g. happiness or epicureanism for pleasure's sake[2]. Those modes normally anticipated an approach of ethics sometimes separated from faith or religion. On the other hand the ethical code accepted by the religious conviction have often accentuated ideals that donot emphasis our presence in the cosmos. This may be understood in the Christianity with its over prominence on monasticism

[1] Al Quran 3:104, The Holy Quran Translation by Abdullah Yusuf Ali, (Kuala Lumpur: Islamic Book Trust, 1994). The translations of the Quranic Ayah referred in this paper were taken from Ali's translation unless specifically mentioned.

[2] R.I. Beekun, "Islamic Business Ethics", Human Development Series No. 2, (Herdon, Va: IIIT, 1997): 3–9.

heightening its advocacy to retire from the hustle and bustle of day to day life. But Islamic way of life emphasises the connection of Man to His Creator. According to the Islamic concept, God is Perfect and All-knowing. Muslims maintain a code of conducts that is neither it is time bound nor prejudiced by human whims[3]. Some of the key factors of the Islamic ethical system as follow [1][4]:

1. Decisions and actions are arbitrated to be ethically conditional on the intention of the private. God is Omniscient and comprehends every intention perfectly and completely.

2. Good intents followed by good actions are deliberated as acts of worship in Islam. Lawful (*halal*) intents cannot make unlawful and similarly unlawful (*haram*) actions cannot make *halal*.

3. Islam permits an individual the freedom to believe and act however he or she desires, but not at the cost of justice and accountability.

4. Belief in God bestows the individual with comprehensive freedom from anybody or anything except God.

5. Choices that provide benefit the minority or majority are not essentially ethical in themselves. So Islamic ethics is not at all a numbers game.

6. Islam business ethics routines an open system method to ethics, not a sealed, self-oriented system. Selfishness has no provision in Islam.

7. Ethical choices are centered on a concurrent interpretation of the Quran and the natural world.

8. Unlike the moral systems encouraged by several creeds, Islam inspires humankind to practise *tazkiyah* (self improvement) through vigorous involvement in the Islamic way of life. By performing decently in the middle of the tests of worldly life (*duniya*), Muslims demonstrate their importance to God [2].

The Islamic ethical system is neither fragmented nor uni-dimensional. It is a part of the Islamic view of life and therefore complete. There is internal consistency or equilibrium (*adl*), about which Qur'an says:

Hence have we created of you a community (*ummah*) rightly balanced that you may be eyewitness throughout the states and the Apostle an eyewitness over yourselves[5]. (Al Qur'an: 2–143).

The area of Islamic business ethics is extensive with varied dilemmas and issues. One of the important Islamic ethical issues have, for several years, established substantially less consideration than it deserved- the accountability of business or economic organisations to scrutinise the subject of sustainable development in the social order. Business organisations globally have faced and created resource depletion and pollution. Interest on questions of 'environmental and sustainable' activities began after the United Nations Conference on Environment and Development (UNCED) assembled at Rio de Janeiro in 1992. After a span of time, in

---

[3] H.M. Lefcourt, "Locus of Control: Current Trends in Theory and Research", (Hillsdale, NJ: Erlbaum, 1982), 2nd edition.

[4] R.I. Beekun, "Islamic Business Ethics",Human Development Series No. 2, (Herdon, Va: IIIT, 1997)3–21

[5] Al-Quran 2:143

2002, the matter on 'sustainable development' sustained to offer the themes at the Johannesburg World Summit on Sustainable Development (WSSD)[6]. These gatherings have laid a glut of groups motivated on the matters of environmental social responsibility and sustainable development.

This paper is organised as follows. First section provides introduction. Second section discusses on the notion of sustainable development. Then section three lead us the discussion on Islamic perspectives of sustainable development. Section four agues the point of view that sustainable development is an Islamic ethical issue. Section five focuses on the sustainable development attempts for business. Paper concludes in the section five,

2. Notion of sustainable development

"Our Common Future' a declaration of the World Commission of Environment and Development circulated in the year 1987 presented the most extensively mentioned explanation of 'Sustainable Development'. In its canter is the simple concept of confirming a fairer class of life for everybody, now and for generations to come[7]. It describes 'Sustainable Development' as: 'development that meets the needs of the present without compromising the ability of future generations to meet their own needs[8]. Even though the concept is straightforward, but the task is significant. It entails addressing four goals simultaneously, all over the world:

- Societal improvement which grants the demands of everybody;
- Efficient safeguard of the natural environment;
- Wise utilisation of environmental resources; and
- Upkeep of high-pitched and steady degrees of economic development and generate employment.

Corresponding to Islamic teachings, the sustainable development is an essential element to the humankind [3]. Both societies and individual are duty assured to promote and promote its natural possessions, including air, water, seas, climate, flora and fauna and desist from any action likely to cause damage or pollution to the environment resources or distract the balance [4, 5]. As per Islamic ethics, the basic reasoning of the link between humans, God and the natural environment is initiated on the belief that God created when entire universe and rendered it subject to human race but not merely for the later on to take advantage of it for their substantial benefit. Rationally, humankind's eventual objective on the earth is to pray to God, hence not only all their collaborations with the world are subject to God's laws but also by maintaining sustainability in developing the earth [4, 6].

In view of the above, it seems that the idea of sustainable development looks to be relatively simple, however the subjects 'breadth and depth' generate complications. It is revealed that sustainable development must be commercially feasible,

[6] WSSD FfD UN Summit 2002, A Report on "Financing for Sustainable Development", (London: International Institute for Environment and Development, 2002): 2–29

[7] World Commission on Environment and Development, "Our Common Future", (New York: Oxford University Press, 1987):1–3

[8] Ibid: 2–8

collectively just, and environmentally relevant [7][9]. Several complex and sensitive matters are intrinsic in these explanations and a few of them are:

2.1 'Wants' of the present-day vs. the 'needs' of the present and 'wants' of the future

How can an imaginary upcoming peers be safeguarded as well as to what degree should contemporary civilisation be let go to safeguard future peers! The free market facilitates 'push' the businesses to deliver the goods and services presently required for purchase. Additional the company partly establish future wants and needs of customers via product advancement in reply to current peripheral pressures as well as existing internal capabilities. In replying to these existing pressures or capabilities, many economic companies (businesses) employ life-cycle assessment to evaluate prospective future environmental effects of product layout, production capacity as well as recyclability.

2.2 The perspective of fortitude of economic sustainability

The term under above captioned should be understood in perspective between developed Muslim countries and businesses in developing countries, between business having substantial environmental effects and those having nominal environmental influence or between start up business and the long-stand-up businesses. In the each one of these three circumstances, the cost of sustainable development may generally be more costly to the former businesses than the latter. Therefore, what should be deemed economically feasible for a larger retail outlet in Saudi Arabia may entail financial ruin for a small and micro business in Pakistan. Helman [8][10] contends that there is a obvious trend in the developing area towards superior environmental policies that comprise the quest of the alternatives economic development that may reduce adverse environmental impacts. Additional Pearce and Warford [9][11] say: 'through the technological alteration, replacement between possessions of resources and higher values for goods that adulterate, environmental aims and economic growth which can be made more compatible (p.31).' In respect of technology change, there is no doubt that the advances of technology, it becomes more competent in the development aspect. Underlying one of the causes – because of industrialisation proves in developing Muslim countries often begins with the employing of outdated technology, then in terms production of every aspects should be environmentally expensive. When the advanced technology introduced, the efficiency rises causing an rise in productive movement with fewer flaws and wastes, and consequently a drop in the rate at which resources reduction occurs. Furthermore, as the Muslim countries move ahead, less environmental toxic waste may be allowed. When the economic development reaches the sophisticated stage, business conglomerates use more sophisticated technology, triggering a net drop in resource pollution and depletion. As the per capita income rise, governmental and social awareness about the environment also increase; more anti-pollution rules and regulations are decreed. Therefore, an upturned U-shaped curve may be used to symbolize the shifts in a human society that begins at a point minus environmental

[9] T. Gladwin et al., "Paradigms for Sustainable Development", Academy of Management Review, 20 (1995):974–907

[10] U. Helman, "Sustainable Development: Strategies for Reconciling Environment and Economy in the Developing World", The Washington Quarterly, 18(4, 1995): 43–54

[11] D.W. Pearce and J.J. Warford, "World Without End: Economics, Environment and Sustainable Development", (New York, Oxford University Press, 1993).

value, rapidly improves, and then slow down and turns around when that a human society has the money and time to pay to safeguard the environment.

2.3 Fortitude of the social equity

The dynamics of grit of social equity or social development should vary on who was acquiring the benefit take on, what degree of economic development occurred in the vicinity, whether resources utilised were replenishable and what social and political issues were being confronted or resolved.

2.4 Judgement of environmental friendly development

The environmentally oriented development may be contemplated in such direction so that it should signify the response to whether the natural environment should be safeguarded for its own sake or for the interest of human beings. Al Quran says[12]: "Nuisance has occurred on sea and land because of (the need) that the hands of men have won." The Quran warns man to ward off the mischief by human hands and to seek refuge from all mischief (Al Quran 30: 41 and 113: 2–5). It is clear warning to man to abstain from wrong pursuits and corruption against the ethical norms which God has set in nature for the benefit of man and other creatures. The Prophet of Islam (Peace and blessing be upon him) said: "Ibrahim declared Makkah a sacrosanct city. I do so for the Madina territory between the two *Harrabs* (approximately 12 miles belt). No tree of this City shall be deleted and no animal shall be hunted down" (Hadith: Muslim)[13]. Ecological ethicists like Scherer and Attig [10][14] claim that non-human dwellers are inherently valuable and they be worthy of respect and that creatures have responsibilities of safeguarding towards them. Consequently, the forthcoming sustainability will necessitate a missing of orientation from the human focused anthropological point of view towards more oddball view in consistence with Islamic view on environmental and natural issues. Thus, grit of environmentally suitable action would usually be based further on matters of perspective rather than on one of certain activity [11][15]. A few businesses and individuals may take a wider viewpoint and evaluate the effect of an act on overall future and current environment in the light of the above statement of the Prophet Muhammad (PBUH).

3. Islamic perspective of sustainable development

It is fact that there is no a proper Islamic definition of sustainable development, but, its lack from existing works on Islamic economics- does not imply that such a concept cannot be developed. Asad [12] argues[16]: "In an thought like Islamic -one can not dividing line between the 'spiritual' and the 'material' scopes - and so also should not dividing line between man's faith and his practical life ... " The Quranic depiction of nature, as originate in the many verses, revealed both in Makkah and Madina, is multi-layered. God creates environment, the Al-Quran categorically declares[17]. Where God is portrayed by Unity (*Tawhid*), but nature is described by

[12] Al-Quran 30: 4

[13] The six Sahih Hadith Collection, Arabic and Translation.

[14] D. Scherer and T. Attig (eds), "Ethics and the Environment", (Englewood Cliffs, Prentice Hall, 1983)

[15] D.A. Payne and C.A Raiborn (2001), "Sustainable Development and The Ethics", Journal of Business Ethics, 32, (2001):157–168

[16] Muhammad Asad, This Law of Ours (Gibraltar: Dar al-Andalus, 1987): 133

[17] Al -Quran 3:191; 38:27: 46:3

duality[18], but then duality in the meaning of complementary counterparts, or as pairs, as represented by the term in Arabic '*zawj*'. One more feature of nature discovered in the Al-Quran is balance or order[19]. The concept of a divinely organised tranquillity in nature that it has been observed in the Al-Quran that may be said to describe to the concept that nature is the decisive creation of an omniscient and omnipotent God and is therefore wholly structured ordered[20]. Wicked human powers do not interrupt the order of structure and its nature is prolonged. In this regard, the Al-Quran mentioned[21]: "... Do not spread corruption on earth after it has been so well ordered" (Al-Quran 7: 56), which well articulates such a notion of nature.

As Asad said [12], the Islamic doctrine proclaims that: "Man is an animal in the sense of naturally belonging to that cluster of living beings which are gifted with the faculties of perception, sensation and movement, as well as in the wisdom of being reliant on physiological desires and functions more or less approximating those of other animal existences"[22]. Man's aspect lies in 'trust of volition and reasons' (Al-Quran translated by Asad)[23] whereby man was granted the ability to use choice between evil and good. This rational realisation gives man to consequence the 'ability to form concepts and to bring them together in uncountable mixtures by means of psychological processes which can be directed and absorbed by his will.'[24] Subsequently, whereas other animals acclimatise to their environment or suffer the fatal consequences, man has become increasingly skilful in adapting his environment to suit his own ends, through animal husbandry, agriculture, medicine, human settlements, or more generally we might say, though science and technology. Islam approves all these actions and thus in Islamic perspective, the environmental change is an foreseeable element of life[25]. However, according to Islam, man should not perform these activities arbitrarily. The sayings of the Prophet Muhammed (PBUH) frequently exhort man to be compassionate towards animals[26]. Therefore, the Quran, as well as setting up a idea of nature in connection to God and man, also sets out an moral code to guide book to man: waste is abhorred[27], as is arrogance and all its manifestations in boastful exhibitions of wealth. As a substitute, Islam encourages fairness and distributive justice[28]. Also there is in existence a body of Islamic source of law, courting from the period of the Prophet Mohammad (PBUH) which forbids private proprietorship of shared property resources such as grassland, wildlife, woodland and water, which should be handled for the common good. Sardar [13] said that forests and wildlife are protected in *hima* or reserves, which are formed solely for conservation reasons. Islamic jurisdictions rule which can be

18 Al-Quran 13:3, 31:10; 36:36; 53:45

19 Al-Quran 7:56; 14:33; 15:19; 16:10–15; 54:49; 55:3–13; 67–3

20 Ilyas Baker, "Flight of Time Ecology and Islam," Islam and Environment, ed. Harfia Abdel Haleem, (London: Ta-Ha publishers,1998):80

21 Al-Quran 7:56

22 Asad 144

23 Al-Quran; 30:72,3

24 Asad 146. In order to avoid giving a truncated version of Asad's, conception of man, the following passage should also be quoted: 'The Quran makes it clear that our comprehension of reality can certainly be deepened and widened by what we describe as "mystical experience": in other words, through an intuitive, spiritual contact with the Divine and, hence, with those truths which are neither open to our self-perception nor can be fully grasped by analytical thinking.'

25 Illays Baker, "Flight of Time Ecology and Islam," Islam and Environment, ed. Harfiah Abdel Haleem, (London:Ta-Ha publishers, 1998):83

26 Hafiz BA al- Masri, "Islamic Concern for Animals",(Hants, UK: The Athene Trust, 1987)

27 Al-Quran 7:31

28 Al-Quran; 9-60; 59:7

harnessed to the management of natural resources[29]. It is known fact that Islam promotes earning for the cause of living through hard labour which is considered as an act of worship. A Muslim must adopt any profession that does not contravene the *Shariah*. This implies: (i) businesses should be conducted truthfully, because cheating and fraud, and other habits such as hoarding, adulteration, false advertising, speculation, bribery and paying interest in financial transaction are forbidden; (ii) some professions like prostitution, gambling, manufacturing and selling of pornography, narcotic drugs, alcoholic beverages as well as manufacturing and selling of statues are forbidden [5].

Chapra [14] argued that a Muslim's belief is put first because it gives the worldview which impacts the whole human persona - behaviour, tastes, life-style and preferences, and mindsets towards human beings, environment and resources. It seeks to stimulate a balance between the spiritual and material urges of the human self, enhance family and social solidarity, promote peace of mind in the human being and avert the development of anomalies. A Muslims' faith delivers the moral filter which aims at keeping self-centredness within the boundaries of social interest by varying personal preferences as per social urgencies and eradicating or lessening the use of possessions for the purposes that aggravate the realisation of the social vision[30]. All these elements which fulfil the goals of the *Maqasid al Shariah* (objectivity of Islamic laws) and sustainable development falls within the concept of *Maqasid al Shairah*.

4. Sustainable development as an important Islamic ethical issue

A free-market industrial economy employ market-defined prices as a purifying mechanism to allocate resources. The usefulness of the price scheme only, nevertheless, can hinder the fulfilment of socio-economic objectives. Under a structure of state influence, the distribution of resources is in the big hand of a bureaucracy, which is unwieldy and ineffective. According to Chapra [15][31], the Islamic worldview suggests that the market structure have to be preserved, but that the mechanism of price be matched with a mechanism that minimises excessive claims on properties. This tool is the 'moral filter'. It means that people should pass their possible demands on resources all through the 'filter of Islamic values system' so that several claims may be eliminated before being stated in the market. Siddiqi [16][32] claims that the resources should not be authorised to redirect to the production of extravagance goods until the manufacture of necessary goods are guaranteed in sufficient amounts. The classification of extravagant or luxurious is associated to the basic requirement. of consumption in the society. This suggestion being significant departure from the norms which are not acceptable. Keynes [17][33] argues that even though 'the desires of human beings may well seem to be avid,' ... 'they fall into two types-those requirements which are utter in the sense that we feel them whatever the situation of our fellow human beings possibly, and those

[29] Ziauddin Sardar, "Islamic Futures: The Shape of Ideas to Come", (Kuala Lumpur: Pelanduk,1998)

[30] M.U. Chapra, "The Future of Economics: An Islamic Perspective", (Leicester, UK: The Islamic Foundation,2000).

[31] M.U. Chapra, "Islam and the Economic Challenge", (Herdon, VA: International Institute of Islamic Thought and The Islamic Foundation, 1992).

[32] M.N. Siddiqi, "Muslim Economic Thinking: A Survey of Contemporary Literature," in K. Ahmad (ed.), Studies in Islamic Economics,(Leicester, UK: The Islamic Foundation, 1981)

[33] J.A.M.Keynes, "The Collected Writings of John Maynard Keynes," (London: Macmillan for the Royal Economic Society, 1972)

are relation ones in the logic that their gratification lifts us over/above or makes us feel greater than others. Desires of the second class, which meet the aspiration for superiority, might indeed be voracious; for the greater the general level, the higher still are they'(p.67). However it is not so true of the utter needs, but' Islamic jurists' classifications of conveniences (*hagiyyat*), necessities (*daruriyyat*) and refinements (*tahsiniyyat*) may fall into Keynes' first class of wants.

Further, the Islamic intellectuals who dispensed with the subject of sustainable development that people need to know that it is not a brand new idea. The dilemmas of unsustainable development has been identified in the religious rules like in Al-Qur'an nearly 1400 years ago are argued as follows:

4.1 Eminence on natural resources and balance in Islam

Almighty God has designed the universe with perfect order and balance [18]. Also God has designed all with a plan and the whole univers belongs to God: "See you not that God formed the earth and the heavens in Truth? If He so will, He can eliminate you and set (in the right place) as a new formation?" (Qur'an 14:19). "To Him feel right what is on earth and in the heavens and all between them, and all underneath the soil" (Qur'an, 20:6) "...do not damage on the planet after it has been put in order; that would be the most excellent for you, if you have faithfulness". (Qur'an, 7: 85). Further in the Qur'an God has stated this over and over that the plants, animals and the natural resources are specified for the entire benefits of men and whole human being should usage them in appropriate order for their betterment: "Who has made the earth your couch, and the heavens your canopy; and sent down rain from the heavens; and brought therewith fruits for your sustenance; then set not up rivals unto God when you know (the truth)" (Qur'an, 2:22). This verse of Al-Qur'an plainly asserts the significance of natural resources for nourishment of mankind. Hence, men should make sure of what God has established and they must realise the reality that the whole thing in the cosmos world belongs to God and men donot have right to misappropriate no matter what he possess the wealth. Misappropriating of resources is not allowed in Islam. In this regards Al-Qur'an states that "O Children of Adam! Dress you with beautiful clothing at every time and perform your prayer: eat and drink: but waste not by excess, God adores not the wasters." (Qur'an, 7:31) So, conferring to these Quranic learning, it is the responsibility of mankind to protect and keep the nature as usual and make use of the resources in a wise and balanced way.

4.2 Islam emphasis on reducing economic inequality

The conventional idea of development was largely involved with the issue of economic development by accepting into matter the ideas of Gross National Product (GNP) and Gross Domestic Product (GDP). As per Islamic economic ethics, the GNP and GDP are not appropriate indicators to emphasise whether a balanced development took place or not [5]. The economic inequality between rich and poor is widened. The major problem in this issue is that, though there is enormous earning, but the distribution was not equitable. In this matter, Islam chooses a different method by taking both distribution and earnings under care. Also Islam stresses on the honest earning from productive sources. The strong devotion of Islam to brotherhood and justice needs that richest people of the society take over care of the essential requirements of the underprivileged. Individuals are obligated to work for a living and simply when this is impractical where the state intercede. The *zakah* (alms) is a type of compulsory wealth tax containing y charitable offering for specially selected people in society, enables the care of all parts of society. The wealthy people are not the actual holders of their wealth; but they are simply trustees. Therefore they must perform duties as per the terms of the trust, one of the most vital of which is accomplishing the needs of the poor. The code word '*zakah*' means cleansing and as such, weal redistribution is not only an economic requirement but also a way to spiritual deliverance. Thus, economy is essentially assimilated with ethics[34] and therefore zakah helps to eradicate the poverty which has become a huge social problem and zakah is an essential tool to get rid of poverty.

Another social organisation which helps to reduce poverty is called *Waqf* (organised charity) According to Ali, '*Waqf* is a unique kind of voluntarily run charity that has solidity and capability to make income'. So the income flow of Waqf can be utilised in achieving the requirements of the poor people and thus it guarantees the society's socio-economic prosperity, p. 23. So, it is understood from this discussion that Islam supports philanthropy.

4.3 Significance of business ethics in Islam

At the time when every action of humanity has come in the sphere of business, ethics in commerce has come to be an essential concern all over the globe. Corporate scam has come to be a common issue. Performance of business initiatives are urged in Islam. But Islam stresses on doing business in an ethical and just manner. Islam underlines on consumer privileges by encouraging the businessmen to deliver with just product at proper weight to the consumers. Following are some of the verses in the Qur'an which endorse of this issues:

i. "Provide right amount and weight, nor deny from the people the items that are owing; and do not harm on the ground after it has been put in order". (Qur'an, 7:85)

ii. "Give full gauge when you assess, and weigh up with a sense of balance that is in a straight line; which is the highly fitting and not most disadvantageous in the final fortitude" (Qur'an, 17:35)

iii. "Give full measure and affect no failure (to others by deception)" (Qur'an, 26:181)

"Despair to those who trade in cheating, Individuals who, have to be given by measure have to be offered exact just measure. But when they will give by measure or weight to men, give a smaller amount than due. Do they not believe that they will be asked with accountability?- On a great (dooms) day, a day when (all) humankind will stand in front of the Lord of the Planets?" (Qur'an, 83:1–6)

From the above mentioned verses of the Qur'an, it turn out to be sure that Islam does not endorse fraudulent actions. Islam despises those who are dishonest and illegal in their dealings. God prompts men that they are responsible for all their own actions. What men act will be measured and reported. It will be recalled here that Islam does not endorse revenue from any fruitless source [3, 5].

Question might evolve why does or will the company or an economic establishment put into exercise the sustainable development and in what way to execute 'moral filter' without despotism or coercion. The filter process of values should be socially consented and some way it has to be conceived to motivate the consumers and, business men to bear these values. In Islamic view point, social transformation must be slow and should not be attained through force. The Quranic restriction,

[34] S.N.H. Naqvi, "Ehics and Economics An Islamic Synthesis," (Leicester: The Islamic Foundation,1981)

"There is no force in religion" (Al Quran 2:256) is pertinent here. Eaton [19][35] contends that change can happen by encouraging people to modify their ways and by establishing an example. Usually this is how Islam speedily spread through a larger part of the globe in the 7th and 8th centuries. For an example, when the Muslim traders travelled to remote lands, the people of those places where fascinated by the merchants' business and social conduct and so turn out to be curious about their faith. Several of these people subsequently converted in Islam. A similarity exists today with regard to the 'green' activities, which persists to spread around the world. The implementation of environmentally awareness behaviour is following through instance, education and encouragement, as well as by regulation. Certainly, in the environmental perspective, regulation is insufficient. Just when the political support and will of the populace are robust then it is necessary to impose environmental regulations adequately.

The stakeholders engaged are all the planet's denizens, both non-human and human. Sustainable development should make the highest fair or least destruction by letting those dwellers to survive in the world where there is breathable air and drinkable water, fertile soil and renewable resources prosper. It is hard to use traditional monetary cost an benefit analysis to establish whether sustainable development is useful. Firstly, many present and future costs may be assessed and lowered back to current values; it is perhaps difficult to even realise what types and quantities of costs may be necessary in the forthcoming. Secondly, the advantages of sustainable development are considerably extra qualitative than monetarily quantitative; for an example: the value of a live species cannot be assessed. At the same time with no finances involved, the end result would be unquestionably convincing; no matter how higher the costs of sustainable development are, the advantages of existing and continued presence by the planet's species must go beyond that cost. In Islamic ethics, the advantages of life be greater than the costs to get it.

Thus, Islamic scholars recognise that sustainable development ((refinements (*Tahsiniyyat*) and necessities (*daruriyyat*)) should be considered as part of the interconnected agenda of Islamic business ethics [20][36]. The companies, as compilations of human beings, have a duty to take part in sustainable developments events so as to alleviate their environmental effects and help in delivering, safeguarding and sustaining pleasant environment.

5. Sustainable development attempts for business

In Islam, the commercial activities are deemed to be a socially beneficial act. Prophet Muhammad (peace be upon him) was engaged in business for much of his life. Huge importance is connected to views concerning to consumption, ownership and purposes of a business initiative and the code of conduct of several agents. Islamic socio-economic approach comprises comprehensive analysis of certain economic variables such as circulation of wealth, consumption, taxation, and fair-trading. Shariah originated from the Quran and custom (*Sunnah*) of the Prophet (PBUH) includes business connections between sellers and buyers; employees and employers; and lenders and borrowers [21][37]. Thus, Islam permits people to fulfil all their desires and to go beyond. The goal must not be to build

[35] G.Eaton, "Islam and The Destiny of Man," (Cambridge: The Islamic Texts Society, 1994)

[36] Ismail Hobson; "Islam's guiding Priciples for a Solution to Environmental Problems," Islam and Environment, ed. Harfiah Abdel Haleem (London: Ta-Ha publishers, 1998):33–42

[37] N.H.M.Keller; "Reliance of the traveller: A Classic Manual of Islamic Sacred law" (translation), original written by Ibn Naqib Al Misri, (Evanston, IL: Sunna Books, 1994)

a monotonous homogeneity in Muslim high society. Islam urges to take part in economic endeavours such as lawful enterprise and to take the par in life through easiness in consumption, which may be achieved in life patterns alongside innovation and multiplicity. Neither does Islam imply lack of economic liberalisation. Here there is a distinct form of liberalisation: one in which all public and private sector economic choices are first gone through the filter of ethical values well before they became subject to the control of the market. Undeniably, to execute the 'moral filter' in practice entails the commitment of a huge number of market contributors. Thus, these businesspeople can affect consumer actions. Their economic organisation or company can help to reduce or eradicate pollution affects (through research a brand new product development). Enterprise can also impact how social development will happen and what should be the impact of that development would be through their geographical location and high-tech investment options. Companies can accept a strategy to engage in sustainable development in combination with cost-effectiveness and durability to the benefit of all organisational shareholders. Such a plan would emphasis on both future and current eco-efficiencies.

Islam is a complete code of conduct that impacts on the moral, legal, social economics and environmental aspects. Its enormous impact in institutional form through the Shari'ah law(guidance derived from the Qur'an and Sunnah traditional of the Prophet Mohammad). For that reason, research efforts in the Muslim countries with strong religious institutions such as Islam should consider the importance of religion with business issues [22, 23]. Khan and Karim [24] assert that Islam motivates business, socio-economic and environmental life in the Muslim countries and in the society in a way which can be associated with the sustainable development with clear codification of ethical standards and its enforcement mechanisms. Atan and Halim [25] argue that features of sustainable development and social justice deeply rooted in the Qura'n and the Sunnah, as these resources oblige companies or businesses to execute their guidelines in society and environment. According to Dusuki [26], Shari'ah is an important source with significant value in the Islamic paradigm, offers a religious bond that exceeds the notion of development and sustainability. Katisioloudes and Brodtkourb [27] endorse this statement by pointing out that Islam gives basic knowledge upon which sustainable development methods can be developed.

A study investigated by Koleva [28] on the role of Islam for the practice and understanding of sustainable development with reference to CSR and by relaying on empirical evidence collected from business organisations in the three GCC countries- Saudi Arabia, Oman and UAE. Their findings suggest that Islam as religion is very important for the 63 participants in this survey and stated that their religion helps in realising that makes logic to replication the concept of sustainable development in their business as well and CSR. With this end it ventures Islam as a vital part in the formation and re-formation of the sustainable development spectacle within the observed sample. Consequently, the empirical results show in the study done by Koleva [28] which suggest that contextual specifications of developing countries (Islamic region) might lead to different perception and thoughtful in the matter of sustainable development and also different dynamics in the business-society affiliation.

The prospect for participating in environmentally 'correctness'-a corporation should decide its participant methods in the sustainable development actions. One likely technique may be the usage of the chain of command of ethical behaviour advocated by Des-Jardins [29][38]. The hierarchy comprises of four levels of success:

[38] J.DesJardins< "Corporate Environmental Responsibility", Journal of Business Ethics, 17 (1998): 825–838

5.1 Fundamental level of behaviour

A specific economic activity functioning at the basic stage of behaviour should merely conform by the rules of the territory in which it runs. Such an economic movement would make no sustainable development works since the idea is not embedded into the regulation in any country in the world. This economic efforts would persist within legally appropriate pollution levels, even though it would probably look at those levels as impediments to productive actions. Such movement or organisations may be more likely to obtain certifications for pollution as they should operate 'close to the edge' of suitability. Executives of such organisations could have the view that the expenses of pollution management and ecology are bigger than the immediate gains; this executive may be very 'bottom line' orientated. Furthermore, such executives would certainly perceive the money spent on environmental elements not as investment but then as a cost that corrodes effectiveness. Mission declarations of these movement or organisations may never declare a concern for or emphasis on the real environment. They should bend on the letter of the directive that entails the use of 'top existing technology' or 'top existing management technology.' Thus, these corporations' behaviours should be deemed as legal, religious as well as technological.

5.2 Theoretical level of behaviour

An economic organisation or corporation managing a notional level of conduct would have included the concept of sustainable development concerned in its structural strategy. As Hart[39] [30] claims that there should be no haphazard projects intended at preventing or controlling pollution. Concentrating on sustainability entails putting business policies to a new test. Taking over the whole planet as the framework in which it does business, enterprises must ask question whether it is the part of the resolution to environmental and social problems or component of the problem. In this matter the business organisations should include specifically mention of sustainable development at their mission statements and may have recognised and exposed highly noticeable and eloquent environmental supervision policies. Several of these companies may be quick to layout, develop, and execute environmental management techniques as stipulated by ISO 14001 and to ask for accreditation or self-affirmation within that standard. Company or firms do claims that will be deemed to be operational at the theoretical stage of behaviour in connection to sustainable development and environmental policy. Their polices evidently draw attention to the point that the business viewpoints and its devotion to the environment as one that is vital to the organisation's fundamental values. These businesses are not engaged in sustainable development or environmental protection related activities since some bureau has legally authorised such contribution; they are engaged because they consider those actions to be largely sound. Companies working at this stage of behaviour appreciate that their firms and those in the downstream and upstream value chain may not be successful in a world with out reusable resources or polluted water and air. Consequently, as the organic ecosphere of the planet is battered, the capability of the left over ecosystems to boost the firm's value chain partners declines-leaving a business with no capacity to conduct business. Therefore, participating in sustainable development is the single 'right 'choice. An extra gain is that the sustainable movements also produce a good business idea in the long run.

[39] S.L. Hart, "Beyond Greening: Strategies for a Sustainable World", Harvard Business Review, Jan-Feb, (1997):67–76

5.3 Achievable level of behaviour

An economic or business organisation functioning at the presently attainable level of conduct would recognise that some gains may arise from participating in environmentally-friendly actions that are not lawfully mandated. These companies, however, possibly take part in such events for the 'wrong' causes: revenue enhancement, cost reduction or reputation enhancement. In further words, the activities are to be expected to gain short-term monetary profits larger than their costs. Therefore, these corporations are likely to fix improved pollution control strategies than are mandatory by law, to involve in clean-up projects that should be showcased by their public relation department and to implement programmes and catchphrases that emphasis on environmental 'perfection.' Some cases the Executives of this firms may not involved in the sustainable development projects as they are too unclear and may create a huge current cost whose upcoming profit is quantitatively unidentified. Mission statements of these companies might cite a concern for or emphasis on the physical environment, but then more than possible any such conversation would be given in a management letter or in the explanations of business products, production locations or product lines. These companies may be considered by society as environmentally sensible businesses that are functioning for the more good- but in actuality, the larger good is mainly that of the business organistion[40].

5.4 Rational level of behaviour

An economic or business organisation functioning at the practical level of conduct would admit that advantages arise from participating in environmentally responsive events. These business organisations, however, may strive to make sure of the 'right' matter in relation to the environment since it is 'right' rather than in good reputation or short-term profit. These business organisations and their executives appreciate the requirement for, and significance of environmentally friendly production and changing their activities, to take part in environmental modernisations that may be costly but that may prove extremely beneficial of upcoming outcomes. In performing so, the businesses should anticipate that consumers should appreciate the benefits of such pioneering practices which are worth acquiring at a greater cost than those of a fewer environmentally sensitive contenders. There should be no question that these businesses are profit motivated: management has a fiduciary duty towards a number of groups such as shareholders, creditors, employees, and consumers- to maximise profits and, therefore efficiency. Gwilliam [31][41] claims that, for both services and infrastructure, it is required to be conceded that private sector contribution will be attained only on the basis of an appropriate projected revenue scheme. Indication from a study done by Margretta [32][42] shows that concerned about the economic consequences, business or companies working at the practical level of behaviour are genuinely concerned about the environment and stakeholders. Therefore, the sustainable development is an idea that is heralded and recognised by the business organisations or companies. Companies operating at the practical level of behaviour may strive to find out ways to generate services and products in a way that signifies the principles of the green market. An indisputable fact in favour of business obligation and the free market value in the vicinity of

[40] D.M. Payne and C.A. Rainborn, "Sustainable Development and the Ethics", Journal of Business Ethics, 32, (2001):157–168

[41] "Financing for Sustainable Development", A Report on WSSD FfD UN Summit 2002, (London: International Institute for Environment and Development, 2002):2–29

[42] J. Margretta, "Growth Through Global Sustainability," *Harvard Business Review*, (Jan-Feb) (1997).

sustainable development is a shift in consumer inclinations based on a intensified consciousness about the environment. This change is the central act that regularly stimulates and promotes businesses as well as changing behaviours and thoughts in favour of environmentally sound systems. Increasingly, the consumers are achieving their individual obligations in the field of environmental value. The assumption that business alone is to blame for degradation, or is actually the protector of the environment is illogical- a company only sells what consumers are willing to buy. In the dearth of a appropriate market, the businesses would merely go out of enterprises. Consumers eventually control the disappointments or achievements of firms and their products.

6. Conclusion

The objective of Islamic commercial approach is to eliminate all residues of injustice, inequality, oppression and manipulation from the high society. An individualistic point of view on the sacred destiny of humankind is a counter balanced by an arduous understanding of society and societal collaboration [33][43]. In this argument this paper emphasised that the strong dedication of Islam to wellbeing and justice of human beings insist that Islamic community should contribute in the sustainable development events. This paper explained that with their chains of dealers across consumers, many businesses are developing more awareness of the sustainable development/environmental aspects and effects of their businesses. Perceived as a variety of behaviour, business environmentalism may range from just compliance of laws with recognising and passing on a sustainable development goal (SDG) of the UNO. The view point on the scale at which a firm prefers to operate is manifested in its environmental policies, strategy and action plan.

The theory of 'sustainable development' come to be the slogan in the development literature. By revealing the teachings of a religion (Islam), this paper emphasises that even though the notion of sustainability is a fresh matter in the development literature, Al-Qur'an essentially underlined all the concerns of sustainable development about 1400 years ago. In Islam economic inequality is disliked and for this reason, the notions like *Zakah, Waqf*, charity etc. are urged in Islam. Misuse of natural resources is also forbidden in Islam. Again and again, in the Qur'an mentioned about the order of the universe and the significance of natural resources for humanity. Extravagance is discoursed in Islam. It also identifies the contemporary global businesses are distancing from the principles ethical behaviour. When the businesses have become the part and parcel of contemporary lifestyle, corrupt habits from the component of the global businesses will build big problems for humanity. Islam encourages ethical business activities and disallows all sorts of unethical behaviours in earnings, trading and acquisition of assets in immoral way. In view of this, the concept of sustainable development in Islam is not a brand new issue. Yet after obtaining all the principles of sustainable development in the in the Qur'an, the Muslim countries need to adopt the concept in proper manner.

The economic rewards of moving in the quickest flourishing economic markets and commercial organisations in the world, the sustainable development approaches can offer Muslim countries with the generous of investment if they want to recover health care, civil rights, education and economic prospects. An symmetry in human activities is essential in the businesse vents to safeguard social wellbeing. The sustainable development is a part and parcel of Islamic economic

[43] Mohammed I. Ansari, "Islamic Perspective on Sustainable Development", *American Journal of Islamic Social Sciences*, 11(3), (1994): 394–401

developmental actions, which will fill up the gap of the society's serious issues, like economic opportunities, health care, education and sustainable strategies which will pressurise the track of the businesses and trades ansd directly effect on privileged circumstances and technology of the ecological matter. By describing to the teachings of Islam -one of the monolithic religions in the world that the idea of sustainable development is not ambiguous to religious beliefs specially Islam as a religion. The similar study may be done with the doctrines of other two monolithic religions (Judaism and Christianity) to find out whether religions and development are conflicting to each other or not. It may be mentioned here this study did not consider to make any solution to this issue rather it made an attempt to wide up a new way of idea: are the doctrines of Islam as religion can provide guidelines to the businesses on sustainable development model in the current world?

Author details

Abul Hassan
Centre of Research Excellence for Islamic Banking and Finance, KFUPM Business School, King Fahd University of Petroleum and Minerals, Dhahran, Saudi Arabia

*Address all correspondence to: ahfarooqi@kfupm.edu.sa

References

[1] Beekun R. *Islamic Business Ethics*. Verdon: IIIT; 1997

[2] Ahmad K. *Studies in Islamic Economics*. Leicester: The Islamic Foundation and KAAU; 1980

[3] Rice G. Pro-environmental behaviour in Egypt: Is there a role for Islamic environmental ethics? Journal of Business Ethics. 2006;**65**:373-390

[4] Ansari A, Jamal P, Oseni U. Sustainable development, Islamic divension with special reference to conservation of the environment. Advances in Natural and Applied Sciences. 2012;**6**(5):607-619

[5] Hossain D. Sustainable development and Islam: Is religious teaching invalid. Middle East Journal of Business. 2014;**9**(1):10-17

[6] Khalid F. The environmental crisis and modernity: An Islamic perspectives. Islamic Perspectives. 2008;**1**:40-45

[7] Gladwin T. Paradigms for sustainable development. Academy of Management Review. 1995;**20**:974-907

[8] Helman U. Sustainable development: Strategies for reconciling environment and economy in the developing world. The Washington Quarterly. 1995;**18**(4):43-54

[9] Pearce DW, Warford JJ. *World without End: Economics, Environment and Sustainable Development*. New York: Oxford University Press; 1993

[10] Scherer D, Attig T, editors. *Ethics and the Environment*. Englewood Cliffs: Prentice Hall; 1983

[11] Payne DA, Raiborn CA. Sustainable development and the ethics. Journal of Business Ethics. 2001;**32**:157-168

[12] Asad M. *This Law of Ours*. Gibraltar: Dar al-Andalus; 1987

[13] Sardar, Z; "Islamic Futures: The Shape of Ideas to Come", (Kuala Lumpur: Pelanduk,1998)

[14] Chapra MU. *The Future of Economics: An Islamic Perspective*. Leicester, UK: The Islamic Foundation; 2000

[15] Chapra MU. *Islam and the Economic Challenge*. Herdon, VA: International Institute of Islamic Thought and The Islamic Foundation; 1992

[16] Siddiqi MN. Muslim economic thinking: A survey of contemporary literature. In: Ahmad K, editor. *Studies in Islamic Economics*. Leicester, UK: The Islamic Foundation; 1984

[17] Keynes JAM. *The Collected Writings of John Maynard Keynes*. London: Macmillan for the Royal Economic Society; 1972

[18] Hassan, A & Chachi, A (2004), "Role of Islamic banks in sustainable development" in the book titled *Sustainable Development in Islamic Perspectives*, edited by Iqbal, M., London: Palgrave

[19] Eaton G. Islam and the Destiny of Man. Cambridge: The Islamic Texts Society; 1994

[20] Hobson I. Islam's guiding principles for a solution to environmental problems. In: Haleem HA, editor. *Islam and Environment*. London: Ta-Ha publishers; 1998

[21] Keller NH. Reliance of the Traveller: A Classic Manual of Islamic Sacred Law, (Translation), Original Written by Ibn Naqib Al Misri. Evanston, IL: Sunna Book; 1994

[22] Syed J, Van Buren I. Global business norms and Islamic views of women's employment. Business Ethics Quarterly. 2014;**24**(2):251-276

[23] Terjesen S, Sealy R. Board gender quotas: Exploring ethical tension from a multi-theoretical perspective. Business Ethics Quarterly. 2006;*26(1):23-65*

[24] Khan FR, Karim N. Corporate social responsibility: Contemporary thought and Islamic perspectives. Thought on Economics. 2010;**21**(1):45-55

[25] Atan R, Halim NAA. Precipitation of Muslim consumers towards CSR. British Journal of Economics, Finance and Management Services. 2012;**4**(20):65-80

[26] Dusuki AW. What does Islam says about corporate social responsibility? Review of Islamic Economics. 2008;**12**(1):5-12

[27] Katisioloudes M, Brodtkourb T. Corporate social responsibility: An exploratory study in the United Arab Emirates. Advanced Management Journal. 2007;**72**(4):9-20

[28] Koleva,P; Towards the Development of Empirical Model of Islamic CSR : Evidence from Middle East. *Journal of Business Ethics*, 2020, February, ULR Link: https://doi.org/10.1007/s10551-020-04465-w (access date October 21,2020)

[29] Des-Jardins J. Corporate environmental responsibility. Journal of Business Ethics. 1998;**17**:825-838

[30] Hart SL. Beyond greening: Strategies for a sustainable world. Harvard Business Review. 1997:67-76

[31] Gladwin T. Paradigms for sustainable development. *Academy of Management Review.* 1995;20:974-907

[32] Margretta J. Growth through global sustainability. In: *Harvard Business Review*, (Jan-Feb). 1997

[33] Ansari MI. Islamic perspective on sustainable development. American Journal of Islamic Social Sciences. 1994;**11**(3):394-401

Chapter 10

Teacher Professional Competencies in Education for Sustainable Development

Xiaoyao Yue and Ruixuan Ji

Abstract

At present, combining sustainable development with education has become one of the school's missions. Students must master sustainable development skills. In order to explore the ideal method of K-12 teachers' professional competence in Education for Sustainable Development and determine the talent leadership strategy can enhance the professional competence of teachers in the 21st century sustainable development education, this study uses content analysis. The author systematically reviewed and analyzed related research work on sustainable development education, teachers' professional abilities and talent leadership strategies. According to the comprehensive results of content analysis, the ideal way for K-12 teachers to achieve professional sustainability is as follows: content focuses on sustainability with 21st century skills, collaboration with peers, active learning, and application of learning sustainability in practice Model, peer guidance, feedback and evaluation, duration, and teacher professional development. In order to achieve the second research goal, the authors found that talent leadership strategies can enhance the sustainable development of K-12 teachers' professional capabilities, including K-12 teacher professional development methods, K-12 teacher professional capabilities, student performance and focus on student performance.

Keywords: education for sustainable development, teacher professional competencies, talent leadership strategies

1. Introduction

In the 21st century, new trends in technology, economy, and politics affect people's social life, workplace, and lifestyle, especially environmental and resource challenges. In this case, education needs to be changed to adapt to these emerging trends. Traditional K-12 education is not popular, and educators call on us to reform the curriculum and teaching methods to teach students sustainability, such as poverty, citizenship, peace, democracy, security, human rights, social and economic development, health, gender Equality, cultural diversity, environmental protection, natural resource management, urban and rural development, production and consumption patterns, and corporate responsibility. Teachers must master all this knowledge before teaching students. In order to achieve this goal, school leaders must improve teachers' professional abilities to meet students' needs.

2. Literature review

2.1 Related concepts of education for sustainable development

2.1.1 Sustainable development

Sauve and Montreal [1] proposed that education reform should be the main task according to the UNESCO's sustainable development document. What is Education for Sustainable Development (ESD)? The report of the ESD program was written by McKeown et al. [2], describing the Education for Sustainable Development focusing on the sustainability of the school. Linking education to sustainable development is a central task. Their research summarizes four aspects:

1. Promoting basic education

2. Re-orienting current direction to promote sustainable development

3. Addressing public knowledge and understanding

4. Training

This research will develop education through talent leadership strategies to enhance teachers' professional ability education to achieve sustainable development in the 21st century.

2.1.2 Education and sustainable development

Sustainable development includes three pillars of environmental ecology, economy and society [3]. Education is the most basic element and plays an important role (see **Figure 1**).

On the other hand, education can contribute to common interests, promote national development, and provide help to families, communities, and communities that remain unchanged. When faced with economic, environmental and social challenges, education is more important in the 21st century than in the past. Whether students are future citizens, employees, managers, parents and leaders, they must face future challenges [4], especially their contribution to sustainable development. Jerald [5] believes that new trends in technology, economy, and

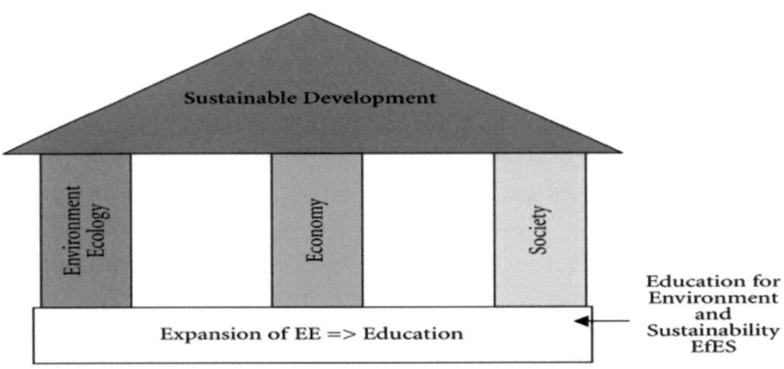

Figure 1.
Education as the foundation of the three pillars. Source from: Nikolopoulou et al. [3] education for sustainable development. California: Sage.

politics affect people's communities, workplaces, and lifestyles, and sustainable development becomes more and more necessary. Facing all challenges, education needs to be reformed to meet the demands of the world. Traditional education cannot adapt, and educators call on us to innovate courses and teaching to teach students sustainability.

2.1.3 Content of education for sustainable development

According to Nikolopoulou et al. [3] *Education for Sustainable Development*, the content of education for sustainable development is discussed, involving poverty, citizenship, peace, democracy, security, human rights, social and economic development, health, gender equality, and cultural diversity, gender, environmental protection, natural resource management, urban and rural development, production and consumption methods, and corporate responsibility.

2.1.4 21st Century skills enhancing sustainability

For education, student achievement and success are the ultimate goal of education. Kozma [6] believes that if students master 21st century skills, their academic performance will be high. 21st century skills can enhance students' ability to learn sustainable development knowledge. The 21st Century Learning Framework [7] draws the following conclusions: critical thinking and problem-solving skills-students can think critically and have problem solving skills; Intercultural understanding-students learn different cultures and have a good understanding of mixed culture; creativity and innovation ability-students have creativity and innovation ability in future study and work; exchange students can communicate well with others; Information Students know how to search for information and choose useful and effective information. Media literacy students have sufficient media literacy to protect privacy, identify the truth, and prevent being deceived; computers and ICT literacy-students have the ability to understand and use computers, classroom technology, etc. 21st century skills can be used for sustainable development education.

2.1.5 Characteristics of sustainable schools

Students need 21st century skills [8], which can be used for sustainable learning. In order to meet the requirements and needs of sustainable development education in the 21st century, schools must provide teachers with 21st century skills learning sustainability services by providing practice, human resource support and related infrastructure now [9]. Sustainable schools also provide professional development activities to stimulate teacher collaboration [10] to learn sustainability.

3. Methods

This article uses a content analysis method to achieve the goal-to explore the ideal method of K12 teachers' professional ability in the 21st century sustainable development education; determining talent leadership strategies can enhance teachers' professional ability in the 21st century sustainable development education.

The author reviewed the related researches, used the key words to search the published articles since 2000, which in Sage, Eric and Springer, such as, "sustainable development education", "teacher professional competence" and "talent leadership". The keywords determined according to the goal of the thesis are related to the effective K-12 teacher professional competence method in the 21st century

Categories	Sum	Percentage
Professional competencies of K-12 teachers	19	31.7%
Teacher's competences for the 21st century education	14	23.3%
Teacher professional development towards the 21st century education	16	26.7%
Talent leadership towards teacher professional development	11	18.3%
Total	60	100%

Table 1.
Results of content analysis.

education. Based on the theme of K-12 teachers' professional ability method for sustainable development education and talent leadership method, the word frequency count of each identified keyword was collected and classified (**Table 1**). The data was collected and summarized in response to the goal of the paper. Through the analysis of sustainable development education, teachers' professional ability methods and talent leadership, the 21st century sustainable development education and teacher leadership.

Obviously, in order to answer the first research question, the author has determined the ideal and effective method of teacher professional development in K-12 educational institutions in the 21st century. According to the analysis of online research publications, the ideal way to follow the professional competence of K-12 teachers for sustainable development in the 21st century is as follows: the content focuses on sustainability with 21st century skills, collaboration with peers, active learning, and application in learning Learn sustainability model exercises, peer guidance, feedback and evaluation, duration, and teacher professional development. To answer the second research question, the author found that talent leadership strategies can enhance the professional competence of teachers in the 21st century sustainable development education, including K-12 teacher professional development methods, K-12 teacher professional competence, student performance and student performance attention.

4. Analysis and discussion

4.1 Professional competencies of K-12 teachers

4.1.1 The trend of teacher's professional competencies

What are competencies? It is certain that people must master the knowledge, skills and experience in daily activities, and can use these knowledge, skills and experience to engage in future work. Another definition is that a person's knowledge, skills, attitudes, values, motivations and beliefs can convince him or her to succeed in his career [11]. Selvi [12] mentioned that the general content of professional competence includes three parts: inland competence, pedagogy competence and cultural competence. Apart from three main aspects, teachers' professional abilities are in different fields.

The second model states learning is preparation for the future-the competencies in Education for Sustainable Development (ESD)—this model shows developing teacher profession to meet student needs in the future. Although the two kinds of teacher professional competencies model look very different, they are also effective to improve teacher professional competencies.

Bertschy et al. [13] found that teacher professional competence includes two models. The first one is "Curriculum, Sustainable Development, Competence, Teacher Training (CSCT) Model". This model illustrates that teachers' professional abilities can improve the sustainability of the curriculum, stimulate teachers' abilities and develop teacher training practices. The second model points out that learning is preparing for the future-the ability of sustainable development education (ESD), the model shows the development of teacher careers to meet the needs of future students. Although these two kinds of teacher models look very different, they are also effective for improving teacher professional competences.

4.1.2 Professional competencies of K-12 teachers enhancing students' learning

The professional ability of K-12 teachers will affect students' achievement and motivation. In this regard, Kunter [14] pointed out that it is obvious that teachers have a good understanding of subject content, high quality of beliefs, original motivation and direction, and can control themselves regularly, which will promote student achievement and motivation. In other words, teachers' knowledge level and constructivist beliefs can predict students' motivation and achievements. Specifically, teachers' motivation and self-regulation ability can predict students' performance and motivation.

4.2 Teacher's competences for the 21st century education

4.2.1 Teachers' competencies for the 21st century schools

Caena [15] pointed out that K-12 teachers' professional ability content includes the following characteristics: teachers should have tacit and explicit knowledge, practical knowledge and cognitive thinking ability. Especially teachers should have higher motivation, positive beliefs, correct values and be able to handle their emotions. Based on these abilities and skills, teachers can solve more difficult problems and apply them to disciplines to solve teaching problems. These emotional skills will also affect the teacher's career in different situations, thereby helping the teacher complete the task and meet the requirements. In addition, as we have seen, in the 21st century education, the trend of using technology and information is developing. School leaders require teachers to learn ICT (information, communication, technology) skills [16].

4.2.2 21st Century teachers' competencies affecting students' learning outcomes

Teachers have adopted innovative methods in the curriculum and teaching to provide students with opportunities to improve critical thinking and problem-solving skills. And students can learn content knowledge that can remember a long-life experience [17]. Teachers choose practical learning methods to enter the classroom to teach the subject. For example, there are some new subjects, such as the physics subject, and the new course "Science, Physical Education, and Me." In this creative course, students can physically check their athletic performance.

Kozma [6] described that students learn the skills and knowledge of the 21st century, which is beneficial to students who have high academic achievements and a better life and work in the future. Teachers with educational capabilities in the 21st century will greatly improve students' academic performance and achievements. 21st century skills such as critical thinking skills and problem-solving skills are good for students' academic performance [18].

4.3 Teacher professional development towards the 21st century education

4.3.1 Theories of teacher professional development

Linda [19] concluded that there is not enough literature discussion on the definition of teacher professional development (TPD), and even experts have tried to find the ideal definition, but this has failed. Some literary works on teacher professional development are called TPD, which are used by teachers to improve their content knowledge, pedagogy knowledge, critical thinking and problem-solving skills. These skills and knowledge can be formed through learning and communication with peer teachers. Therefore, the definition of teacher professional development is the process of improving teacher characteristics. One can grow into a professional process. Teacher professional development is divided into two types: functional development and attitude development.

Attitude development is about the process of the attitude formed by teachers in their work, while functional development is about the process of the transformation of teachers' intelligence and motivation.

Haßler [20] pointed out that teachers who apply active learning strategies to the classroom will become reflective practitioners. In this class, students learn content by solving problems, communicating critically, asking questions, and using logical thinking. Therefore, teachers must learn this method by participating in professional development activities. He also suggested that "teacher education" or "teacher professional development" is better than "teacher training". Educators have built a communication learning environment for teachers, conducted high-quality discussions with learners and conducted practical activities. Learners can answer questions openly will actively engage students in the learning process. When learners ask other teachers to speak about their critical thinking, they can obtain useful information from other teachers' thoughts. Usually applying technology in education can enhance interaction and collaboration. Educational technology has the most beneficial impact on students' learning. Schools should support teachers in using technology in the classroom, which requires an adaptable professional development plan.

Another study by Postholm [21] shows that teacher professional development is related to teacher learning. This is how professors learn and how they use knowledge, abilities and skills to teach students how to learn. When teachers participate in coaching or learning activities in school, they can acquire knowledge and skills. They can also improve their professional skills through classroom research and learn from their peers through collaboration. Teachers can learn when attending learning and assessment meetings. When teachers reflect and plan activities in learning teaching and knowledge, they can learn from peer groups.

Linda [22] presented three main research reports from the Stanford Educational Opportunity Policy Research Center of the United States, which introduced teachers' professional development opportunities in learning. First of all, teachers hope to gain more professional learning experience, focusing on disabling students, subject background, classroom leadership and the use of technology. The second is that teachers do not have enough opportunities to participate in professional training of duration (less than 8 hours), nor do they have enough time to participate in seminars. The third report says that the state improves the professional development of teachers, including the following: professional development standards, accountability and supervision of professional development efforts, various intermediary offices that provide infrastructure and support for regional professional development; and schools and Areas can be used to strengthen professional development resources.

Blank [23] determined the content of teacher professional development, which provides teachers with knowledge of subject content and related skills. He also described that active learning methods have been used in teachers' professional development activities, thus providing teachers with opportunities to improve themselves. Generally speaking, teacher professional development requires teachers to learn together with their peers at school; mother tongue courses are also used as learning materials for teacher professional development; sufficient time is important for teacher professional development activities. The final and critical factor is feedback and evaluation. In order to achieve the purpose of feedback and evaluation, these metrics point out that: attention should be paid to the implementation of the quality of the development process; the teacher's knowledge has been increased; the teacher's classroom practice has changed, and the student's performance has also been improved.

To a certain extent, duration plays a vital role in career development education. If the professional study time is short, not dedicated and disorderly, then teachers will not get great help in development activities, just like students. To encourage teachers to change their habits in the classroom, school leaders should provide sufficient time for teachers' professional development [24].

In summary, the keywords for effective teacher professional development are content-focused, active learning, developing collaboration, applying models in practice, providing coaching and expert support, and feedback and evaluation on teacher professionalism and duration [21, 23–26].

4.3.2 Teacher professional development for the 21st century education

In today's world, education is changing [27]. In the 21st century, society has undergone tremendous changes and stimulated changes in the education system. In the education reform, teacher professional development has become one of the important components. Educators pointed out that the most important thing to note is that teachers work as professional teachers. Professional development is a person's professional role. Teacher professional development is the result of teachers gaining experience and systematically evaluating teaching. Professional development includes formal and informal experience. Effective professional development will profoundly affect the work of teachers in and out of school. Professional development also affects the relationship between teachers' beliefs and behaviors and the quality and practice of teachers in the classroom, thereby affecting students' learning and performance. The higher the degree of professional development, the better the student's performance.

High-quality teacher professional development refers to the main contents of TPD activities, themes, pedagogy and courses, and was discovered by Pedemonte [28]. The author's research implies that the focus on the subject is carried out with a greater degree of collective participation, active learning, collaboration and a longer duration. It is related to classroom practice teaching and is an effective TPD method for teacher reporting. In his research, teachers adopted a method of collective participation, requiring students to do some homework at least within a week, and arrange them into small groups for collaborative learning.

4.4 Talent leadership towards teacher professional development

4.4.1 Talent leadership theory

Talent management and leadership skills seem to be one of the most important themes of organizations in the 21st century. Obviously, research on talent leadership in organizations is limited. In fact, talent management often draws attention to industrial organization (I-O) theory and human resources (HR) professional fields, which include identifying, selecting, and developing and retaining high-quality and suitable employees [29]. Talent is a key element of school success. Those who change their organizational performance through short-term work or long-term development of the best potential and values [30, 31]. As the organization discovers, leads and develops current and future members, talent management can be determined [30, 31]. Talent leadership theory mentions that in school planning, leaders should explore strategies for organizational performance to meet current and future needs and establish the necessary processes to measure the school's ability [32].

4.4.2 Talent leadership enhancing teacher professional development

The Organization for Economic Co-operation and Development (OECD) has broadly determined the professional development of teachers, which is a process of improving teachers' skills, knowledge, practices and other areas. Professional leadership should respond to teachers' major career transformations, develop their talents, and strength professionally [33]. Indeed, focusing on talent leadership can help teachers determine their talents and put them into practice. The American Institute presents a talent development framework that mentions three key elements: school leaders should meet the requirements of your students by arranging enough talents in their careers; school leaders should develop future talents Teachers and administration prepare to meet student needs; school leaders can support your student needs with support, and retain teachers who can continue to maintain high-quality teaching and use their talents for practice. In addition, the Ministry of Education and Training stated that school leaders should establish a link between high-quality teaching and student achievement and promote educational skills and knowledge in the development of professional teachers. As an education leader, designing and implementing effective professional development is their main job [22].

4.5 Deming circle

Deming circles are used to implementing quality management and continuous improvement. W.E. found this method of organization. Deming (Deming) and named PDCA (Planned Examination Action) circle [34]. Planning to develop a vision is the mission of the organization. Do the steps, methods, strategies to achieve the goal. Check the assessment and access the results. The bill identifies areas for improvement (**Figure 2**).

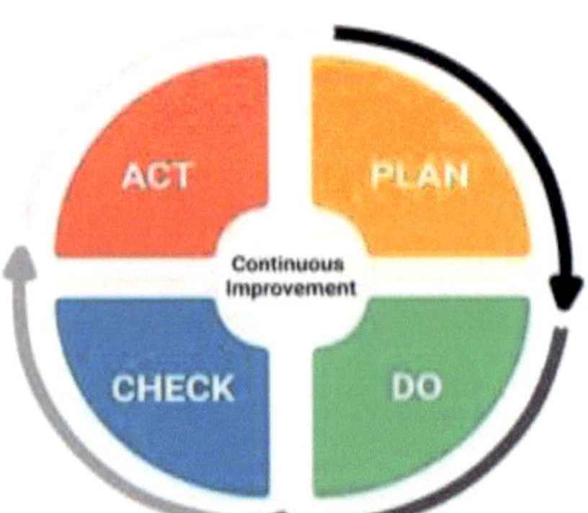

Figure 2.
Advanced PDCA circle. Source: https://kanbanize.com/lean-management/improvement/what-is-pdca-cycle.

5. Results

In the 21st century, it is expected that K-12 students will learn the skills of the 21st century. School leaders should find appropriate educational leaders to develop teachers' professional abilities. School leaders will develop personal talents, skills and 21st century skills to meet students' current needs and future needs. In **Table 1**, K-12 school leaders enable each teacher's 21st century skills, abilities and knowledge to make the school a success. Talent leadership school leaders use these seven methods to improve teachers' professional abilities (**Figure 3**).

5.1 For answering the first research question

Based on the comprehensive results of content analysis, the ideal method for K-12 teachers' professional abilities in 21st century education is as follows: content focuses on 21st century skills, collaboration with peers, active learning, model exercises to learn 21st century skills, coaching, feedback and evaluation, duration. Content Focus on Sustainability of 21st Century Skills Focusing on the main content and teaching strategy models of 21st century skills are the key to teachers' professional development, helping teachers master the sustainability of 21st century skills and how to teach students.

Collaboration with peers. Cooperation with colleagues and subordinates. Each teacher has his own talents, learn from the same learn, and preside over the demonstration class; management team cooperation and discussion, the teacher can also discuss the work of students with other teachers. Apply technology in interaction, collaboration, and work. **Active learning.** Active learning methods have been used in teachers' professional development activities, thus providing teachers with better opportunities for self-improvement. **Apply learning sustainability models in practice.** Teachers apply teaching theories, concepts and models of sustainable development skills to actual classrooms. They must learn how to teach students the skills of the 21st century. **Peer guidance**. In talent leadership strategies, leaders use peer guidance rather than traditional expert guidance. Some teachers have 21st century skills. Some people dominate critical thinking and problem solving, some shine in creativity and innovation, and some do well in computing and ICT literacy. These teachers may be tutors. **Feedback and evaluation.** The feedback and evaluation

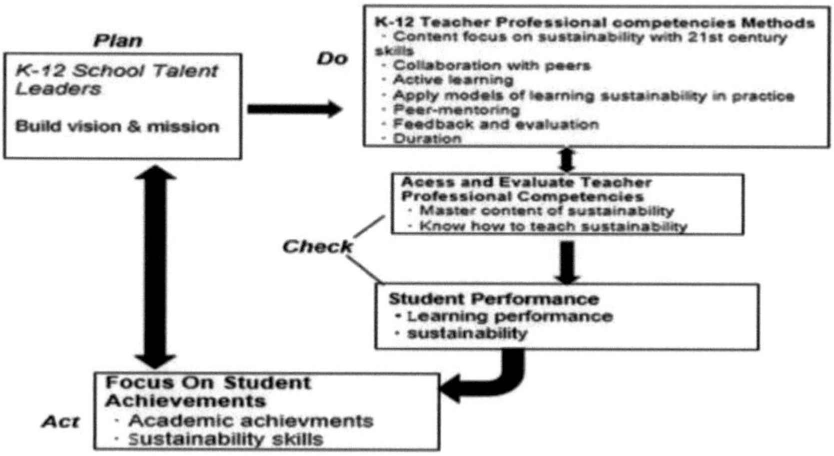

Figure 3.
Talent leadership strategies enhance teacher's professional competencies in 21st century education for sustainable development.

of TPD is very important. The purpose of feedback is to achieve the quality and efficiency of TPD. In addition, the feedback should confirm that the teacher's ability has been developed, the teacher's classroom practice has been changed, and the student's performance has been improved. Sufficient time is essential for teachers' professional development activities. Teachers should have enough opportunities to participate in professional training of continuous duration (for example, more than 8 hours), and have enough time to participate in seminars.

5.2 For answering the second research question

Talent leadership strategies include K-12 teacher professional development methods, K-12 teacher professional capabilities, student performance, and attention to student achievement. K-12 teachers' professional development process is inefficient, they must improve their professional abilities, master the content of sustainable development skills, and know how to teach students sustainable development skills. Students master it and show better academic performance. Of course, students' academic achievement and sustainability skills will be improved. Students' grades reflect the value of the model.

6. Conclusion and implication

K-12 school leaders can use these effective methods to develop the professional skills of K-12 teachers to develop sustainability with 21st century skills, including focusing on the sustainability of 21st century skills and collaborating with peers, active learning, applying learning sustainability model in practice, peer guidance, feedback and evaluation, duration. Teacher professional development. Teachers participate in open subject content courses at professional development schools to provide content knowledge mastered by teachers. Talent leadership strategies for K-12 teachers' ESD professional capabilities, including K-12 teachers' professional development methods, K-12 teachers' professional capabilities, student performance, and attention to student performance.

Acknowledgements

Our sincere appreciation goes to three researchers: Nikolopoulou, Abraham and Mirbagheri creatively positioned education as the foundation of the three pillars. In addition, we would also like to thank all friends for their keen and powerful academic observations, which not only inspired this research paper, but also inspired our future research.

Author details

Xiaoyao Yue[1] and Ruixuan Ji[2*]

1 Higher Education Research Institute, Yunnan University, Kunming City Yunnan Province, China

2 Faculty of Education, College of Arts, Law, and Education, University of Tasmania, Hobart, Australia

*Address all correspondence to: ruixuan.ji@utas.edu.au

References

[1] Sauve, L & Montreal, U. Q. (1996) Environmental Education and Sustainable Development: A Further Appraisal. Canadian Journal of Environmental Education. 1(7).

[2] McKeown, Hopkins, Rizi and Chrystalbridge (2002). Education for Sustainable Development

[3] Nikolopoulou, Abraham & Mirbagheri (2010), *Education for Sustainable Development.* California: Sage.

[4] Pellegrino, J. W., & Hilton, ML. (2012). *Education for life and work developing transferable knowledge and skills in the 21st century.* Washington: The National Academic Press.

[5] Jerald, B. D. (2009). *Defining a 21st century education*. Center for Public Education.

[6] Kozma R.B. (2008) Comparative Analysis of Policies for ICT in Education. In: Voogt J., Knezek G. (eds) International Handbook of Information Technology in Primary and Secondary Education. Springer International Handbook of Information Technology in Primary and Secondary Education, vol 20. Springer, Boston, MA. https://doi.org/10.1007/978-0-387-73315-9_68

[7] Partnership for 21st Century skills. (2007). Professional development: a 21st century skills implementation guide. Retrieved from http://www.p21.org/storage/documents/p21stateimp_professional_development.pdf.

[8] Wan, G., & Gut, D. M. (2011). *Bringing the school into the 21st century.* New York: Springer.

[9] Dewey, J. (2008). *21st Century learning environment*. Partnership for 21st century skills. http://www.21stcenturyskills.org

[10] Bellanca , J. A. & Brandt, R. (2010). *21st century skills: rethinking how students learn*. Solution tree press. ISBN: 9781935249900

[11] UNESCO. (2010). *Strategic planning: concept and rationale: education sector planning working papers working paper 1.* International Institute for Educational Planning.

[12] Selvi, K. (2010) Teachers' Competencies. International Journal of Philosophy of Culture and Axiology. 7(1):167-175

[13] Bertschy, F., Künzli, C. & Lehmann, M. (2013). Teachers' competencies for the implementation of educational offers in the field of education for sustainable development. Sustainability 2013, 5, 5067-5080; doi:10.3390/su5125067

[14] Kunter, M., Baumert, J., Voss, T., Klusmann, U., Richter, D. & Hachfeld, A. (2013). American Psychological Association. Journal of educational psychology. Vol. 105, No. 3, 805-820

[15] Caena, F. (2014). Teacher competence frameworks in Europe: Policy-as-discourse and policy-as-practice. *European Journal of Education*, 49(3), 311-331.

[16] UNESCO (2011). ICT competency for teachers. Version2.0. Paris: UNESCO

[17] Ennis, D. C. (2013). *Reimagining professional competencies in physical education*. University of North Carolina at Greensboro. Motriz, Rio Claro, v.19 n.4, p.662-672.

[18] American Association of Colleges for TeacherEducation(AACTE). (2010). An emerging picture of the teacher education pipeline.Washington D,C: Author.

[19] Linda, E. (2008). *Professionalism, Professionality and the Development of Education Professionals*. British Journal of Educational Studies. 56 (1). pp. 20-38.

[20] Haßler, B., Hennessy, S., Cross, A., Chileshe, E. & Machiko, B. (2014). *School-based professional development in a developing context: Lessons learnt from a case study in Zambia.* London: Professional Development in Education.

[21] Postholm. M. B. (2012). *Teachers' professional development: a theoretical review.*

[22] Darling-Hammond, L. (2014). Strengthening clinical preparation: the holy grail of teacher education. Peabody Journal of Education, 89(4), 547e561.

[23] Blank, R.K., Alas, N.D. & Smith, C. (2008) *Does Teacher Professional Development Have Effects on Teaching and Learning? Analysis of Evaluation Findings from Programs for Mathematics and Science Teachers in 14 states.* Washington: Council of Chief State School Officers. ISBN: 1-884037-25-9.

[24] DeMonte, J. (2013). *High-quality professional development for teachers: supporting Teacher Training to Improve Student Learning.* Washington: Center for American Progress.

[25] Gökmenoğlu, T. & Clark, C. M. (2015). *Teachers' evaluation of professional development in support of national reforms.* Issues in Educational Research. 25(4), 442-459. http://www.iier.org.au/iier25/gokmenoglu.pdf

[26] Darling-Hammond, L., Hyler, M. E., & Gardner, M. (2017). Effective teacher professional development. Palo Alto, CA: Learning Policy Institute.

[27] Reimers, E. V. (2012). *Teachers' professional development: a theoretical review.* Programme for Teacher Education. Norwegian University of Science and Technology. Norway: Vol. 54, No. 4, December 2012, 405-429.

[28] Pedemonte, F. B, (2016). *"High-Quality Teacher Professional Development and Classroom Teaching Practices: Evidence from Talis 2013"*. OECD Education Working Papers, No. 141, OECD Publishing, Paris. http://dx.doi.org/10.1787/5jlpszw26rvd-en

[29] Slizer, R.F., & Dowell, B.(2010). *Strategy-driven talent management.* New Jersey: Wiley.

[30] Ford, J., Harding, N & Stoyanova, D. (2014). *Talent management and development: an overview of current theory and practice*. Bradford University School of Management.

[31] Davies, B. and Davies, B. (2011) *Talent Management in Education*, London: Sage

[32] Cannon, J. A. & McGee, R. (2010). *Talent management and succession planning.* Published by the Chartered Institute of Personnel and Development, 151The Broadway, London SW19 1JQ. SBN-13 978 1 84398 173 2

[33] CAMBRIDGE international examinations (2015). *Professional development.*

[34] Sokovic, M., Pavletic, D., & Pipan Kern K. (2010). Quality Improvement methodologies – PDCA Cycle, Radar Matrix, DMAIC and DFSS. Journal of Achievements in Materials and Manufacturing Engineering, 43(1), 311-329.

Chapter 11

Driving a Sustainable University-Industry Partnership

Zainuddin Abd Manan and Sharifah Rafidah Wan Alwi

Abstract

There has been a lot of emphasis on the need for academia-industry collaboration. A successful and sustainable academia-industry partnership can result from a university's efforts in driving values in its collaboration with industry. This chapter describes a model for mainstreaming a sustainable university partnership with industry through the university's academic curriculum. The University-Industry Innovation eXchange (UNIX) internship program is a project-based industrial training scheme that is integrated with research projects to provide students with an engaging experience of working with industry for up to one year to solve practical industrial problems. Successful implementation of UNIX projects within the Universiti Teknologi Malaysia's (UTM) work-based curriculum contributes toward nurturing life-ready and job-ready graduates, development of resilient and sustainable organisation through improved operations, and enhanced university-industry partnership.

Keywords: work-based learning, sustainable partnership, university-industry innovation eXchange (UNIX), sustainable organisation, industrial training

1. University's role in driving sustainable partnership with industry

Among the key roles of a university is to educate and empower people with knowledge and skills so that they will become prosperers of lives. To effectively achieve this mission, universities must formulate a sustainable partnership with industry, government and community, apart from with other universities. In order to foster and drive a sustainable partnership, a university must begin by building a compelling case and unique offerings on how the partnership could benefit collaborators. This chapter presents the strategies and unique offerings of Universiti Teknologi Malaysia (UTM) in creating a sustainable partnership through a work-based curriculum that contributes toward nurturing life-ready and job-ready graduates, development of resilient and sustainable organisation through improved operations, and enhanced partnership with industry.

At UTM, the traditional practice of having a short industrial training or odd career days toward the end of a degree program has undergone sweeping transformation toward a customised and immersive *UTM-Industry Innovation Exchange* (UNIX) project that includes up to 50% work-based learning elements that is implemented in close collaboration with UTM industry. The partnership combines industrial training, trans-disciplinary action research and design projects that embed contemporary challenged-based topics including elements of Fourth

Industrial Revolution (4IR) as part of student learning time (SLT) to enable students to be inclusively involved in real-life problem solving that benefits industry and community.

2. UTM-industry innovation eXchange (UNIX) program

The School of Chemical and Energy Engineering, Universiti Teknologi Malaysia (UTM-SCEE) founded the "UTM-Industry Innovation Exchange" (UNIX-Internship) project back in 2010 as one of its signature global branding through creativity and innovation (GBCI) project. UNIX is aimed at value-adding, expanding and maximising the benefits of the industrial training program to university, students and the industry.

Since 1983, UTM-SCEE sends an average of 150 undergraduate students to undergo a ten-week Industrial Training (InTra) program. The purpose of InTra is to provide students with industrial exposure and experience before they graduate. This training is also designed to meet the accreditation requirements for the engineering program by the Engineering Accreditation Council of Malaysia (EAC) of Malaysia.

Over the years, UTM-SCEE received numerous feedbacks from stakeholders, especially from the industry and students regarding InTra. Most companies found that they were not able to assign InTra students with reasonably challenging projects because of the short ten weeks duration of the InTra. Most industries typically accept students for InTra just to fulfil their corporate their social responsibility (CSR) goals. Except for providing students with exposure to day-to-day industrial operations, industries generally do not expect any added-value or contributions from universities through the InTra program. As a result, there is no commitment from the industry to provide students with the opportunity to apply their knowledge to solve industrial problems.

In some cases, there are mismatches between internship training provided by the company and the students' industrial training programme requirement. In a paper reported by Ayob et al. [1], some engineering students were given tasks such as the promotion of business product and management of foreign workers, which are not related to their studies. According to the article by Feijoo et al. [2], it is emphasised on the need to introduce a more in-depth study of specific topics that could be included as an additional project scope to improve industrial training.

Many universities generally regard the InTra program as not more than a means to provide short industrial exposure to students. Students generally appreciate their short industrial exposures but found that they were not able to fully benefit from undergoing InTra. The minimum of eight weeks internship period (according to the Engineering Accreditation Council guide [3]) is typically too short for them to be immersed in projects to solve industrial problems and does not allow them to deeply apply the theories and knowledge that they have learnt over the period of their studies. Phang et al. [4] stated that a longer industrial training duration can increase the job-readiness and the future career development of engineering undergraduates. According to the authors, many parties regard the standard 10–12 weeks internship period as being too short and should be reviewed. The need for a longer industrial training duration is also supported by the study of Jamaluddin et al. [5]. In addition, Filho et al. [6] stated that, to enhance sustainability in the curricula, academia needs to develop a more engaging collaborative approaches in working with industries.

SCEE fully recognised the limitations of the traditional InTra program and the importance of offering a practical and mutually beneficial cooperation program for the industry. In October of 2010, SCEE established the UNIX-Internship project as one of SCEE's global branding projects through creativity and innovation (Global Branding through Creativity and Innovation - GBCI).

UNIX is an innovative program to foster and facilitate a win-win" collaborative partnership via human capital development, research as well as consultancy services between UTM-SCEE and the industry. UNIX integrates three core courses offered by the UTM- SCEE, namely the (i) Industrial Training (IT) and (ii) Undergraduate Project 1 and II (UGP1 & UGP2). Integration of professional work placement and engineering research project was also introduced by Cork Institute of Technology, Ireland [7]. Their industrial attachment model includes four months of professional work placement, followed by seven months of engineering research project involving the company where the students are placed.

The objectives of the UTM-SCEE UNIX project are to:

i. enhance graduate employability via industrial/government, project-oriented internship programs,

ii. form a vibrant, symbiotic, and sustainable linkage between UTM and the industry/government/community

iii. create a market-driven as well as technology-driven R & D ecosystem.

To ensure the success and effectiveness of the program, a pilot-scale UNIX-internship at SCEE was initiated by selecting 10% of the total students to undergo InTra via the UNIX program. Selected students were placed in industries that have become members of the UNIX consortium and will conduct training/activities related to pre-agreed research projects. During the InTra, students will be co-supervised by the industry as well as by a research project supervisor from SCEE. The UNIX program spans across one academic year involving UGP 1 (Semester 1), ten weeks InTra and UGP 2 (Semester 2).

2.1 Stages of UNIX implementation

The SCEE UNIX-Internship program involves three stages of implementation:

Stage 1: Project Conception

This stage involves a discussion between the UTM team comprising of the UNIX committee and the prospective research leader, and the industry. The UTM team begins by presenting the possible research topics, the offer for collaboration initiatives and UNIX as one of the possible collaborative programs for the company to consider as a starting point. The meeting is aimed to identify possible areas of collaboration and specific projects of interest to companies.

Stage 2: Appointment of Academic and Industrial Supervisors

The second stage of UNIX involves the appointment of the research and industrial supervisors with expertise relevant to the needs and interests of the industry, and in line with the academic requirements. This stage involves more detailed discussions between the supervisor and the company to come up with a project proposal that will address the needs of all parties involved.

Stage 3: Selection of students

In this stage, the UNIX committee identifies students to participate in the UNIX program based on (i) the project topics agreed upon by UTM research supervisors and UNIX consortium companies, and (ii) the performances of students in the academic as well as extra-curricular activities.

	Semester 1				Industrial attachment			Semester 2			
Plan/Month	**F**	**M**	**A**	**M**	**J**	**J**	**A**	**S**	**O**	**N**	**D**
Technology/process review & screening	■	■	■	■							
Industrial attahcment (on-iste) – data collection					■	■	■				
Data analysis, optimisation and economic studies								■	■	■	■

Table 1.
UNIX-internship timeline.

Typically, between 10 and 15% of the total students undergoing IT will be selected to undergo the UNIX program. Selected students will be placed in companies that have become members of the SCEE-UNIX consortium to conduct market-driven as well as industry-driven research projects that typically begins with state-of-the-art literature and technology screening during their Undergraduate Project 1 (from February until May of the academic year). This is followed by the student undergoing industrial internship attachment that involves industrial data collection and analysis by the student from June until early September. The project closes with the compilation and presentation of results and proposed solutions to the company in December. During the one-year course of UNIX, students will be supervised by an academic and an industrial supervisor. **Table 1** shows the typical UNIX-Internship timeline.

2.2 Benefits of UNIX

From the feedbacks and evaluations conducted on the industry, students, and supervisors, it has been found that the UNIX-Internship program has provided a positive learning experience that has significantly impacted the cognitive and affective domains of learning in students. Students developed problem-solving, time management, communication and team working skills during the 1-year course of continuous communication and engagement with industry. This allows them to function more effectively in learning together and in producing high-quality engineering solutions. The feedbacks also show that there is significant inculcation and drive toward sustainable development practices from the aspect of knowledge as well as behaviour. One of the most vital points of UNIX is the effectiveness of collaboration between faculty and industry in successfully solving complex and practical industrial problems. Such collaboration enriched participating students and faculties, and contributed toward sustainable development of organisations. All in all, the program has become an innovation that can sustainably provide a comprehensive and dynamic learning environment that had enhanced deep learning and instill positive behaviours among students and collaborating parties.

Follow are the multiple benefits of the UNIX program:

2.2.1 To industry

The human resource support to perform cutting-edge R & D provided by UNIX has enabled industries to:

- Gain competitive technical and commercial advantages and allow industries to achieve sustainable industrial operations. To date, UNIX has led to improved industrial processes, productivities, and profitability as well as enhanced safety and environmental practices for more than 100 local and multinational companies in Malaysia and abroad.

- Gain access to human resources with high-level generic as well as technical skills to solve complex problems encompassing optimal operations, sustainable development, safety-health-environment, economics & project management.

- Gain access to academic resources such as R & D grants, research expertise and facilities toward enhancing a company's competitive edge.

2.2.2 To the academia, and the nation

UNIX enables:

- The university and the nation to create an ecosystem of market-driven R & D through synergistic industry-academia-government-community engagement.

- Students and staff to gain extended exposure and experience working and engaging on collaborative projects with industry.

- Students' employability, and faculty members' skills to be enhanced. This will ultimately contribute toward industrial and national productivity.

2.3 Sample of UNIX projects

Table 2 shows the list of industry collaboration projects that have been successfully implemented since 2006.

2.4 International Paper publication from industrial cooperation

Some samples of collaborative projects related to the sustainable development of organisations published in high impact magazine articles and journals include:

- Article in 'Chemical Engineering' magazine published with MIMOS Semiconductor Sdn Bhd [8].

- Article in 'Chemical Engineering Progress' magazine published with MIMOS Semiconductor Sdn Bhd [9].

- An international journal published with MIMOS Semiconductor Sdn Bhd in the Journal of Environmental Management, which currently has an impact factor as high as 5.65 [10].

- An international journal published with the Malaysia Energy Center (MEC) in the Renewable and Sustainable Energy Reviews Journal, which currently has an impact factor as high as 12.1 [11].

2.5 Awards & recognitions

UNIX has also led to recognition and awards such as Prince Sultan Abdul Aziz International Prize for Water [12] which is the "spin-off" results of the

Company	R&D projects	Year started	Student involvement
BERNAS	Toward a Resource-Efficient, Integrated Rice Mill Complex – Optimisation of Rice Supply Chain	2009	1 PhD
	Optimisation Rice-Husk Based CHP System	2008	1 undergrad
CCM	Development Of Math Models for Retrofit based on Minimum Water Network Technique and considering multiple contaminants	2009	1 undergrad 1 MSc
	Combined Mass and Heat Exchange Networks	2009	1 MSc
TITAN Petchem	Computational Fluid Dynamics Modelling of Ethylene Cracker Furnace	2008	2 undergrads
	Development of Soft Sensor for Ethylene Cracker	2009	1 PhD
	Steam Trap Optimisation	2008	1 MSc
Mechmar Boiler	Techno-Economic Feasibility of CDM Project from Palm Oil Waste	2008	1 MSc (part time)
Malaysian Energy Centre & Malaysian Venture Capital	Optimal-Audit, Optimal-Heat, Optimal-Water Software Development	2006	5 undergrads, 2 MSc, 2 programmers
Pan Century Oleo Chemical (PCOC)	Maximum heat recovery network and hydraulic system analysis	2007	1 undergrad
	Maximum Heat Recovery System (Pinch Analysis)	2007	1 undergrad
FELDA Oil Products	Heat recovery network retrofit	2008	1 undergrad
MIMOS Semiconductor (MySEM)	Cost Effective Minimum Water Network using graphical approach	2006	1 PhD 1 undergrad
Malaysian Newsprint Industry (MNI)	Maximum water recovery with regeneration targeting using numerical method	2006	1 MSc
	Optimisation of CHP system	2008	1 MSc
Polycore	Electrical Energy Management	2008	2 undergrad
Infineon	Overall Plant Utility Optimisation	2008	1 MSc (part time)
Ethylene Malaysia	Power recovery network	2006	1 MSc
TITAN Polymer (M) Sdn Bhd	Modelling The Product Quality and Production Rate of Propylene Polymerisation in Industry Reactors Formulation of Modelling and Simulation Algorithm for Propylene Homopolymerization Loop Reactor Artificial Neural Network Modelling of Propylene Polymerisation in Industrial Loop Reactors Development and Simulation of Hybrid Model for Propylene Polymerisation in Industrial Reactors	2008	3 MSc 4 undergrads
Kempas Edible Oil Sdn Bhd	Develop a prediction model for: Phosphoric acid and bleaching earth dosage for degumming and bleaching process, respectively,	2009	2 undergrads

Company	R&D projects	Year started	Student involvement
	in palm oil refinery. Product quality of the refined oil from degumming and bleaching process.		
Mensilin Holdings Sdn Bhd	Optimisation of decentralised electricity generation from biogas and biomass.	2010	1 PhD
Kerry Ingredients	Modelling and optimisation of Industrial Spray Dryer	2010	1 undergrad
Kerteh Petronas Gas Bhd	Modelling of Benfield CO2 removal system Integrated reformer Methanol with natural gas plant Life cycle analysis (LCA)	2010	2 undergrads
PPNJ, Kahang, Kluang	Performance Study of POME Treatment using SBR	2008	1 undergrad
PPNJ, Kahang, Kluang	Performance Study of POME Treatment using MBR	2009	1 undergrad
PPNJ, Kahang, Kluang	Cost Benefit Analysis of Producing PHA from POME	2010	1 undergrad
Agensi Nuklear Malaysia	Characterisation and Properties of Ethylene Vinyl Acetate/ Sepiolite Nano Composite Preparation of Polyamide-6 Polypropylene EFB Composite	2012	2 undergrads
Lembaga Minyak Sawit Malaysia (MPOB)	Study of Polylactic Acid (PLA)/Empty Fruit Bunch Fibre (EFBF) Compatibilizer With Maleic Anhydride Low Density Polyethylene/Oil Palm Mesocarp Fibre Composite Effect of Inorganic Plasticiser On Low Density Polyethylene/Palm Pressed Fibre Composite Film Polyurethane/Oil Palm Biomass Fibres Composite Foam	2012	4 undergrads
PGEO Edible Oils SdnBhd	Blending of Polymer with Shea Latex for Plastics Applications Blending Of Polymer with Shea Latex for Plastics Applications	2013	2 undergrads
Agensi Nuklear Malaysia	Suspended Solid Removal by Natual Adsorbent Oil Removal from Superabsorbent For Waste Treatment	2013	2 undergrads
Lembaga Getah Malaysia	Preparation of Nanoparticle Assembly Using Natural Rubber Latex	2013	1 undergrad
Lipidchem Sdn Bhd	Formulation of Water-soluble beta carotene powder palm oil.	2013	1 undergrad
Lipidchem Sdn Bhd	1. Formulation and pilot prototype of Water soluble MCT powder from coconut oil	2014	1 undergrad
Naturemedic Supply Sdn Bhd	1. Anti-inflammatory properties of herbal supplement for gout, R-38. 2. Anti-inflammatory and antioxidant properties of botanical drinks	2014	2 undergrads

Company	R&D projects	Year started	Student involvement
Pantai Medivest	1. Detailed Design of Heat Recovery System and Fuel Switching	2009	2 Master
Malakoff R&D Sdn Bhd	1. Feasibility of study of steam demand requirement in Tanjung Langsat industrial area	2011	1 UG
Jabatan Alam Sekitar	1. Development of Environmental Impact Assessment (EIA) guidelines for solid waste incineration plant	2011	1 PhD
Pertamina	1. Maximising heat recovery for retrofit	2011	1 PhD Student, 1 Undergrad Student
Middle Distillate Plant	1. Retrofit of Middle Distillate Refinery Plant for Utility Conservation Using Pinch Analysis	2012	3 PhD Students
Synthomer	1. Sustainable energy management system.	2012	1 MSc student
	2. Cooling load optimization	2012	1 Undergrad student
	3. Batch heat integration with exothermic reaction	2012	1 Undergrad Student
Mudra Tropika	1. Water reuse and rainwater harvesting design	2012	1 Master
UTM	1. Carbon emission reduction in UTM	2012	1 Master
Iskandar Malaysia	1. Low carbon society	2012–2015	5 PhD, 8 Master, 2 UG
Institute Development Bank	1. Draft-1 of the Green Technology Blueprint for the OIC Countries	2013	4 PhD
Evyap Sabun Sdn Bhd	1. HAZOP analysis and 3-D pipe modelling Design Gap Analysis	2013 and 2014	3 PhD students
AMR Sdn Bhd	1. Cogeneration feasibility study for hospital clinical waste heat recovery	2014	1 PhD
Johor Port Authority	1. Ships emission analysis at Johor Port and Port of Tanjung Pelepas	2015	1 Master
Sterling Engineering Sdn Bhd	1. Heat pipe operability study	2015	2 UG
UTM	1. Energy factor analysis for university	2015	1 UG
Malaysian BioXcell Sdn Bhd	Greenhouse Gas Emission Reporting System Software	2015	1 undergrad
Total			113 students

Table 2.
List of industry on our UNIX-internship program.

collaboration with MIMOS Semi-Conductor and Sultan Ismail Mosque in UTM (see **Figure 1**). **Table 3** shows the list of water savings from UNIX projects.

In addition, SCEE also won USD 100,000 Islamic Development Bank (IDB) Prize of Excellence in Science and Technology 2017, cited as an Institution having achieved outstanding contribution to a given scientific discipline" (**Figure 2**).

Figure 1.
Prince Sultan Abdul Aziz international prize for water as a result of the UNIX program.

UTM's Sultan Iskandar Mosque	FW reduction: 95.3% WW reduction: 64.7% Savings = USD 5, 400/yr. Payback period = 5 years
MIMOS Semi-conductor (Near) Zero-Discharge Semi-Conductor Plant	FW reduction: 85.1% WW reduction: 97.7% Savings = RM 190, 000/yr. Payback period = 4 mths
CCM Chemicals Holistic Water Minimization	FW reduction: 35.8% WW reduction: 100% Savings = USD 105,000 /yr. Payback period = 1.87 yrs

Table 3.
List of water savings from UNIX projects.

Figure 2.
SCEE was awarded the Islamic Development Bank (IDB) prize of excellence in science and technology 2017.

2.6 Consultancy spin-off as a result of UNIX

UNIX has also spin-off to bigger industrial collaboration after the spin-off either in the form of R&D grants or consultancy projects as listed in **Table 4**.

Company	Consultancy projects	Outcomes
Greentech Malaysia	Baseline study of Energy efficiency and renewable energy award in Malaysia	A full report with extensive literature review and stakeholder analysis for energy efficiency and renewable energy award in Malaysia
Pantai Medivest Sdn Bhd	Improvement of Heat Recovery System and Fuel Switching for Pantai Medivest Sdn Bhd (PMSB) Incinerator Plant	The savings for the heat recovery system and fuel switching results in savings of RM 983, 386/year for fuel oil and RM63,612/ year for electricity. The total investment is RM141, 000 with a payback period of less than two months.
Padi Beras Nasional Berhad	Design of cogeneration system for rice mill	The proposed cogen scheme manages to satisfy the total drying heat requirement as well as the boiler turndown ratio constraint while generating a maximum of 582 kW power and making full use of the limited available rice husk quantity of an average 2.3 ton/hr. The total annual power saving for this scheme is RM 547,485, and yearly diesel savings is RM 3,312,276. The project payback period is 3.34 years.
Greentech Malaysia	Development of a Hazard & Operability Studies (HAZOP) for Biomass-Based Power Generation System for Palm Oil Mills	A 3 days training module for Biomass-Based Power Generation System HAZOP for Palm Oil Mills
Greentech Malaysia	Development of UTM-GTM Energy Audit Software for Malaysian Industries and Buildings	An energy audit software that consists of macro (e.g. fuel switching, cogen) and technical level (e.g. motor, fan, chiller, compressor) analysis for current equipment/system benchmarking.
IOI Groups	Retrofit for Energy Efficiency Improvement	A detailed study that includes benchmarking, data validation and sampling, hydraulic analysis, heat integration, system troubleshooting. The cooling water pump has successfully been reduced to two from three.
MIMOS Semiconductor	UTM-MIMOS Water Minimisation Project	Savings of freshwater and wastewater bills worth RM 50 k per month with two years payback period. This is a reduction of more than 80% of freshwater consumption.

Table 4.
Consultancy projects from UNIX.

2.7 Companies' responses

Below are some sample feedbacks from the UNIX-Internship Invitations:

Response from Petlin (PETRONAS):

Dear Prof. Zainuddin,

Unfortunately, this year (2011), our student quota is pretty occupied. As per email below, we are interested with the sandwich course as below, especially now that we are embarking Energy Loss Management System (ELMS). Good to study back our energy and mass balance throughout the plant (after eight years running). Maybe to study the water balance as well. This also will benefit the student and PM Sdn Bhd very much.

2012 then? When usually the best month to start the planning? Please advise. Will put it in my calendar. So when the month comes, will trigger the need for communication and will directly communicate with you.

Regards,
Process Safety Technical Department
PM Sdn. Bhd.

Response from Indah Water Konsortium:

Dear Prof Zainuddin,

Yes, we accept students for their industrial training subject to review and acceptance by the relevant department in IW Sdn Bhd. For this, we would advise that a written letter applying for the industrial training is submitted to our Human Resource Department. The letter shall include the details of the student, discipline, faculty, etc.; training dates and duration; the name of UTM coordinator and his/her details. Should there be any preferred area for the training (e.g. Engineering Design, Environmental Management, R&D, Planning, etc.), please state it in the letter. Our HR Department will reply accordingly. Kindly ensure adequate notice period is given for IW to process the application and reply accordingly. Thanks.

Regards, Manager

Response from PL Sdn Bhd

Dear Dr. Sharifah Rafidah,

I had received a good response from my boss. He is very interested with F2C program, especially for Chemistry or Polymer majors. If you do not mind, can I arrange you to do a presentation of the F2C program at our workplace.

Here is the tentative date:
Date: 30/12/2010 or 31/12/2010
Venue: PL Sdn Bhd
Time: Please advise us.
Enclosed here is the map to our plant. Your reply is highly appreciated.
Thanks.
| Human Resource Assistant | Human Resource
| PL Sdn Bhd

3. Examples of impactful UNIX programs to contribute toward sustainable organisation

UNIX has resulted in impactful outcomes for companies driving toward a sustainable organisation. Below are some examples:

3.1 Middle distillate company

A PhD student was attached in a middle distillate company in Sarawak, East Malaysia. The company requested a study on their existing heat integration system and proposed possible measures to further improve their thermal energy recovery systems, reduce emissions and minimise utility costs. The student performed a comprehensive 'Pinch Analysis' study for the company and proposed heat recovery retrofit measures. The study has helped the company improved its heat integration network and resulted in a reduction in 1.6 MW of energy, with annual savings of USD4.1Million. The study has also contributed to a more sustainable energy system for the company.

The student received the Vice-Chancellor Award during the 55th UTM Convocation Ceremony. In addition, he was also selected as the National Young Scientist Representative during the 65th Lindau Nobel Laureate Meeting 2015 (see **Figure 3**). He was also chosen as the top 3 finalists for the European Federation of Chemical Engineer (EFCE) Excellence Award in Recognition of an Outstanding PhD Thesis on Computer-Aided Process Engineering (CAPE).

The work also resulted in software called Optimal Site which won the Jury and Gold Award in the 16th Industrial Art and Technology Exhibition (INATEX), UTM and Silver Medal in the 14th International Conference and Exposition on Inventions by Institutions of Higher Learning (PECIPTA).

3.2 MIMOS semiconductor Sdn Bhd

Another PhD student was attached in MIMOS Semiconductor. She performed a feasibility study on water sustainability programs for MIMOS. The study predicted savings of freshwater and wastewater bills of worth Ringgit Malaysia (RM) 50 k per month with two years payback period. The savings represent a reduction of more than 80% of freshwater consumption. The water minimisation strategies holistically included measures for water elimination, reduction, reuse, outsourcing and treatment. The work produced a UTM commercial software, Optimal Water, that won several national and international product innovation awards, and resulted in joint collaborative international publications involving UTM and MIMOS. The work also won prestigious international awards such as the Saudi Prince Sultan bin Abdul Aziz International Prize for Water 2008 (Water Management Category), the Germany

Figure 3.
Liew Peng yen selected as National Young Scientist Representative during the 65th Lindau Nobel laureate meeting 2015. The picture was taken with Steven Chu, former United States secretary of energy. He is the winner of the 1997 Nobel prize in physics.

Figure 4.
Sharifah rafidah Wan Alwi (front row, second from left) was selected as one of the green talents 2009 by the government of Germany.

Green Talent Award (see **Figure 4**) [13] and the Malaysia's Sarawak State 2008 Maal Hijrah Outstanding Achievement Award.

3.3 Synthomer

One undergraduate and one postgraduate student were attached in Synthomer Malaysia under the UNIX program. The undergraduate student developed software to monitor the cooling duty and scheduling of reactor for polymerisation reaction (see **Figure 5**). The software has helped the company to reduce its reactor downtime, minimise cooling requirement and optimise production.

The master student was assigned to develop a sustainable energy management system and performed an energy audit for the company. The feasibility study

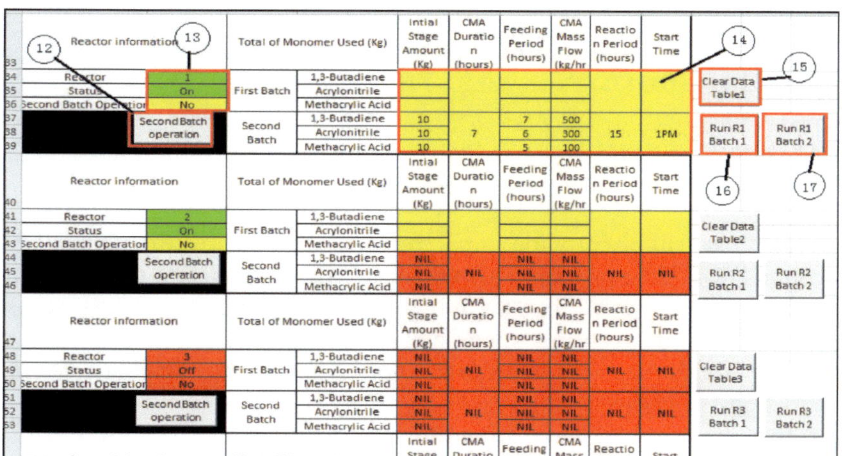

Figure 5.
Output of UNIX - software for cooling duty monitoring & reactor scheduling of semi-batch free radical emulsion polymerisation.

conducted by the student managed to identify scope for annual energy savings of up to RM740,000 and recommended a sustainable energy management program for the company. UTM collaboration with Synthomer has also resulted in a memorandum of understanding (MOU) [14] that provided placement for more students to undertake various other UNIX projects.

4. Conclusion

Over the years, more than 100 public and private institutions had benefited from UNIX collaboration with UTM. Having access to UTM's R&I ecosystem, network, resources, technology, and know-how allow collaborators to add value, improve efficiency, raise competitiveness, and drive innovation that ultimately enhances the image, profitability and sustainability of their businesses. The UTM-Industry Innovation Exchange Internship Program (UNIX-Internship) transformed a routine university's conventional short exposure industrial training programs into a 1-year, value-laden, industry-oriented, project-based internship programs. It has huge potential to be a game-changer to the teaching and learning ecosystem in the following major ways:

- Sharpening of student's generic skills, including lifelong learning, problem-solving, communication, teamworking, and leadership skills, while positively impacting the cognitive and affective domains of learning among students.

- Providing students with vital practical industrial experiences of project execution and management and the skill to solve complex problems encompassing sustainable development, safety-health-environment, economic analysis & project management.

- Providing students with better career prospects through prolonged exposure and experience working and engaging with the industry.

- Providing affordable R & D support to companies toward the development of sustainable organisations. To date, UNIX has benefitted more than 100 local and multinational companies.

- Forming a vibrant, synergistic, and sustainable linkage between UTM and stakeholders (SDG17 – Partnerships for the Goals).

- Creating a culture and an ecosystem of market-driven R & D among the young students.

The works particularly provide impactful contributions toward advancing Quality education (SDG Goal #4) and Partnership for the Goals (SDG Goal #17) of the Sustainable Development Goals. The numerous UNIX projects with industries, among others, also address other specific SDG goals related to energy and water sustainability and climate action, industry innovation and sustainable consumption and production.

Apart from successfully benefitting more than 100 organisations, the UNIX project-based industrial internship program has enhanced UTM graduate employability. In addition, UNIX has formed a vibrant, synergistic and sustainable linkage between UTM and stakeholders, and created a culture and an ecosystem of market-driven R & D for universities.

Acknowledgements

The authors acknowledge the contributions of the academic and industrial supervisors and appreciate the facilities and resources provided by all the companies involved in the UNIX program.

Conflict of interest

The authors declare no conflict of interest in this written chapter.

Author details

Zainuddin Abd Manan* and Sharifah Rafidah Wan Alwi
Process Systems Engineering Centre (PROSPECT), Research Institute for Sustainable Environment (RISE), School of Chemical and Energy Engineering, Universiti Teknologi Malaysia, Johor, Malaysia

*Address all correspondence to: dr.zain@utm.my

References

[1] Ayob A, Osman SA, Omar MZ, Jamaluddin N, Kofli NT, Johar S. Industrial training as gateway to engineering career: Experience sharing. Procedia - Social and Behavioral Sciences. 2013;**102**:48-54. DOI: 10.1016/j.sbspro.2013.10.712

[2] Feijoo G, Arce A, Bello P, Carballa M, Freire MS, Garrido JM, Gómez-Díaz D, González-Álvarez J, González-García S, Mauricio M, Méndez R, Moreira MT, Mosquera-Corral A, Navaza JM, Palacios MC, Roca E, Rodil E, Rodríguez H, Rodríguez O, Sineiro J, Soto A, Torres MD, Moreira R. Potential impact on the recruitment of chemical engineering graduates due to the industrial internship, Education for Chemical Engineers. 2019; 26: 107–113. DOI: ISSN 1749–7728.

[3] Engineering Accreditation Council. Engineering Programme Accreditation Manual 2012. Board of Engineers Malaysia. Available from: http://www.eac.org.my/web/document/EACManual2012.pdf [Accessed: 2020-08-23]

[4] Phang FA, Yusof KM, Saat MM, Yusof NM. Perceptions of engineering students on industrial training in Malaysia, QScience Proceedings (World Congress on Engineering Education 2013). 2014:20 http://dx.doi.org/10.5339/qproc.2014.wcee2013.20

[5] Jamaluddin N, Ayob A, Osman SA, Omar MZ, Kofli NT, Johar S. Undergraduate industrial training experience: A win-win situation for students, industry and faculty. Procedia - Social and Behavioral Sciences. 2013;**102**: 648-653. DOI: 10.1016/j.sbspro.2013.10.783

[6] Leal Filho W, Raath S, Lazzarini B, Vargas VR, de Souza L, Anholon R, et al. The role of transformation in learning and education for sustainability. Journal of Cleaner Production. 2018;**199**: 286-295. DOI: *10.1016/j.jclepro.2018.07.017*

[7] Lenihan S, Foley R, Carey WA, Duffy NB. Developing engineering competencies in industry for chemical engineering undergraduates through the integration of professional work placement and engineering research project, Education for Chemical Engineers. 2020. 32: 82–94. DOI: 10.1016/j.ece.2020.05.002

[8] Manan ZA, Wan Alwi SR, Samingin MH, Misran N. Assess your Plant's true water-saving potential. Chemical. Engineering. 2006;**113**(12): 42-49

[9] Manan ZA, Wan Alwi SR, Samingin MH, Misran N. Retrofit water systems the SHARPS way. Chemical Engineering Progress. 2006;**102**(11): 20-27

[10] Wan Alwi SR, Manan ZA, Samingin MH, Misran NA. New holistic framework for cost effective minimum water network in industrial and urban sector. Journal of Environmental Management. 2008;**88**:219-252. DOI: 10.1016/j.jenvman.2007.02.011

[11] Manan ZA, Shiun LJ, Wan Alwi SR, Hashim H, Kannan KS, Mokhtar N, et al. Energy efficiency award system in Malaysia for energy sustainability. Renewable and Sustainable Energy Reviews. 2010;**14**(8):2279-2289. DOI: 10.1016/j.rser.2010.04.013

[12] Prince Sultan Bin Abdulaziz International Prize for Water. Water Management & Protection Prize (Co-Winner). 2008. Available from: https://psipwevaluations.org/index.php?option=com_content&view=article&id=302&Itemid=132&lang=en [Accessed: 2020-08-23]

[13] Green Talents. Dr. Sharifah Rafidah Binti Wan Alwi (Malaysia). Federal Ministry of Education and Research Germany. 2009. Available from: https://www.greentalents.de/awardees_awardees2009_sharifah-rafidah-binti-wan-alwi.php [Accessed: 2020-08-23]

[14] Utusan Malaysia. MOU UTM-SSB Collaborate to Share Expertise (In Malay). 27 October 2011. Available from: http://akhbar-utusan.blogspot.com/2011/10/utusan-online-johor_27.html [Accessed: 2020-08-23]

Chapter 12

Exploring a Culturally-Responsive Model and Theory for Sustainable Development in Education Based on Cebuano Context

Reynaldo B. Inocian

Abstract

This paper explores a culturally-responsive model and theory for sustainable development in education that intertwines a seamless juxtaposition of cultural knowledge, mastery, reflections and understanding, and innovations in the Cebuano context. A multiple case analysis of selected quintains of Cebuano culture in literature reviews, and past travel observations and experiences were used as the methodology of the study. Results revealed that studies on cultural knowledge reflected a Cebuano identity of indigenous worldviews and reverence to nature. Cultural knowledge served as a basis for cultural mastery in the formulation and implementation of government policies as exemplified in the *Bayanihan* to Heal Act, the creation of the Inter-Agency Task Force, and other decisions of government and non-government agencies to protect people's welfare. Cultural reflections ignited how people responded to these policies, with contrasting views and ambivalence. To prevent the furtherance of these views that would heighten possible conflict and violence, cultural innovations through a KRSP Model offers vibrant opportunities to promote and realize ESD Goal No. 4 by 2030.

Keywords: quintain, cultural knowledge, cultural mastery, cultural reflection, cultural innovation, KRSP model, quadrivium theory

1. Introduction

"Black Lives Matter" became a popular mantra among Black Americans after George Floyd died on May 25 this year. This dramatic scene resorted to rallies, looting, and destruction of properties that resulted in violence despite COVID-19 protocols [1]. This racial clamor of assertion reawakens a historical struggle of a cultural divide between the Blacks and the Whites in American history. Racism is crucial to unity, progress, and sustainable development not only in the United States of America but to other countries as well. Come to think of it, are the lives of the whites, the Asians, the Indigenous Peoples, and other races do not matter only because of this mantra? This question challenges racial dominance against racial equality that jeopardizes peace, unity, and sustainable development across the globe during this COVID-19 pandemic. Regardless of race, ethnicity, gender, culture, and religions, all lives matter for sustainable development. It is through education that this cultural divide polarizes to an end and continuously creates a better world for humanity, guided by the democratic principles of freedom, equality, and the pursuit of human happiness.

How can the institution of education achieve this humanitarian goal? Education can start recognizing the country's most important resource – the human population. It is through education, training, mentoring, seminars, conferences, and workshops that make the human population acquire knowledge [2]. Thomas Malthus in his essay once said: "as the human population multiplies geometrically, food supply increases arithmetically" [3]. This quote may result in a disequilibrium of supply and demand in the market that impacts demographic studies. This demographic situation threatens humanity's existence that touches environmental, public health, socioeconomic, and political concerns vital to sustainable development. Curbing the rising number of human populations by the government is insufficient to provide enough opportunities for a sustainable future.

Historically, during the trying times of war (World Wars I and II), terrorism (religious, state, international) [4], and pandemic (Black Death, Spanish Flu, and now COVID-19), the world has been unprepared to manage sustainability, despite its efforts to maintain peace and order, alleviate hunger, and lighten the people's burdens. Natural upheavals and other forms of disturbances produce tensions to humanity's existence; the chain of poverty and hunger continues, undermining people's safety. Abuse, use of power and competition for supremacy and global dominance is obvious. Struggle for hegemony in global politics and the world market becomes one of the visible culprits on why these upheavals happen, setting back the essence of sustainable development.

One of the 'antidotes' in responding to these disturbing challenges is Education for Sustainable Development (ESD). The United Nations Educational, Scientific, and Cultural Organization (UNESCO) mandates 17 goals for ESD. Among these goals, this chapter limits its discussion to goal number four on quality education that ensures inclusiveness and equitability of quality education and the promotion of lifelong learning opportunities for all [5]. This is one of the targets of ESD by 2030, with an emphasis on cultural contributions [6]. However, the broadness of this goal allows the author to pick 'world heritage sites and local cultural properties' as one of ESD's eight themes, using the principles of tolerance and cultural relativism in the educational system. There is a potential for the Philippines to support this mandate in consonance with the finding of National Commission for Culture and the Arts (NCCA) that education ranked 4th in the executive survey on Filipino values with the essential capacity to ensure a brighter future, learn values, promote human rights, challenge values education, and improve its delivery [7].

This chosen ESD theme narrows down to specific aspects of the cultural properties of a Cebuano worldview that juxtaposes to secret knowledge, collective values and behavior, festivals, and reverence to the natural environment. In these contexts, this paper explores how ESD intertwines a juxtaposition to create culturally-responsive model and theory in the Philippines that may promote inclusive quality education and national identity in the ASEAN region. This goal desires to promote reduction, if not elimination, of racism, prejudice, and other forms of intolerance that creates bigotry and stronger stigma than the effects of COVID-19 pandemic in many parts of the globe. This happens when there is a lack of cultural knowledge, mastery, understanding, and reflections in cultural contexts that hamper creative cultural innovations for sustainable development, as the four important quintains or case conditions of this paper.

2. ESD using culturally responsive innovations or models

During this time of pandemic where it is impossible to conduct face-to-face interviews and observations to gather data, document reviews of literature in referred journals served the primary methods of this paper. A recollection of past experiences and travel observations in some parts of Cebu, before the onset of the pandemic, provided sufficient grounding of the paper. A multiple case analysis of selected document reviews of culture studies and culture-based ESD was used as the primary method in this paper. A multiple case analysis is a comparative method of research that deals with a small number of observations, interviews, and document reviews in a selected quintain or a target collection [8]. Literature scanning in the previous works on culture studies and culture-based innovation in education was archived, analyzed, and contextualized to provide a thorough analysis of this paper. The quintain focused on the paper was a condition studied on how a local culture can be used in enhancing ESD based on NCCA's survey on 19 values of a Filipino.

Ned Hermann's Brain Dominance Theory served as the fundamental framework in the presentation and analysis of the paper. This theory suggested that students can benefit from the teacher's delivery of instruction if lessons effectively stimulate both the thinking (cerebral) and feeling (limbic) parts of the brain [9]. Hence, to observe a vivid contextualization of this theory in the investigated quintain of the paper, **Figure 1** shows the four elements of a culture-based ESD framework.

The first element of the culture-based ESD framework is cultural knowledge (CK). This element refers to the knowledge of facts, concepts, principles, generalizations,

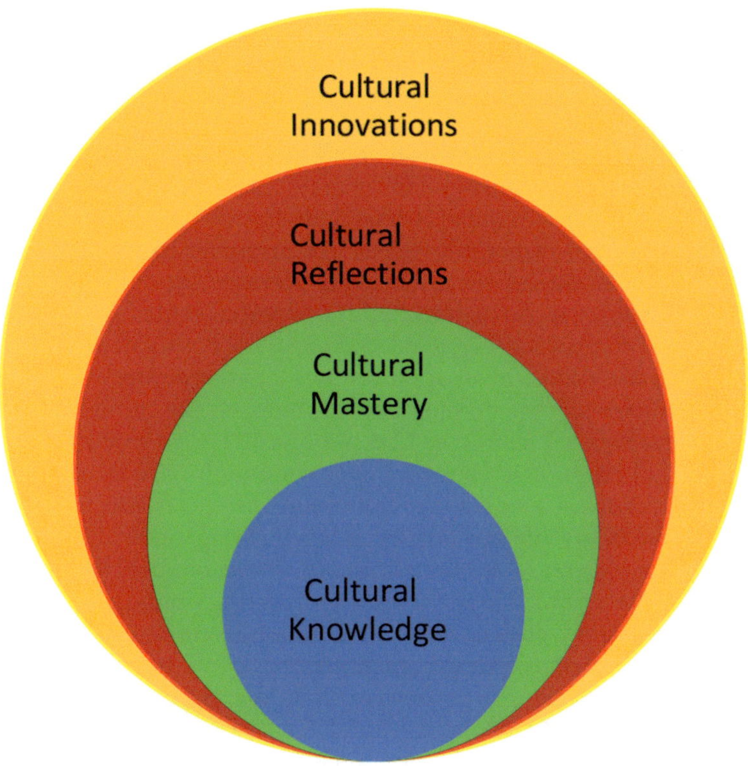

Figure 1.
Elements of culture-based ESD.

and theories on local cultures, which are essential in ESD. The second element is cultural mastery (CM). CM is the repetition of the learned competencies. This is classified into cognitive, fine and gross motor, and appreciation skills. Both the first and second elements emphasize convergent, linear, and objective analysis of cultural quintains. When learners' CK and CM are in place, they are ready to hurdle the third and fourth elements in the framework. The third element is the cultural reflections (CR), which utilizes the understanding and decision-making for further actions. This includes the process of doing integration, collaboration, and revision of what has been learned in the CK and CM. This collaboration requires participation by stakeholders [10]. The framework completes with cultural innovations (CI) as its fourth element. CI includes cultural innovations in the contexts of the languages, traditions, mores, folkways, and other cultural elements and properties in the community. Unlike the CK and CM, the CR and CI emphasize the divergent, cyclical, and creative synthesis of cultural orientations in a specific locality.

2.1 Quintain for cultural knowledge

The dynamics of human society depends on the culture of its people. Issues on gender, race, religion, and diet are avoided when society has an awareness of cultural knowledge. Cultural knowledge (CK) does not only include how people behave and act, but this also includes secret knowledge which is often regarded as taboos in other societies. CK also includes the people's worldviews on how they look at their social environment and the way they respond to it [11]. Concepts of cultural relativism, tolerance, justice, and peace may dispel a wrong understanding of cultural diversity and distorted worldviews when there is a vibrant interplay of education for sustainable development in the community, with the support of other social institutions as well.

2.1.1 The knowledge of Cebu's traditional healing

The indigenous knowledge of *panambal* or healing allows the people of the community to use folkloric modalities and become responsive in using medicinal plants available in the natural environment to heal their illnesses [12–15]. This local culture of healing allows the community to become sustainable and be relieved from expensive medicines in drugstores and hospital services [16]. It also opens various studies on these medicinal plants that exhibit a potential value for laboratory trials by pharmaceutical companies [17], to contribute to the production of medicine and increase business and employment opportunities for community members.

This also promotes tourism development to showcase the culture of *panambal* in the Philippines. **Figure 2** shows the 12 common cultural practices of *panambal* in Cebu, Philippines [16]. *Hilot* is a body massage commonly used by old folks in rural areas. The advent of the spa for stressed individuals promotes *hilot* in most urban areas that make masseurs' life sustainable. *Palina* is fumigation commonly used by faith healers for patients to smell the aromatic smoke of burnt herbs, myrrh, frankincense to relieve pain; and to drive out evil spirits. Vendors earn an income of these materials for *palina,* provide relief on middle-income earners' sickness, and supply Catholic churches for use during masses.

Himolso is a pulse-checking of patients to determine the blood pressure and diagnose ailments so that the *albularyo* (faith healers) can find the necessary herbs and plants to treat them. *Palakaw* is a petition for healing used by the *albularyo* to implore the spirits to heal patients. *Pasubay* is a diagnosis of ailments and its possible means for cure [16], utilizing *himolso*, viewing crystals, card reading, rituals, and psychic powers. *Tutho* is a saliva-blowing at the head of the patient; while the *tayhop*

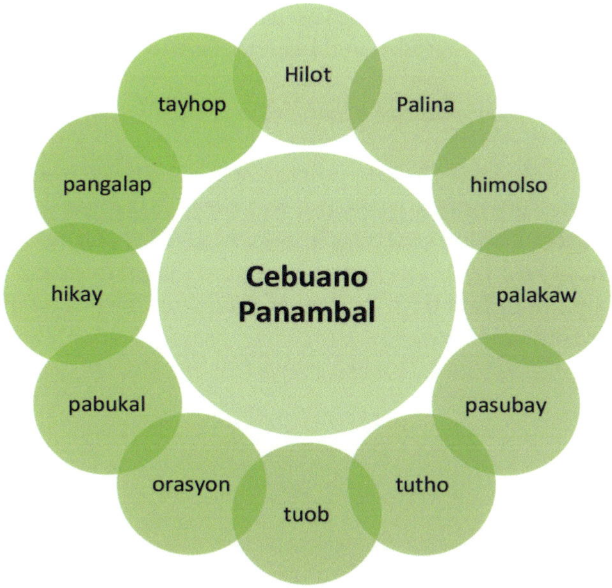

Figure 2.
Traditional healing practices in Cebu [16].

is a gentle-blow of the affected part of the patient's body to experience relief of pain. *Tuob* is a steam inhalation commonly used in rural areas to treat colds, cough, fever, and influenza using herbs, spices, and salt in a boiling pot. *Pangalap* is the searching of the medicinal herbs and plants for the intended *palina*. *Albularyo* uses the roots, leaves, bark, and juices of these medicinal flora for healing. *Pabukal* is a decoction of herbal plants [12], which will be served as a traditional tea that provides a catharsis of pain. *Orasyon* is the mystical prayers of the *albularyo* with God or with the spirits of the underworld to grant healing.

Hikay is a feast to please the spirits of nature or offer thanksgiving to the souls of the departed ancestors to protect family members from harm. *Hikay* is also used to heal one's ailment after having offended with any spirit of nature in a form of *hikayan* (a ritual celebration) such as *harang* (ancestor worship); *huhat silung* (ritual for good fortune and thanksgiving for abundant harvest); *tigpo* (atonement of sins of the spirits of the underworld); *sagangsang* (ritual for abundant wine); *damit* (ritual for abundant harvest); *balangkisaw* (ritual for atonement after having offended with the spirits of the water gods); and *bug-os* or *pamisa* (offering for the souls of the departed) using *puso* (cooked rice in pouches) [18]. **Figure 3** shows the six designs of *puso* used during the *hikay* celebration [18–21].

Figure 3 visualizes the six types of rice pouches used during the *hikayan* or *offrenda* celebration – an animistic ritual offering. Native animism is a belief that post-mortals being depended on sacrifices offered up by the living [22]; and the belief that the materialistic and the spiritual worlds remain inseparable [23]. These rice pouches are offered to the spirits of the underworld to provide farmers with an abundant harvest, safety from natural calamities, healing their sickness, achieving a healthy and abundant life, and fulfillment of their dreams. *Binaki* (froglike shape) and the *Manan-aw* (blooming phalaenopsis) represent a replication of the beauty of nature. These pouches are offered with great intentions of healing and for a successful harvest. *Binosa* (shot glass shape) and *Tinigib* (chisel-shape) symbolize the perceived utilitarianism in the ritual offering for the success of the *hikayan*. *Badbaranay* (wad-like shape) and the *kinasing* (heart-shape) are used for self-glorification in union with the spirits of nature. These pouches represent the intimacy of man, nature, and spirit.

The recent NCCA survey that ranked 8th on health and wellness among the19 values of a Filipino [7] reflects the 12 traditional healing practices of a Cebuano.

2.1.2 Knowledge of Cebuano collective behavior and act of kindness

Another lens to look into cultural knowledge is examining how people behave and act in the community during good and bad times. **Figure 4** mirrors this lens into five Cebuano cooperation practices known as TAYTU (*tagay, alayon, yayong, tambayayong*, and *unong*) [24]. The friendliness and gregariousness of everybody prove that they are not in isolation. As part of social culture, Cebuanos are sensitive and cooperative to other's needs.

Figure 3.
Six Puso designs.

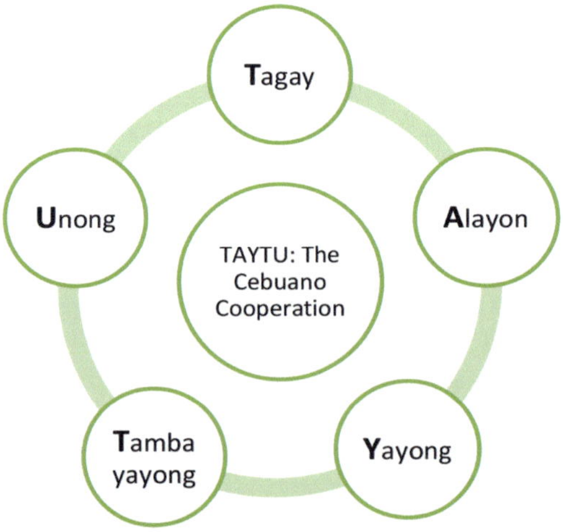

Figure 4.
Cebuano cooperation.

Either in good times or in bad times, *tagay* (social drinking) is a refuge of *barkada* (friends) to share their emotions either for comfort or for fun. This Cebuano culture survives with time and it is sustainable. Before, *tangero* (drinkers) used *hungot* (smoothened coco shell) as a local shot glass to be shared among the members of the spree on the porch or at the corner. As time evolves, bars provide several shot glasses, i.e. one glass for each drinker to use to prevent viral infection. Regardless of the time, drinkers share their successes, fears, pains, and failures to seek comfort and piece of advice over a bottle of beer or wine matched with a *pulotan* (appetizer) and a *kantahan* (singing).

To speed up the task at hand, the Cebuano people engage with an *alayon* (working as a team). In rural areas, farmers do *alayon* on the farm among each member of the team. Their survival depends on the efforts of others [25]. They decide to participate in the *alayon* and work cooperatively on the farm for a week; take turns working on another farm for the succeeding weeks until they finish or decide to have another *alayon* cycle. *Yayong* is an act of helping each other by lifting a heavy object, fetching water, changing tires, and doing laundry. This act of kindness extends to help the person during the time of crises like the death of a loved one, loss of a job, and easing of someone's burden.

When *yayong* is extended to several members of the family, friends, and members of the community, it becomes a *tambayayong* (a collective effort) to make the community more sustainable and achieve development. The fishermen in the coastal areas of Cebu use *tambayayong* in casting nets for fishing and by pulling these nets with heavy loads of catch on the shoreline. When *yayong* becomes well-established, an individual is ready to help others. This act of kindness is called *unong*. This *unong* is more than the act of sympathy, but empathy extended during wake and burial to the families of a departed loved one. *Unong* is extended to people who are victims of natural calamities and human atrocities in a form of donations and other humanitarian services to alleviate their suffering. *Unong* also includes the support extended to welfare homes for the aged, child-care centers, correctional centers, street families, street children, persons with disabilities (PWDs), and other minority groups. Generally, TAYTU is reflective with *pakikipagkapwa* (social relations) that ranked 3rd in the national survey of Filipino values, which includes *Bayanihan* (cooperation), empathy, reciprocity, and hospitality [7].

2.1.3 Knowledge of Cebuano cultural festivals

In the NCCA survey of Filipino values, culture, arts, and sciences ranked 9th among the 19 Filipino values [7]. This means that the expressions of the Cebuano festivals shape their soul and identify as a Filipino. The province of Cebu is the most highly celebrated in the Philippines because of her 32 known festivals among the 44 towns and six component cities. A festival is a celebration of a particular event with the maximum participation of everybody in the community [26]. **Figure 5** shows the distribution of the 32 celebrated festivals with five types: environmental (38%), socio-anthropological (25%), economic (22%), historical (9%), and religious (6%) reflect cultural gratitude and pride. **Tables 1–5** present the origins of these festivals.

The cultural knowledge of festival celebrations in Cebu is reflective of the experiences, stories, and folklore of the 32 towns and cities covered in the study. As shown in **Table 1**, the festivals with environmental origins have greater convergence in the south and eastern part of the province, which constitutes 38% among the over-all festivals celebrated annually. This implies that Cebuano festivals in the studied locations have greater animistic beliefs and traditions, reflective of their experiences and interaction with the environment. This connection between man and nature creates a profound intimacy that promotes Cebuano cultural identity

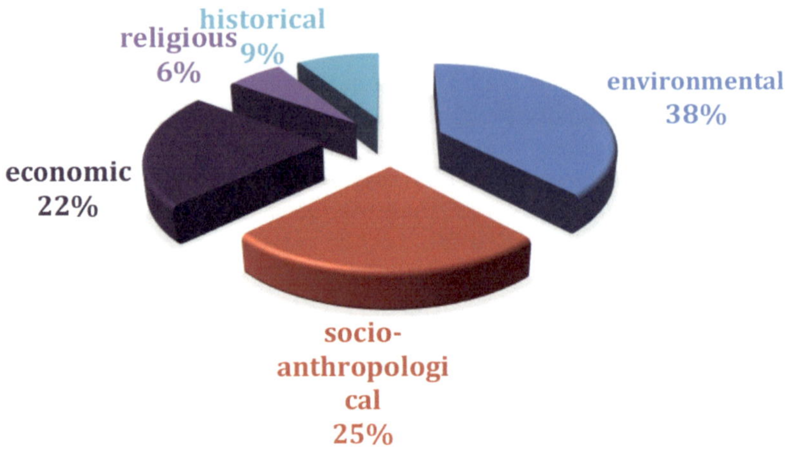

Figure 5.
Origins of cultural festivals.

Festivals of Cebu	Towns & component cities	Location	Origin
Sinulog	Cebu City	East	Sulog (water current)
Silmugi	Borbon	Northeast	Silmugi River
Soli-soli	San Francisco, Camotes	Northeast	Soli-soli (grass)
Kabkaban	Carcar City	Southeast	kabkab (native fern)
Mantawi	Mandaue City	East	Tawi (grass)
Kinsan	Aloguinsan	Southwest	Kinsan (a type of fish)
Kaumahan	Barili	Southwest	Uma (farm)
Dinagat	Cordova	East	Dagat (sea)
Siloy	Alcoy	Southwest	Siloy (black shama)
Bonga	Sibonga	Southeast	Bunga (fruit)
Bolho	Boljoon	Southeast	Bolho (water sprout)
Kawayan	Alegria	Southwest	Kawayan (bamboo)

Table 1.
Festivals with environmental origins.

and pride. For instance, the Siloy Festival of Alcoy is a depiction of pride of the town's locally known siloy or a songbird Black Shama (*Copsychus cebuensis Steere*), as an avian species found only in Cebu, Philippines. Cebuanos in the southern part of Cebu exhibit their profound dependency and cultural gratitude with nature. The various *bolho* (water spouts) of the town of Boljoon provides an abundant supply of freshwater from springs and falls for domestic use. The bounty of nature from the harvest of the *umahan* (farm) and *bunga* (fruits) from orchards makes the towns of Barili and Sibonga one of the 'vegetable and fruit baskets' in the province. Cebu is not only known for farm abundance, but the *dagat* (sea) also provides Cebuanos with rich marine resources like the *bakasi* (eel); and *kinsan* (fish) in the towns of Cordova and Aloguinsan [27].

Trees and grasses shape the identity of the cities of Mandaue and Carcar and the towns of San Francisco and Alegria. The name Mandaue is derived from *tawi,* a Banyan tree from a Ficus family. This tree provides shades for fisherfolks to trade with their catch with farm products on the coast. Carcar is also derived from *kabkab*

Festivals of Cebu	Towns and component cities	Location	Origin
Toslob	Oslob	Southeast	Toslob (plunging into the sea)
Hinulawan	Toledo City	West	Hinaguan (fruits of labor)
Palawud	Bantayan	Northwest	Lawud (deep sea fishing)
Kabuhian	Ronda	Southwest	Kabuhian (livelihood)
Hinatdan	Ginatilan	Southwest	Hatud (an act of good service)
Karansa	Danao City	Northeast	Karansa (dancing in merrymaking)
Sinanggiyaw	Dumanjug	Southwest	Sinanggiyaw (planting & thanksgiving)
Halad	Talisay City	Southeast	Halad (offering for thanksgiving)

Table 2.
Festivals with socio-anthropological origins.

Festivals of Cebu	Towns & component cities	Location	Origin
Sarok	Consolacion	Northeast	Sarok (farmer's hat)
La Torta	Argao	Southeast	Torta (sponge cake)
Pintos	Bogo City	Northeast	Pintos (a local delicacy)
Tagitab	Naga City	Southeast	Tagitab (electrical light)
Budbod	Catmon	Northeast	Budbod (millet suman)
Utanun	Dalaguete	Southeast	Utanun (vegetables)
Tostado	Santander	Southeast	Tostado (local cookies)

Table 3.
Festivals with economic origins.

Festivals of Cebu	Towns & components cities	Location	Origin
Tag-anito	Tudela	Northeast	Anito (spirits)
Kabanhawan	Minglanilla	Northeast	Banhaw (resurrection)

Table 4.
Festivals with religious origins.

or *kabankaban* (*Drynaria quercifolia Linn*), an epiphyte that grows within the branches and trunks of trees [28]. *Kabkab* enhances natural beauty and provides lush canopies to shade farmers and fisherfolks in trading their products. The importance of *soli-soli* (*Typha latifolia*) in San Francisco [29], and *kawayan (Bambusa vulgaris)* in Alegria recognizes the importance of these grasses, as primary materials for the weaving of bags, baskets, mats, hats, and pouches for local industries.

Recognizing the importance of rivers for trading is unquestionable in history. The Silmugi River of Borbon and the Rivers of Guadalupe and Pahina Central remind the residents of the place of the importance of these rivers to agriculture and trade. The vibrance of the economic life of the Cebuano reflects the *sulog* (current) of water, as they perform annually the grandest celebration of the country – the Sinulog Festival in honor of the Señor Santo Niño de Cebu, for bequeathing His abundant blessings [30].

Table 2 shows the festivals in southwestern and northeastern Cebu with socio-anthropological origins. The Cebuano in these towns and cities exhibit reliance on

Festivals of Cebu	Towns and component cities	Location	Origin
Haladaya	Daan Bantayan	Northeast	Haladaya (victory offering)
Kadaugan	Lapu-lapu City	East	Daug (winning for victory)
Tagbo	Poro, Camotes	Northeast	Tagbo (to meet)

Table 5.
Festivals with historical origins.

the bounty of nature. The bounty of marine life makes the fisherfolks of Oslob engage in *tuslob,* plunging into the waters either to catch fish or to swim. This is a similar version to the fisherfolks' mundane life on the island of Bantayan as they perform the *palawud,* sailing to the *lawud* (deep seas), looking for a bountiful catch. To meet both ends, the residents of Ronda find ways to survive by relying on their *kabuhian* (livelihood) through farming, fishing, and craft industries. Success in these endeavors is celebrated by the residents of Dumanjug in their *sinanggiyaw*, a celebration of good planting and copious harvesting. The *sinang-giyaw* proves the feasting celebrations of the early Filipinos during planting and harvesting seasons [31, 32].

The resilience of the Cebuano mirrors their *hinaguan,* the golden achievement of success as the residents of Toledo City perform their Hinulawan Festival. The jovial celebration equates to the cheerful celebration of *halad* (offering) by the residents of Talisay City as they showcase their annual Halad Festival. With a joyful mood, the residents of Danao City dance the *karansa* (thrilled dancing) to celebrate the success of the city's local industries. The residents of Ginatilan celebrate a remarkable value of *hatud* (an act of good service) by which *hinatdan* (being given) the town got its name [33]. This is a festival of cultural gratitude and service without cost during times of need.

Table 3 shows 22% of Cebu's festivals with an economic origin. A greater slice of this percentage related to cuisines. Pastries represent a very important aspect of food culture. "Recognizing the story of native foods is a story about history, ecology, and culture that extends well beyond the dining table [34]." This quote reflects how Argao, Santander, and Catmon become proud of their origin as a town. Food becomes the ethnicity marker of a place i.e. used to express affection and demonstrate power and authority [35]. The delicious *torta* (sponge cake) of Argao marks the town's identity in the South. Santander's *tostado* (local cookies) marks the town's reputation as one of its local brands. Native delicacies of the north attract locals and tourists alike too, as Catmon showcases the traditional *bubod* (suman) made of *kabog* (millet) wrapped and cooked with banana leaves. Few kilometers away from Catmon is the city of Bogo, where *pintos* (a local delicacy) made of grated young corn, mix with milk, and sugar, wrap with flesh inner pericarp of corn.

Part of earning income by the residents of Consolacion is the weaving of a traditional farm hat known as *sarok*. This industry reflects the ingenuity of the townsfolks to use dry leaves of bananas and bamboo strips [36, 37]. Farm yields are indicators of sustainable development. The town of Dalaguete showcases its *utanun* or vegetables as a 'vegetable basket' in the south. Naga City, one of the industrial zones in Cebu, recognizes *dagitab* (electrical lights) as these continue to shine through the years symbolizes the existence of the National Power Corporation (NPC) plant in the city for more than two decades, giving its dedicated service to the Cebuano people.

Table 4 shows 6% of Cebu's festival with religious origins. The intimate connection and reverence of Cebuano to nature before the arrival of the Spanish conquistadores reflects a renaissance of the Tag-anito Festival of Tudela. Cultural gratitude of all the favors granted by the spirits of nature (anitos), the residents of Tudela perform the *tag-anito,* a prayer of thanksgiving in festive dancing, and rejoicing. One Castillan heritage that Cebuano Catholics of Minglanilla practice during the Easter celebration is the *kabanhawan.* This festival celebrates the resurrection of the crucified Christ meeting His mother, Mary. This festivity symbolizes the renewal of Cebuano from the bondage of sins.

Table 5 shows the Cebuano festivals with the historical origin. During the pre-colonial times, the residents of Poro, Camotes practiced *tagbo*, which means to meet. This scene manifests the value of reconciliation to settle the tribes' differences on the island. The celebration of victories for defending the territories against the enemies and colonizers is one of the traits of a Cebuano. The *haladaya* (celebration of victory) of Daanbantayan from pirates and the *kadaugan* (victory) of the island of Mactan by chieftain Lapu-lapu in 1521 demonstrate the heroic acts of the Cebuano.

2.1.4 Knowledge on the natural origin of some towns and cities of Cebu

Before the arrival of the Spaniards in 1521, the ancestors of modern Filipinos named their towns and villages with names of everything in the natural environment. Five cities and nine towns in Cebu named after the names of endemic flora and fauna; six named after specific water bodies and its characteristics [38]. This worldview implies a Filipino intimacy and reverence with nature, closely similar to other Southeast Asian neighbors. Early Cebuano adored spirits of nature, worshipped the sun, the moon, and the stars [39]. A 37% of the 51 towns and cities of Cebu derived their names from the bounty of nature. A presumption that 63% of these towns and cities changed their names during the Spanish occupation in the province either by force or consent with the Spanish authorities under the bastion of Christianity.

The changes of these names of the 63% of towns and cities in Cebu were obvious replications of the names of some provinces in Spain like Asturias, Compostela, Toledo, Santander, Cordova, Tudela or naming these places based on names of saints like San Francisco and San Fernando with a historic and religious sense [38]. However, the remaining 37% retained their old names as shown in **Figure 6** either because the Spanish officials never had the interest of changing it or the Cebuano fought for its retention because of its anthropologic value, the pride of place, and sentimentality. **Figure 7** shows the three classifications of the origins of towns and cities in Cebu. Five cities and seven towns have 63% origin with endemic flora. Bogo City is derived from a *bogo* (*Garuda floribunda*) tree, which served as a trading center with traders coming from the islands of Bantayan and Masbate. Carcar City got its name from *kabkab* or *kaban-kaban*, a local fern found abundant in the lush vegetation of tropical Cebu [28]. This epiphyte grows within trunks and branches of trees. Naga City is derived from *naga* or narra (*Pterocarpus indicus*) tree [40]. The town folks name the place because of the available narra tree in the early times. The characteristics of this hardwood are essential in the production of durable pieces of furniture.

As mentioned in the Mantawi Festival, the name of Mandaue city is also derived from a *tawi* tree that commonly grows in the coastal area. The *magtalisay* (*Terminalia catappa*) is a very important tree where the City of Talisay's name is taken [41]. The abundance of this tree that grows on the coast provides shade for fishermen to trade their catch, and for the residents who spend time swimming during holidays and other special occasions. The town of Argao comes from *sali-abgaw* (*Premma vestilla*) [42], which is known to have a curative element for healing. The town of

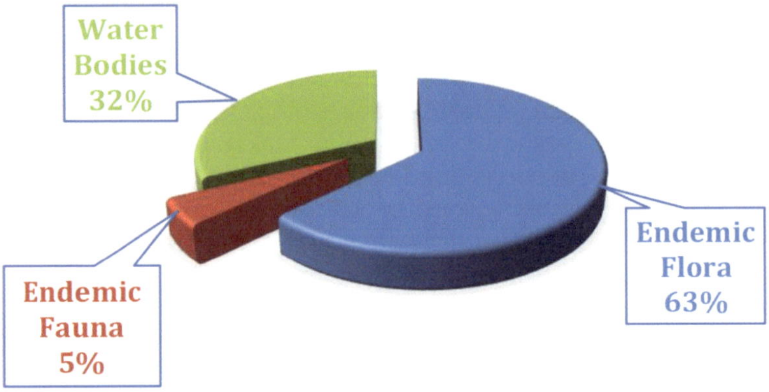

Figure 6.
Natural origins of towns and cities in Cebu.

Badian comes from *badyang* (*Alocasia macrorrhizos*) [43], which large leaves resemble like a heart-shape commonly used to wrap leafy vegetables and flower harvests from the farm.

Barili is derived from *balli* (*Echinochloa stagnina Retz*) [44], a grass that is used to feed cattle in the fields. Catmon is derived from a catmon (*Dilleniaccaea philippinensis*) tree [45], one of the endemic rare species of trees in the Philippines. Dalaguete is taken from a *dalakit* (*Ficus benjamin linn*) tree [46], i.e. often

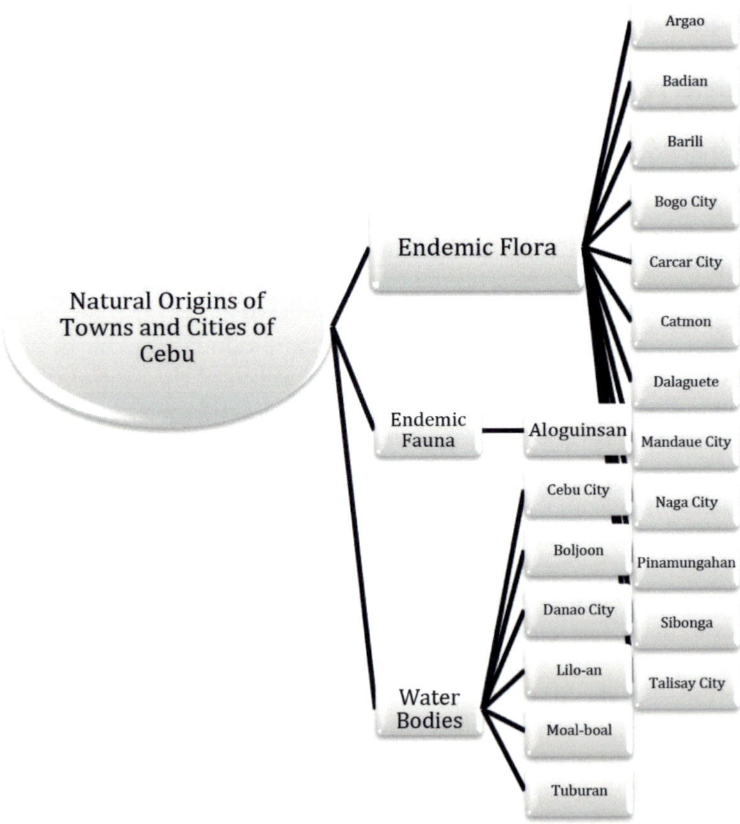

Figure 7.
Origins of towns and cities of Cebu.

mentioned in Cebuano folklore. The towns of *Pinamungahan* and *Sibonga* derived their names from a betel palm (*Areca catechu*) [47, 48]. Wrapped with the leaves of *buyo* (*Piper betel* L.), the nut of this palm is an essential element to ancient rituals like in the *hikayan* celebration.

The only town named after an endemic fauna in Aloguinsan. As mentioned in the Kinsan Festival, the name of the town is derived from *ulo* (head) and *kinsan* (big fish) [27]. Freshwater is one of the very important resources for survival. The towns of Boljoon, Moal-boal, and Tuburan got their names from abundant springs and water spouts like in Boljoon from *bolho* (water spout) [49], Moal-boal from *mual* (spring or well) and *bual* (bubbling water) [50], and Tuburan from *tubod* (spring) [51]. Residents of these towns use springs for household consumption and agricultural use. The City of Danao got its name from *danaw* or *danawan* (a marsh pond) [38], which is used by farmers for their water buffalos to plunge after the day's toil of plowing. Lilo-an got its name from *lilo* (whirlpool) [38], which is risky for fishermen's fishing expeditions. The old name of the City of Cebu was Sugbu that got its name from *sug* (current) of the river or stream adjoining the Mactan Channel, which is a busy waterway for maritime trade and harbor. With the NCCA survey, Filipino values related to the environment ranked 13th [7]. This finding intertwines a connection on how Cebuano values the environment is indicative of the socio-anthropological nostalgia of the natural origins of towns and cities. This connection represents a cultural ecology that man, nature, and spirit are closely related [23].

2.2 Quintain for cultural mastery

What is central in the study of culture is a shared knowledge [11]. This is the way how to make a culture of a place sustainable, by mastering and sharing it for dissemination. There are different ways on how to engage in cultural mastery. First is by embracing and appreciating its worldviews and the essential benefits these bring to community life. Second is by engaging it through constant practice to learn the culture. The third is by supporting cultural advocacies and foundations to achieve the real essence of culturally responsive sustainable development. Fourth is by monitoring and regulating people's cultural competence through ESD cultural frameworks. The fifth is by evaluating cultural programs to ensure sustainability.

2.2.1 The mastery of traditional healing

For poor and middle-income families who cannot afford to seek hospital help during the COVID-19 pandemic use *tuob* (steam inhalation) as home remedies; despite the disapproval of the Department of Health because of lack of scientific studies. *Pabukal* (decoction) is also used as another remedy to enhance the immune system during this time of COVID-19 pandemic. In the decoction, pulverized dried leaves of *kamunggay* (*Moringa oleifera*) and *kamias* (*Averrhoa bilimbi*) or ginger powder with lemon juice, and crushed garlic are boiled for 15 minutes. Some use *pabukal* with salt to experience comfort. The Department of Health (DOH) in the Philippines encourages the public to eat moringa to help protect from the COVID-19 virus because nutritionist Salina Teo explains that moringa contains vitamins C and E, calcium, potassium, and iron to boost the immune system [52]. *Hilot* is integrated into health and wellness in spa services. The promotion of herbal medicine and the propagation of herbal plants through the creation of herbal gardens for home remedies [53]. The recognition and production of virgin coconut for medicinal use by some pharmaceutical companies is another example of cultural mastery [17]. Along this vein, the Department of Science and Technology (DOST) in the Philippines through the Philippine Council for Health Research and Development

(PCHRD) prepares a set of policies that welcome traditional healing practices into the mainstream of medical science [14].

2.2.2 The mastery of Cebuano collective behavior and act of kindness

How is the culture of collective behavior and acts of kindness mastered? The willingness to help is a prime value of a Cebuano to sympathize with by extending their donations during the times of calamities either in cash or in kind. *Unong* or empathy is an act of kindness in times of someone's grief of a loss of someone. During the COVID-19 pandemic, the Philippine government has created the Inter-Agency Task Force (IATF) to manage cases of COVID −19 infections. As deputized by the government under the Bayanihan to Heal Act, IATF functions as a *tamabayayong* unit with members from other government agencies. This initiative of the government recognizes cultural knowledge of the Filipino collective behavior of *Bayanihan*. The term *Bayanihan* is a derivative word of *bayani*, which means hero. Hence, *Bayanihan* is a heroic act of kindness. A successful marriage of a couple succeeded because they do *yayong* (partnership) in building a family. Successful cooperatives in Cebu are living witnesses of *tambayayong* (cooperation) efforts of its members. Following the protocols of staying home, wearing masks, washing of hands, and observing a meter of social distancing during community quarantines exemplify a *tambayayong* spirit with the government, to reduce contagion.

2.2.3 The mastery of the Cebuano cultural festivals

The celebration of annual festivals has been a part of Cebuano's cultural life. The grandest Sinulog Festival is supported by the Sinulog Foundation, Inc., the Cebu City government, the private sectors, and the faithful. Festivals with economic origins promote the products of towns and cities through the government's One Town One Product (OTOP) policy by the Department of Trade and Industry (DTI). Festivals with environmental origin are used to promote the preservation of the endemic species of flora and fauna. The Dinagat Festival recognizes the *bakasi* (*Anguilla japonica*) as the popular exotic street food of the town of Cordova that promotes tourism attraction of the town. The Siloy Festival of Alcoy becomes a grand slam winner in Sinulog competition because of its message to conserve the endemic Black Shama. In 2012, BirdLife International, the Official Red List Authority for Birds for International Union for Conservation of Nature (IUCN) classified the Black Shama endangered [54]. The local communities know the existence of the Black Shama and recognize the efforts of the government through the Department of Environment and Natural Resources (DENR) for its preservation. However, there is still the need for a concerted effort for both government and non-government organization programs to inform, educate, and communicate these conservation policies and programs [54], for sustainable development.

2.2.4 Mastery regarding the natural origin of towns and cities

How can the natural origins of towns and cities impact cultural practice? In the case of the local governments of Bogo City and Catmon, Cebu. They initiated the planting of the *bogo* and the *catmon* trees in their locality to remind the residents of the nostalgia in the socio-anthropological origins of their town and cities. Nurseries run by government and non-government organizations propagate these species for the pride of place and historical sense. With the origins of the towns of Boljoon, Malabuyoc, and Tuburan derived from bodies of water, domestic and farming life is made possible. The pristine waters of these towns promote local tourism development. These mastery efforts reconnect the profound intimacy, love, and reverence of nature by the Cebuano folks during the pre-colonial periods, which are vital in shaping, cultural and ecological gratitude, Cebuano identity, and pride of place.

2.3 Quintain for cultural reflections

In understanding cultural contexts, reflection is a common tool to process a person's ideas, feelings, and actions. **Figure 8** shows the types of cultural reflections. *Reflections On* refers to someone's insights on the cultural contexts, in a form of positive or negative impressions, positive or negative observations, and comments. *Reflections In* refers to someone's feelings or emotions about his or her experiences, gut feeling, and affirmation for acceptance or rejection of a specific cultural context. *Reflections About* refer to someone's right decisions and right actions in a specific cultural context.

2.3.1 Cultural reflections on traditional healing

Despite the government's response to COVID-19 pandemic, contact tracing of possible infected residents is difficult with no enough health workers to facilitate, hospital bed capacity exceeded, suspected COVID-19 patients have no choice to wait in a long queue to be swabbed or to hop from one hospital to another to find their luck and get admitted; the unlucky ones accept their fate to perish. These sad realities create fear and some of those who have insufficient income resort to traditional Cebuano healing as an alternative. The Cebu provincial government through its memorandum encourages the use of *tuob* as home remedies. Issues between culture and science on the efficacy of *tuob* crop up between health workers and the people who believe it. A reflection on this, the Department of Health (DOH) does not

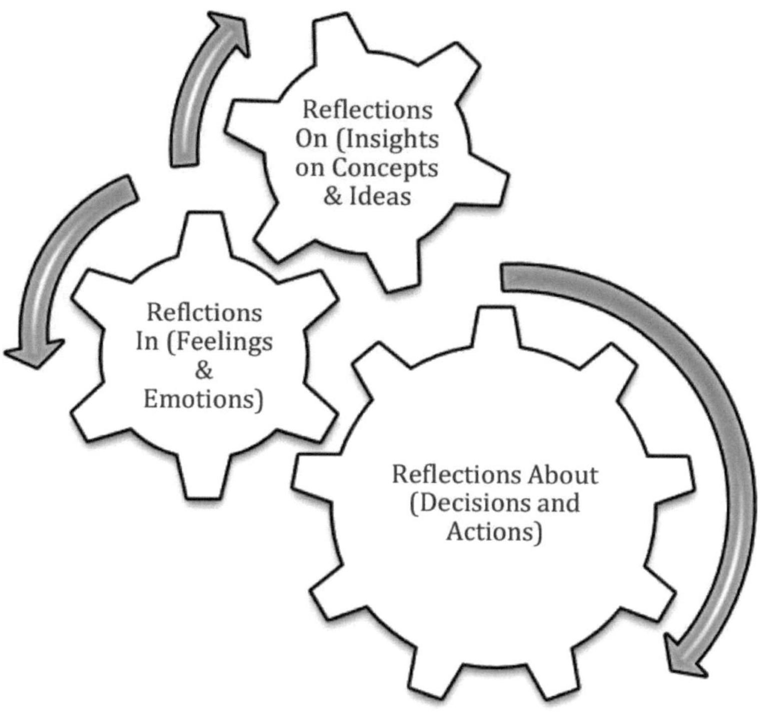

Figure 8.
Types of cultural reflections.

recommend it because of a lack of scientific studies to prove its claim. DOH officials further explain its danger that its heat can damage the patient's lungs and eyes and can spread viral contamination within the family members by its liquid droplets or by its aerosol. A reflection in contextualizes this, while those who support *Tuob* claim for healing, the rest feel the ambivalence – whether to accept it or not. This ambivalence may result in mixed emotions and worries about their health conditions. A reflection about why a concrete action may not be initiated by the government and other private companies to provide further studies to investigate the efficacy of *tuob* or explore the other forms of Cebuano *panambal* (healing), instead of destroying a cultural practice like this. Doing it will eradicate the ethnocentric bias of a peripheral culture, who knows this is one way to support sustainable development in local public health in the future.

2.3.2 Cultural reflections on Cebuano Collective behavior and act of kindness

Collective behavior shapes people's identity through their cultural knowledge and practices. In times of natural calamities and in trying times of need, a Cebuano can extend his or her helping hand as contextualized in the TAYTU. During this time of the pandemic, it is irreconcilable that an official of the country labels a Cebuano as *gahi'g ulo* (hard-headed) because of a lack of support or cooperation to prevent the rise of COVID-19 cases in Cebu. While it is true to some, there are some Cebuano who managed to stay home for four months of quarantine measures. A reflection on downplaying the extent and danger of COVID-19 by some local government officials, and their laxity to lead affect the rising cases of COVID-19. Residents can never be blamed as hard-headed because they simply go out to buy their provisions when aids of government remain insufficient for the longest duration of lockdown. Along with TAYTU, a reflection about retorts that Cebuano residents are compliant to cooperate with government protocols provided that the necessities of their families are provided. How can this be done when some of them work daily, some lost their jobs, some left with no savings? How can they survive? Being hard-headed is a risky decision for their loved ones because they have to go out and buy their provisions including medicines for the family. This concern validates the NCCA survey that Filipinos most highly valued the family [7]. They take risks in 'meeting both ends meet' for the security and safety of their families. A reflection about these questions. Where is the act of kindness when people are lining up under the heat of the sun claiming their financial assistance? How sure that social distancing and wearing of masks are strictly followed to prevent them from being infected? Why can the local government not request help from their constituents to help in the distribution of these food packs to the residents' houses? When systems and good governance are observed, the potentials of a Cebuano *alayon*, *yayong*, *tambayayong*, and *unong* can never be underestimated. These collective behaviors can build successful cooperatives and merge partnerships to bigger corporations, which if these would succeed, a *tagay* celebration is possible to enjoy a lighter side of life.

2.3.3 Cultural reflections on Cebuano cultural festivals

A reflection on the tapestry of cultural festivals that speak the cultural, historical, and natural identity of the towns and cities of Cebu. Festival is a colorful pageantry for product promotion and tourism marketing strategies. A reflection narrows down the religious purpose of festival celebrations is overshadowed by business motives for marketing strategies, to gain profit, and to ensure economic sustainability. However, a reflection about the internalization of these festivals in the cultural fabric of the Cebuano souls for unity and harmony in the entire province.

2.3.4 Cultural reflection of the natural origins of towns and cities

The naming of towns and cities in Cebu after an endemic flora and fauna and bodies of water is unique in the Philippines and perhaps the rest of the world. A reflection on upholds an ethos of Cebuano intimacy and reverence to nature – cultural and ecological gratitude given to Mother Nature – the source of everything that people need. A reflection makes the Cebuano proud about the origins of their towns and cities. Concern for conservation efforts of these endemic flora and fauna and the preservation of the bodies of water remain one of the important reflections about this quintain to improve sustainability.

2.4 Quintain for cultural innovations

After all the discussions on cultural knowledge, mastery, and reflections, the greatest challenge is how to innovate culture and integrate it with ESD. Cultural innovation is a process of integrating cultural knowledge, skills, and reflections into another concept, product, and system for development. The previous works of the author and company on culture-based pedagogies support cultural innovations [24, 37]. As contextualized in the culture of healing, a cultural knowledge about *panambal* (healing) using herbal medicine includes finding out the different herbal plants including its parts, and its processes of utilization for healing. Its cultural mastery includes the practice of using these herbal plants. Believing and sharing the testimonies and claims based on scientific studies on the efficacy of these herbal medicines presupposes cultural mastery. Cultural reflection is both the process of 'doing things right' (efficiency) and 'doing the right things' (effectiveness), to ensure public health safety. Thinking beyond about it to improve healing is a cultural innovation that includes: propagation of herbal plants, creation of traditional healing centers, the production of bottled herbal products approved by the Food and Drug Administration (FDA) for safe use, and the creation of the concept of *panambal* to education like making a *panambal* teaching strategies that would improve localized and contextualized learning. Therefore, there is a need to incorporate sustainable initiatives in innovative development [55]. Harmonizing these elements into a desired framework of action is known as the KRSP Model for a Culture-based ESD. How does this framework work for sustainable development?

2.4.1 The KSRP model for a culture-based ESD

To make culture-based education sustainable and achieve its desired goals by 2030, KRSP (**K**nowledge of culture, **S**kills in cultural practice, **R**eflections to cultural contexts, and **P**erformance in cultural innovations) Model facilitates the holistic ESD. **Figure 9** shows 13 intricacies of the KSRP Model for a Culture-based ESD in four phases. The first phase is the quadrivium of knowledge (K), skills (S), reflections (R), and performance (P) in a seamless and nurturing delivery of instruction as shown in **Figure 1**.

This primary phase emphasizes the basic notion of learning from easy to difficult, i.e. from concrete to abstract or from specific to general in a linear and sequential form of instruction. The second phase is the blended quadrium of knowledge and skills (KS), knowledge and performance (KP), skills and reflections (SR), and reflections and performance (RP). The connection between knowledge and skills (KS) enhances individuals' left-brain potentials for critical analysis such as comparing and contrasting, classifying, analyzing, inferring, supporting a statement, ordering and ranking, evaluating and critiquing, and decision-making, to become more rational [53]. The connection between reflections and performance

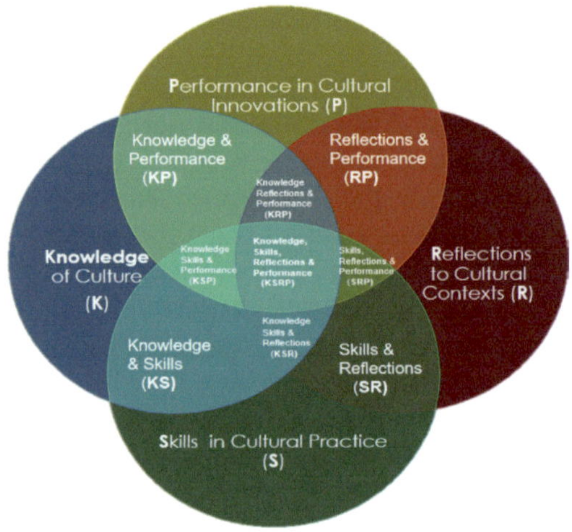

Figure 9.
KRSP model for a culture-based ESD.

(RP) nurtures individuals' right-brain potentials for creativity such as originality, fluency, flexibility, elaboration, brainstorming web, and generating relationships for integration, to become more intuitive [53]. The linking of the skills and reflections (SR) provides opportunities for sensitivity to affect like feelings and emotions and become more instinctive. The connection between knowledge and performance (KP) promotes opportunities for action and experimentation to become more intellectual.

The third phase is the trifocal trivium of knowledge, skills, and performance (KSP); the trifocal trivium of knowledge, skills, and reflections (KSR); the trifocal trivium of skills, reflections, and performance (SRP); and the trifocal trivium of knowledge, reflections, and performance (KRP). KSP indicates more left-brain dominance with creative results on cultural products and performance. KSR implies also with more left-brain dominance with concern for collaboration and team-building. SRP shows more right-brain dominance with an emphasis on self-regulation and competence. KRP projects the likelihood of right-brain dominance with emphasis on critical analysis and logical understanding. The last phase is the connection that integrates knowledge, skills, reflections, and performance (KSRP). The combined fulcrum of KSRP completes the holistic success of a culture-based ESD. KSRP promotes understanding, tolerance, respect, and harmony despite diverse perspectives and cultural orientations.

2.4.2 Quadrivium theory of culture integration for ESD

With the KRSP Model as a lens, a Quadrium Theory of Culture Integration for ESD is generated as shown in **Figure 10**. To make education sustainable for 2030, first educational institutions need to conduct intensive research and archiving of cultural artifacts for curation to establish a cultural knowledge profile of a certain locale.

Second, making use of the curated culture profile, cultural mastery propels for practice according to the person's skills and interest. Third, concerns and issues in the process need further reflections for better action that facilitate cultural innovations for the sustainability and development of ESD. Fourth, deciding for better action supports the eight standards of effective critical thinking such as clarity, accuracy, precision, relevance, depth, breadth, logic, and fairness [10]. Missing one of these elements in the quadrivium, as discussed in **Figure 8**, affects the quality of ESD implementation.

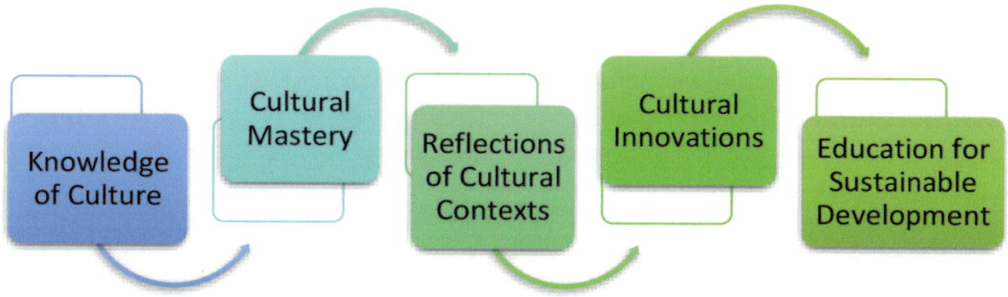

Figure 10.
The four elements in the ESD Quadrivium.

3. Conclusion

Quality and sustainable education underscore the fragments of culture such as knowledge, skills for practice, reflections, and the right actions for innovations. Recognizing Cebu's knowledge of traditional healing, the people's collective behavior, and the act of kindness, the origins of festivals, towns, and cities challenge modernity and science in the mastery and reflection process. This issue thwarts the essence of culture as a 'soul of the nation' to survive, preventing opportunities for creativity and innovation for sustainable development. The four elements of a culture-based ESD dovetails the creation of the KRSP Model that propels the generation of Quadrium Theory of Culture Integration for ESD.

Acknowledgements

Due acknowledgment to the Cebuano writers and scholars who wrote the history of different towns and cities of the province of Cebu that contributed to the scholarly impact of this chapter. Likewise, the same gratitude is given to the Cebu Provincial Government for the number of volumes of this history project given to our university library.

Author details

Reynaldo B. Inocian
Department of Social Sciences and Humanities, College of Arts and Sciences, Cebu Normal University, Cebu City, Philippines

*Address all correspondence to: inocianr@cnu.edu.ph

References

[1] J. Lee, "George Floyd: Five factors behind the UK Black Lives Matter protests," *BBC News,* pp. https://www.bbc.com/news/uk-52997848, 13 June 2020.

[2] J. O. Ohiorenoya and O. F. Eboreime, "Knowledge Management Practices and Performance in Nigerian Universities," *European Scientific Journal, 10* (16), pp. 400-416, 2014.

[3] J. C. Welling, "The Law of Malthus," *The Anthropologist, 1* (1) https://www.jstor.org/stable/658457?seq=1#metadata_info_tab_contents, pp. 1-24, 1888.

[4] A. J. Bergesen and O. Lizardo, "International Terrorism and World System," *Sociological Theory, 22*(1), pp. 38-52, 2004.

[5] National Council for Curriculum and Assessment, "Education for Sustainable Development: A study of opportunities and linkages in the primary," NCCA, June 2018. [Online]. Available: https://ncca.ie/media/3573/esdreport_final_june2018.pdf. [Accessed 3 June 2020].

[6] K. Shulla, W. Leal Filho, S. Lardjane, J. H. Sommer and C. Borgemeister, "Sustainable development education in the context of the 2030 Agenda for," *International Journal of Sustainable Development and World Ecology, 27* (5). https://doi.org/10.1080/13504509.2020.1721378, pp. 458-468, 2020.

[7] A. M. R. Villalon, L. R. Astudillo, J. S. J. Soliman, and M. F. Del Rosario, "National Commission for Culture and the Arts (NCCA) study on Filipino Values," in the National *Conference on Cultural Statistics*, Waterfront Hotel, Cebu City, 2019.

[8] R. E. Stake, Multiple Case Study Analysis, New York: Guilford Press, 2006.

[9] N. Hermann, The Whole Brain Business Book, New York: McGraw-Hil, 1996.

[10] N. Rowan, P. Kommor, A. Herd, P. Salmon, and P. Benson, "Critical Thinking and Interdisciplinary Development Fostering Critical Thinking in an Interdisciplinary Well Coaching Academic Program," *European Scientific Journal, 11* (8), pp. 46-59, 2015.

[11] F. L. Jocano, Filipino Worldview Ethnography of Local Knowledge, Quezon City: PUNLAD, 2001.

[12] R. A. Molina, P. E. L. Esperat, and A. A. J. Gracia, "Traditional Healing Practices in Zamboanga," *EPRA International Journal of Multidisciplinary Research, 6* (5), pp. 81-87, 2020.

[13] R. S. Del Fierro and F. A. Nolasco, "An Exploration of the Ethno-Medicinal Practices among Traditional Healers in Southwest Cebu, Philippines," *ARPN Journal of Science and Technology, 3* (12). http://citeseerx.ist.psu.edu/viewdoc/download?doi=10.1.1.675.8751&rep=rep1&type=pdf, pp. 1182-1188, 2013.

[14] N. R. Rebuya, E. S. Lasarte and M. M. A. Amador, "Medical Pluralism, Traditional Healing, Practices, and the Partido Albularyo: Challenge in Inclusion," *Open Journal of Social Sciences, 8* (?) https://doi.org/10.4236/jss.2020.86007, pp. 72-79, 2020.

[15] L. G. D. Crisol and E. J. J. Oledan, "The Mananambals and Their Functions in Philippine Culture," *CASS Langkit, 7* (?) https://www.msuiit.edu.ph/academics/colleges/cass/research/langkit/2017/Article%205.pdf, pp. 84-94, 2016.

[16] Z. R. J. S. Berdon, E. L. Ragosta, R. B. Inocian, E. B. Lozano, and C. A. Mañalag, "Unveiling Cebuano Traditional Healing Practices," *Asia*

Pacific Journal of Multidisciplinary Research, 4 (1), pp. 51-59, 2016.

[17] I. A. Uy, M. L. G. Dapar, A. T. Aranas, R. A. R. Mindo, C. K. Cabrido, M. A. J. Torres, M. M. E. Manting and C. G. Damayo, "Qualitative Assessment of the Antimicrobial, Antioxidant, Phytochemical Properties of the Ethanolic Extracts of the Roots of *Cocos nucifera* L.," *Pharmacophore, 10* (2), pp. 63-75, 2019.

[18] R. B. Inocian, Lukay Art in the Philippines: Cebu's Pride and Unique Ritual Identity, Germany: Scholar's Press, 2015.

[19] L. T. E. Alix, Hikay: The Culinary Heritage of Cebu, Cebu City: University of San Carlos Press, 2013.

[20] E. I. Nocheseda, Palaspas: An Appreciation of Palm Leaf Art in the Philippines, Quezon City: Ateneo de Manila University Press, 2009.

[21] E. I. Nocheseda, The Art of Puso Palm Leaf art in the Visayas in Vocabularios of the Sixteenth to Nineteenth Centuries, Quezon City: Ateneo de Manila University, 2011.

[22] W. H. Scott, "Prehispanic Filipino Concepts of land Rights," *Philippine Quarterly of Culture and Society, 22* (3), pp. 165-173, 1994.

[23] T. Chaitieng and T. Srisatit, "Spiritual Forest of Phutai People: The Biodiversity of Sacred Plant and the Ecological-Cultural Values in Sakhon Nakhon Basin, Thailand," *European Scientific Journal, 9* (32), pp. 436-447, 2013.

[24] R. B. Inocian, L. C. Dapat, G. B. Pacaña and G. M. Lasala, "Indigenizing and contextualizing the use of cooperative learning," *Journal of Research, Policy & Practice of Teachers & Teacher Education*, *9* (2), pp. 1-18, 2019.

[25] J. M. Castillo, C. G. Fario, J. A. Trinidad and R. P. Bernarte, "National Pride of the Filipino Youth," *Asia Pacific Journal of Multidisciplinary Research, 4* (3), pp. 18-25, 2016.

[26] E. Olaniyan Modupe, "An Appraisal of Osun Osogbo as a Festival Theatre," *European Scientific Journal, 10* (11), pp. 326-336, 2014.

[27] E. Tesaluna, The History of Aloguinsan, Cebu Philippines, 14., Cebu City: Cebu Provincial Government, 2014.

[28] J. Noel, The History of Carcar City, Cebu Philippines, vol. 3, Cebu City: Cebu Provincial Government, 2014.

[29] S. N. Tanduyan, "(Abstract) Soli-soli (*Typha latifolia*) as an industry and as a festival emblem of Pacijan Island, Cebu, Central Philippines: its status, processing and proposed conservation options for sustainability," *DOST SciNET-PHIL, 35* (1), 2013.

[30] E. Oracion, "The Sinulog festival of overseas Filipino workers in Hong Kong: Meanings and contexts," *Asian Anthropology, 1* (?), <https://search.informit.com.au/documentSummary;dn=099428090648631;res=IELHSS> ISSN: 1683-478X., pp. 107-127, 2012.

[31] F. L. Jocano, Filipino Indigenous Ethnic Communities, Patterns, Variations, and Typologies, Manila: PUNLAD, 1998.

[32] L. Junker, Raiding, Trading, and Feasting the Political Economy of Philippine Chiefdoms, Manila: Ateneo de Manila University Press, 2000.

[33] A. Jumao-as, The History of Ginatilan, Cebu Philippines, Vol. 31, Cebu City: Cebu Provincial Government, 2014.

[34] C. Craw, "Gustatory Redemption? Colonial Appetites, Historical Tales and the Contemporary Consumption of Australian native Foods," *International*

Journal of Critical Indigenous Studies, vol. 5, no. 2, pp. 13-24, 2012.

[35] H. V. Kuhnlein and O. Receveur, "Dietary Change and Traditional Food Systems of Indigenous Peoples," *Annual Reviews by the University of Manitoba, 16* (?) pp. 417-442, 1996.

[36] J. M. P. Cuyos, "'Lacion women weave sarok," *Cebu Daily News,* pp. par. 1, https://newsinfo.inquirer.net/39829/%E2%80%98lacion-women-weave-sarok, 11 08 2011.

[37] R. B. Inocian, A. L. I. Callangan, D. R. Medrano and W. G. Gualiza, "Cebuano Cultural Identities: Prospects for a Culturally Responsive Pedagogy," *Journal of Research, Policy & Practice of Teachers & Teacher Education, 10* (1), pp. 44-62, 2020.

[38] J. L. Benitez, "Historicity of City and Town Names in the Province of Cebu," *CNU Journal of Higher Education, 11*(?) https://jhe.cnu.edu.ph/index.php/cnujhe/article/view/162, pp. 1-12, 2017.

[39] M. R. Montebon, Retracing Our Roots: A Journey into Cebu's Pre-Colonial Past, Minglanilla, Cebu: ES Villaver Publishing, 2000.

[40] E. Mongaya, The History of Minglanilla, Cebu Philippines, Vol. 36, Cebu City: Cebu Provincial Government, 2014.

[41] R. Patalinghug, The History of Talisay City, Cebu Philippines, Vol. 9, Cebu City: Cebu Provincial Government, 2014.

[42] T. Sales and P. Gershwiler, The History of Argao, Cebu Philippines, Vol. 15, Cebu City: Cebu Provincial Government, 2014.

[43] M. Tabada, The History of Badian, Cebu Philippines, Vol. 17, Cebu City: Cebu Provincial Government, 2014.

[44] T. Maghanoy and F. Moreño, The History of Barili, Cebu Philippines, Vol. 20, Cebu City: Cebu Provincial Government, 2014.

[45] I. Manticajon, The History of Catmon, Cebu Philippines, Vol. 24, Cebu City: Cebu Provincial Government, 2014.

[46] J. Osorio, The History of Dalaguete, Cebu Philippines, Vol. 29, Cebu City: Cebu Provincial Government, 2014.

[47] M. Beltran, The History of Pinamungajan, Cebu Philippines, Vol. 40, Cebu City: Cebu Provincial Government, 2014.

[48] N. Ponce, The History of Sibonga, Cebu Philippines, Vol. 48, Cebu City: Cebu Provincial Government, 2014.

[49] R. Rigor, The History of Boljoon, Cebu Philippines, Vol. 21, Cebu City: Cebu Provincial Government, 2014.

[50] J. Gabales, The History of Moalboal, Cebu Philippines, Vol. 37, Cebu City: Cebu Provincial Government, 2014.

[51] M. Echica, The History of Tuburan, Cebu Philippines, Vol. 53., Cebu City: Cebu Provincial Government, 2014.

[52] M. C. Layug, "Can Eating Malunggay help Protect you from Novel CoronaVirus?" *GMA News Online,* pp. par. 1-4 https://www.gmanetwork.com/news/, 4 February 2020.

[53] R. B. Inocian, Aesthetic Teaching Pedagogies: A Voice of Experience, London: Cambridge Scholar's Publishing, 2018.

[54] R. B. Parilla, R. P. Laude, A. P. O. De Guia, M. V. O. Espaldon and L. M. Florece, "Local Communities' Knowledge, Attitude and Perception Towards Cebu Black Shama (*Copsychus cebuensis* Steere) and its Habitat Characteristics in Cebu Island,

Philippines," *Journal of Environmental Science and Management, 19*(2), file:///C:/Users/Sir/Downloads/147-Article%20Text-415-1-10-20191113.pdf, pp. 76-83, 2016.

[55] O. Okinono and D. Salleh, "Nigeria Niger Delta: Innovation for Sustainable Development," *Asia Pacific Journal of Education, Arts and Sciences, 2* (4), pp. 41-60, 2015.